# COMPARATIVE GOVERNME

Founding Series Editor: The late Vinc

GU00372933

*Published*

Rudy Andeweg and Galen A. Irwin
**Governance and Politics of the Net**

Nigel Bowles
**Government and Politics of the Un**____ _____ ,____ _____,

Paul Brooker
**Non-Democratic Regimes: Theory, Government and Politics**

Robert Elgie
**Political Leadership in Liberal Democracies**

Rod Hague and Martin Harrop
**Comparative Government and Politics (5th edition)**

Paul Heywood
**The Government and Politics of Spain**

B. Guy Peters
**Comparative Politics: Theories and Methods**
*[Rights: World excluding North America]*

Tony Saich
**Governance and Politics of China**

Anne Stevens
**The Government and Politics of France (2nd edition)**

Ramesh Thakur
**The Government and Politics of India**

*Forthcoming*

Judy Batt
**Government and Politics in Eastern Europe**

Robert Leonardi
**Government and Politics in Italy**

---

**Comparative Government and Politics**
**Series Standing Order**
**ISBN 0–333–71693–0 hardcover**
**ISBN 0–333–69335–3 paperback**
*(outside North America only)*

You can receive future titles in this series as they are published by placing a standing order. Please contact your bookseller or, in the case of difficulty, write to us at the address below with your name and address, the title of the series and the ISBN quoted above.

Customer Services Department, Macmillan Distribution Ltd
Houndmills, Basingstoke, Hampshire RG21 6XS, England

---

# Political Leadership in Liberal Democracies

**Robert Elgie**

Published by
PALGRAVE MACMILLAN
Houndmills, Basingstoke, Hampshire RG21 6XS and
175 Fifth Avenue, New York, N. Y. 10010
Companies and representatives throughout the world

PALGRAVE MACMILLAN is the global academic imprint of the Palgrave
Macmillan division of St. Martin's Press, LLC and of Palgrave Macmillan Ltd.
Macmillan® is a registered trademark in the United States, United Kingdom
and other countries. Palgrave is a registered trademark in the European
Union and other countries.

ISBN 0–333–59758–3 hardback
ISBN 0–333–59759–1 paperback

This book is printed on paper suitable for recycling and
made from fully managed and sustained forest sources.

A catalogue record for this book is available from the British Library.

10   9   8   7   6   5   4   3   2
11   10   09   08   07   06   05   04   03

Printed and bound in Great Britain by
Antony Rowe Ltd, Chippenham and Eastbourne

**Series Standing Order (Comparative Government and Politics)**
If you would like to receive future titles in this series as they are published, you
can make use of our standing order facility. To place a standing order please contact
your bookseller or, in the case of difficulty, write to us at the address below with
your name and address and the name of the series. Please state with which title
you wish to begin your standing order. (If you live outside the United Kingdom
we may not have the rights for your area, in whch case we will forward your order
to the publisher concerned.)
Customer Services Department, Macmillan Distribution Ltd
Houndmills, Basingstoke, Hampshire RG21 6XS, England

To Etain, my family and my friends

# Contents

# List of Tables, Figures and Exhibits

**Tables**

**Figures**

**Exhibits**

# Preface

This textbook aims to provide an introduction to the study of political leadership in liberal democracies. It is part of a series which is designed primarily to be of interest to a student audience both undergraduates and postgraduates. However, it is also hoped that it will be of interest to both the informed general reader and to academics with an interest in some of the issues which surround the study of political leadership. In sum, the intention is to present essential information in a clear, readable and methodical way, while at the same time stimulating further interest in both the study of political leadership in general and the role of political leaders in contemporary politics in particular.

This book provides an introduction to political leadership by analysing the role played by Presidents and Prime Ministers in six liberal democracies – Britain, France, Germany, the United States, Japan and Italy.It focuses on the leadership of the executive. In part, this focus was chosen because it is salient to many of the degree courses that are taken by undergraduate and postgraduate students in English-speaking countries. For good or bad, students have to study the political systems of the above countries and wish to understand why they operate in the way that they do. Less mundanely, this focus has also been chosen because it responds to a widely-perceived gap in the existing academic literature. Perhaps surprisingly, with the exception of the US presidency, there are very few studies of Presidents and Prime Ministers in these countries. For both reasons, it is hoped that this book will serve as a reference for all those people who are interested in learning about the role played by the leaders of these six countries in the context of their respective political systems.

Although this book focuses on Presidents and Prime Ministers, it is not primarily concerned with the role of individuals in the political process. It does not consist of case studies of, for example, Roosevelt, Churchill, de Gaulle, Adenauer, or Thatcher. Reference will be made to all these leaders during the course of the book, but it is not designed as a study of selected personalities, their individual motivations, or the impact they might have had on particular societies. Neither is it the purpose of the book to identify the essential characteristics of different types of leaders. Instead, this book is more concerned with the relationship between leaders and their institutional settings. It examines each country's leadership environment from an institutional perspective so as to determine the dominant leadership pattern that has been present since 1945. By focusing on leadership since this time, it is not concerned with whether or not there is currently a crisis of leadership in contemporary political systems. By taking an institutional perspective, it will not make rational choice assumptions about leader/follower utility maximisation, nor will it adopt explicitly behavioural assumptions about leaders responding to and transforming the wants and needs of group members. Instead, by concentrating on leadership patterns, it attempts to identify whether or not leadership responsibilities have generally been concentrated in one institution, divided between several institutions, or absent altogether.

Political leadership is a huge and amorphous subject. Any book can deal with only a fraction of the issues which might be included under the heading of 'leadership studies'. Nevertheless, this book tries to provide a positive contribution to certain aspects of such studies. In the first chapter, it sets out a framework with which to study the leadership role of Presidents and Prime Ministers in liberal democracies. In the next six chapters, it examines this role in Britain, France, Germany, the United States, Japan and Italy since 1945. In the final chapter, it reflects on the institutional approach to politics and what this study of political leadership can tell us about the strengths and weaknesses of such an approach. In these ways, it is hoped that it will both inform and make a modest contribution to an ever-expanding field of study.

ROBERT ELGIE

# Acknowledgements

In the course of writing this book, I have run up a great number of debts to many people. To begin with, I would like to thank Steven Kennedy, my publisher, for commissioning the book in the first place and then for waiting extremely patiently as deadlines were missed. I benefited from the discussions that I had with him at the start of the project and I am extremely grateful for his support throughout. I am also very grateful to both Andy House and Simon Towler who went to some trouble to provide information for me when I was at a loss to obtain it myself. I would also like to thank Keith Povey and Elizabeth Black for their remarkable efficiency in copy-editing the text.

I owe an especial debt of gratitude to Vincent Wright. Over the past couple of years, he has expended a very considerable amount of effort to ensure the realisation of this book. He has commented in detail on every chapter. He has taken the trouble to see me on a regular basis. He has also entertained me with his wit and stimulated me with his insights into the problems of comparative politics. It would be difficult to overstate how grateful I am for his help and advice during the course of writing this book.

In addition, thanks must also be extended to the other people who read individual chapters and who returned them with comments and advice: Paul Byrne, Mark Donovan, Steve Griggs, Jeremy Leaman, Joni Lovenduski, Ferdinand Müller-Rommel and Alan Ware. May I also thank two unnamed readers whose remarks on the final draft were much appreciated. Finally, as ever, Etain Tannam was a source of particular support, confidence and belief throughout.

By way of these thanks, I hope to have repaid at least some of the debts that I have accrued over the last couple of years. It simply remains to say that the usual caveat applies; all responsibility for the final content of the book is entirely my own.

ROBERT ELGIE

# 1
# Leaders, Leadership and the Leadership Environment

This book focuses on the power and motivation of the central political leaders, whether heads of state or government or both, in liberal democracies and on their interaction with the contemporary leadership environment in which they operate. It uses six detailed chapter-length case studies to illuminate common features and variations in Britain, France, Germany, the United States, Japan and Italy.

It examines the roles of the principal political leaders in these countries – that is, the President in the United States, the head of government in Britain, Germany, Italy and Japan and both the President and the head of government in France – and the ways in which the people who occupy these positions respond to the unique set of institutional, historical and social forces which comprise each country's leadership environment. Each chapter will deal with one country and will identify the dominant pattern of political leadership to be found in that country since 1945. Although each country's dominant leadership pattern is in many ways unique, certain similarities will be identified between three sets of countries: Britain and France; Germany and the United States; and Japan and Italy. The final chapter will construct a comparative picture of these various patterns of leadership and will examine the reasons why these patterns should have occurred.

Before embarking upon the six country chapters, though, it is necessary to set the scene. This chapter will provide an introduction to the study of political leadership in liberal democracies. It consists of four parts. The first part will briefly examine the concept of political leadership. The second part will introduce the interactionist approach to the study of political leadership. The third part will look at

1

political leaders, identifying some of the different ambitions that they exhibit and the ways that they behave in office. The final part will analyse the leadership environment in which political leaders operate, examining the main elements of this environment. Let us begin by looking at the concept of 'political leadership'.

## What is political leadership?

Leadership is the unidentifiable in pursuit of the indefinable. Leadership is unidentifiable in the sense that it has no physical manifestation. It is not an object. It does not have substance in the same manner as the nose on one's face. Political leadership is not the Houses of Parliament, Capitol Hill, or the Elysée Palace. There is no material thing which we can touch or see and then unambiguously declare that we have identified 'leadership'. Instead, 'leadership' is an abstraction. It is a social science concept. It is a concept whose meaning is socially constructed. Individuals may have their own preferred definition of leadership. At best, there may be common agreement that one definition of leadership is better than all others. Whatever the case, 'leadership' is an essentially contested concept. In this sense at least, the concept of 'leadership' is indefinable and closely resembles other related social science concepts, such as 'power', 'influence', authority' and 'control'.

As with these other concepts, 'leadership' has been the subject of considerable theoretical and empirical investigation across a wide range of social science disciplines. Excellent work on leadership has been conducted in the fields of social psychology, education, anthropology, sociology, theology and business studies amongst others. Yet, despite the large amount of work that has been undertaken, there is no consensus of opinion in any of these fields, never mind across all of them, as to which definition of leadership most successfully captures the essence of the term. All told, there are thousands of competing definitions of 'leadership' (Rost, 1991, pp. 37–95). In the field of political science too, a great deal of extremely rewarding work has been undertaken. There are many books and articles which explicitly tackle the concept of political leadership. (See, for example, Blondel, 1980 and 1987; Burns, 1978; Edinger, 1975 and 1990; Gardner, 1990; Kellerman, 1984; Mughan and Patterson, 1992; Paige, 1977; Sheffer, 1993; Stern, 1993; and Tucker, 1981). Needless to say, this work has resulted in the identification of numerous definitions of political leadership. (A few of the more recent ones may be found in Exhibit 1.1.) Once again, though, there is no single, agreed definition of the concept. The essence of leadership remains as difficult to pin down in the context of political science as it does in the context of all the other social sciences.

---

**EXHIBIT 1.1**
**Some definitions of political leadership**

1. ... [T]he behavior of persons in positions of political authority, their competitors, and these both in interaction with other members of society as manifested in the past, present, and probable future throughout the world (Paige, 1977, p. 1).
2. Leadership over human beings is exercised when persons with certain motives and purposes mobilise, in competition or conflict with others, institutional, political, psychological, and other resources so as to arouse, engage, and satisfy the motives of followers (Burns, 1978, p. 18).
3. Leadership is a process of human interaction in which some individuals exert, or attempt to exert, a determining influence upon others (Tucker, 1981, p. 11).
4. [P]olitical leadership is the mobilization and direction, by a person or persons using essentially noncoercive means, of other persons within a society to act in patterned and coherent ways that cause (or prevent) change in the authoritative allocation of values within that society (Hah and Bartol, 1983, pp. 119–20).
5. We can say that leadership is the process by which one individual consistently exerts more impact than others on the nature and direction of group activity (Kellerman, 1984, p. 70).
6. [I]t seems possible to define political leadership ... as the power exercised by one or a few individuals to direct members of the nation towards actions (Blondel, 1987, p. 3).
7. Leadership is an influence relationship among leaders and followers who intend real changes that reflect their mutual purposes (Rost, 1991, p. 102).
8. [Leaders] are persons who exercise control over the behavior of others so as to move them in a desired direction ... (Edinger, 1993, p. 6).

---

Difficult or otherwise, to the extent that this is a book about political leadership, it would appear that a working definition of the concept is needed in order to make sense of its manifestations in the context of liberal democracies. We need to have some idea of what we mean when we refer to the term. This book, though, will not simply offer a new definition of political leadership. In the knowledge that the concept of 'leadership' is essentially contestable, there is little academic value-added to be gained from such an exercise. As Rost has noted, the nature of leadership studies is such that: '[t]he culture allows anyone to give a definition of leadership, and *ipso facto* it is as accurate and acceptable as anyone else's definition' (1991, p. 6). The incremental addition to knowledge of a new definition would be as near to zero as makes no difference.

Neither will this book simply adopt one of the current definitions of political leadership and try to apply it in the context of each of the six country chapters which follow. This is because, as we shall see, there are many different types and forms of political leadership as well as many different arenas in which political leadership must be exercised. Types and forms of political leadership correspond to the manner in which leaders exercise leadership. They include charismatic leadership, heroic leadership, revolutionary leadership, innovative leadership, transforming leadership, transactional leadership, personal leadership, individual leadership, collective leadership, consensual leadership, reactive leadership and managerial leadership. An individual may have to exercise a combination of these different types and forms of political leadership at any one time. In part, this is because political leadership must also be exercised in many different arenas. There is policy leadership, party leadership, Cabinet leadership, legislative leadership, opinion leadership, bureaucratic leadership, judicial leadership, gubernatorial leadership, mayoral leadership and so on. Once again, an individual may have to exercise political leadership in any one or more of these different arenas simultaneously. Consequently, as one writer has noted: 'Even if one definition of leadership were chosen ... the operational meaning of the definition would change depending on the context in which leadership would be exercised' (Hockin, 1977, p. ix). Choosing a single definition would be both arbitrary and restrictive. It would be unable to capture the variations in the types and forms of leadership that have to be exercised across many different arenas simultaneously.

Instead, this book is concerned with political leadership as the process by which governments try to exercise control over public policy decisions (Edinger, 1975, p. 257). Here, political leadership deals with the question of who controls the outcome of public policy decisions within a state and how they do so (Kellerman, 1984, p. 71). In particular, this book focuses on the extent to which heads of state and heads of government, that is, the individuals who occupy the most prominent positions of authority in the state structure, are able to determine the outcome of the decision-making process. Are they able to shape this process, or is it shaped by forces above and beyond their control? Can they innovate, or do they react? Can they set the government's agenda, or is it set for them? Can they exercise individual leadership, or is leadership collective? Are leadership responsibilities centralised in the office of the President or Prime Minister, or are they shared between either or both of these institutions and others in the wider political system? These are the central questions with which this book is concerned.

## The interactionist approach to the study of political leadership

In addressing these questions, this book assumes that political leaders do matter. It assumes that individuals do make a difference and that they are able to shape the course of the decision-making process. However, this book does not assume that individuals have complete freedom to shape policy outcomes. Instead, it takes as its basic assumption that all leaders are constrained in the extent to which they able to act freely. As such, it adopts an interactionist approach to the study of political leadership.

In the nineteenth century, there was a debate as to the role played by the individual in the historical process. (For an overview, see Taras and Weyant, 1991, pp. 3–5.) One contributor to this debate was the historian, Thomas Carlyle. He was associated with the so-called 'Great Man' school of political leadership (see Exhibit 1.2). Carlyle argued that great leaders were able to change the course of history. They were the agents of social and political change. He depicted them as being people who were morally good and who were endowed with such special personal qualities that they would necessarily triumph against any odds. In this way, nothing could prevent them from exercising political leadership. They were heroes. Needless to say, there were problems with Carlyle's theory. By implication, it excluded the impact of 'Great Women'. It glossed over the question of what was meant by a 'morally good' action. It assumed the existence of God. More importantly, in the context of this study at least, it exaggerated the influence that individuals exerted on the course of events. In the context of modern liberal democracies, with all their complex interplay of institutional, historical and social forces, political leaders are not simply free to act as they would wish. They operate within the confines of a system where their freedom of action is bounded by other factors.

---

**EXHIBIT 1.2**
**The 'Great Man' theory of history**

Thomas Carlyle, writing in 1840:

Universal History, the history of what man has accomplished in this world, is at bottom the History of the Great Men who have worked here. They were the leaders of men, these great ones; the modellers, patterns, and in a wide sense creators, of whatsoever the general mass of men contrived to do or attain; all things that we see standing accomplished in the world are properly the outer material result, the practical realisation and embodiment, of Thoughts that dwelt in the Great Men sent into the world: the soul of the whole world's history, it may justly be considered, were the history of these (reproduced in Kellerman, 1986, p. 5).

According to Carlyle:

1. Some people are born great. Greatness is an innate God-given quality.
2. Such people are objectively great. It is not just that everyone thinks they are great.
3. Their greatness enables them to change the course of history.
4. They change the course of history for the good. They are moral people.

---

Yet, to admit that political leaders are bounded is not necessarily to conclude that they have no freedom of action at all. In the nineteenth century, cultural (or social) determinists, such as Herbert Spencer; set themselves up in opposition to writers such as Thomas Carlyle. Cultural determinists denied that individuals had any significant impact on the course of events (see Exhibit 1.3). They argued that the course of history was determined by the impersonal interplay of social and cultural forces over which individuals had little control. Individual leaders were the product of the times in which they lived. They simply symbolised and reflected the social forces around them. The leadership environment in which they operated shaped their actions, leaving them with little or no opportunity to make a personal impact on historical events. However, as with the 'Great Man' school of history, the cultural determinist school was ultimately unfulfilling. It implied that individuals were powerless and that all people would act in the same way if they were faced with the same situation. The basic problem with both approaches was that they were reductionist. The former assumed that only the individual was important to the historical and political process. The latter assumed that the individual was unimportant and that the changes leaders appeared to bring about were really the result of the interplay of impersonal social processes (Katz, 1973, p. 208).

---

**EXHIBIT 1.3**
**The cultural determinist school of history**

Herbert Spencer, writing in 1873:

If it be a fact that the great man may modify his nation in its structure and actions, it is also a fact that there must have been these antecedent modifications constituting national progress before he could be evolved. Before he can re-make his society, his society must make him. So that all those changes of which he is the proximate initiator have their chief causes in the generations he descended from. If there is to be anything like a real explanation of these changes, it must be sought in the aggregate of conditions out of which both he and they have arisen.

Even were we to grant the absurd supposition that the genesis of the great man does not depend on the antecedents furnished by the society he is born in, there would still be quite-sufficient facts that he is powerless in the absence of the material and mental accumulations which his society inherits from the past, and that he is powerless in the absence of the co-existing population, character, intelligence, and social arrangements (reproduced in Kellerman, 1986, pp. 13–14).

---

The study of political leadership is more complex than either of these reductionist approaches would suggest. The nineteenth-century debate evolved until there was general agreement on a slightly more refined approach. Now, leadership theorists are interactionists (Greenstein, 1992). That is to say, the extent to which political leaders are able to influence the decision-making process is considered to be contingent upon the interaction between the leader and the leadership environment in which the leader operates. How political leadership is exercised depends on the nature of this interaction (see Greenstein, 1992, p. 115). As Sheffer notes:

Most people still believe that leadership qualities are connected to personal attributes, and hence that leadership is a very individual-istic phenomenon. But most scholars in this area agree that in addition to personal attributes, leadership is intimately related to the fabric of the leaders' relevant societies, to social and political organizations, to established institutions, and to leaders' relations with smaller and larger groups of followers (Sheffer, 1993, p. vii).

That is to say, on the one hand, leaders have certain ambitions and they behave in certain ways. It is this personal aspect of the leadership process which is captured by Carlyle's theory. Leaders may have a vision to transform the environment in which they operate and they may even succeed in reforming institutional structures and changing political attitudes. On the other hand, though, the leadership environment consists of relatively fixed institutional structures, long-term historical and social conditions and short-term social, economic and political demands. It is this systemic aspect of the leadership process which is captured by the cultural determinist approach. The interactionist approach combines the personal and systemic aspects of the leadership process. It implies that political leaders operate within an environment which will both structure their behaviour and constrain their freedom of action. At the same time, it also implies that political leaders do have the opportunity to shape the environment in which they operate, so giving them the potential to leave their mark upon the system (see Figure 1.1). Consequently, leaders may change the course of history, but only if and to the degree that the environment permits it. In the context of this study, it will be shown that Presidents and Prime Ministers are able to influence the decision-making process, but only in the ways that and to the extent that the leadership environment allows. Let us now examine the two aspects of the interactionist approach: political leaders and the leadership environment.

FIGURE 1.1   The interactionist approach to political leadership

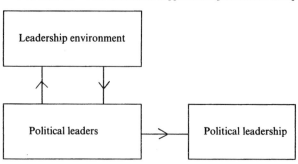

*Source:* Adapted from Greenstein, 1992, p. 109.

**Political leaders**

Political leaders are individuals and, as such, each leader is unique. On assuming office, the leader brings to the job a set of emotions, cognitions and predispositions, which is different from that of his or her predecessor. The individuality of these clusters of personality traits means that each leader has the potential to affect the outcome of the policy process in a different way. There is the possibility that a change of leader will bring about a change in the nature of the governmental decision-making process. It is partly for this reason that voters are sometimes motivated to place their trust in new leaders. There is the belief that a new leader may be better suited to cope with the prevailing leadership environment. There may be a better 'fit' between the personality of the new leader and the environment with which the leader is faced. Nevertheless, despite the uniqueness of each individual, it is still possible to generalise about the impact of the personality of different political leaders upon the decision-making process. There are sufficient similarities between individuals to identify some of the various kinds of ambitions that leaders exhibit and the various ways in which they behave. Let us look at both points.

*The ambitions of political leaders*

Different leaders have different kinds of ambitions. They have different kinds of aims, or goals, that they wish to fulfil. In particular, leaders vary in both the focus and the scope of their ambitions. These variations have the potential to affect the outcome of the decision-making process. For example, individual leaders may focus their attention on certain aspects of this process at the expense of others. It may be that some leaders will concentrate on the procedural aspects of government, ensuring that the business of government runs smoothly, whereas others will be more policy-oriented (Blondel and Müller-Rommel, 1993, p. 14). Moreover, some Presidents and Prime Ministers may naturally steer a course towards 'high' politics and away from 'low' politics. 'High' politics includes areas such as defence and foreign policy as well as matters such as constitutional reform. These areas reinforce the statecraft aspect of the leader's role. They emphasise the difference between the status of Presidents and Prime Ministers and that of the other members of the government. They also usually provide good photo opportunities and the chance to escape the low-life intrigue of party politics. Still, whether they organise or innovate and whether or not they prefer 'high' to 'low' politics, political leaders vary in the focus of their ambitions.

What is more, they also vary in the scope of their ambitions. There are differences in the extent of the policy change that political leaders wish to bring about both within and between different leadership arenas. We are most familiar with 'great' leaders who aspire to leave their mark on all aspects of the domestic political system and even on the world system. Such leaders have a particular vision that they wish to fulfil, or a programme of policy proposals that they wish to implement. They are all innovators. Not all leaders, though, wish to bring about such a great degree of change. Some leaders may have a more restricted set of aims. They may be more policy-neutral and less reformist. In between these two extremes, there are the adjusters (Blondel, 1987, pp. 87–96) or parameter-setters. Such leaders modify policies only to a limited extent and often in a restricted set of areas. As Blondel notes: '[t]hey are agents of moderate change within the context of a more specialized area' (1987, p. 95). In the sense that different kinds of leaders vary in terms of the focus and scope of their ambitions, then the same country may experience different types and forms of political leadership at different times in different arenas simply as a result of a change from one leader to another. In the chapters which follow, some of the ways in which the ambitions of leaders impact upon the leadership process will be identified. In the final chapter, the extent to which these ambitions are determined by the leadership environment in general and by the structure of political resources in particular will be examined.

*The styles of political leaders*

Political leaders differ not only in the focus and scope of their ambitions, but also in the ways in which they try to bring these ambitions about. Although every individual is unique, it is still possible to identify similarities between the kinds of ways that different political leaders behave in office. It is possible to generalise about the behaviour of political leaders and to identify particular leadership styles. These styles may be identified from empirical observations about a person's behaviour in office or they may be constructed on the basis of an individual's total life history using an explicit theory of personality (psychobiography). Whichever methodology is adopted, a leader's style may have an impact upon the decision-making process. In this way, governmental decisions are at least in part a function of the different kinds of leadership styles that political leaders exhibit.

The most basic way of differentiating between leadership styles is to establish a dichotomy of leadership behaviour. In its most rudimentary form, this might involve distinguishing between, say, uncompromising leaders and malleable leaders. That is to say, between those leaders who are habitually willing to fight their corner and those who are willing to cede. In a similar vein, Dennis Kavanagh has distinguished between mobilising and expressive leaders (Kavanagh, 1990, p. 247). The former are said to emphasise decision-making and task-performance, even at the risk of alienating colleagues. The latter emphasise cohesion and the maintenance of the *status quo*, representing and responding to diverse interests. A rather more complex typology has been devised by James David Barber and applied to the character of US Presidents (Barber, 1977). He distinguished between Presidents who had active–positive, active–negative, passive–positive and passive–negative characters (see Exhibit 1.4). He argued that leadership style depended on which type of character Presidents possessed.

It must be appreciated that there are certain methodological problems with Barber's typology (George, 1974). For example, he made the assumption that the presidential character is formed before the person in question comes to office, so Presidents cannot move from one leadership style, say, passive–positive, to another, say, active–positive, during their term in office. As a result, Barber's theory is quite restrictive. On the basis of the same assumption, Barber also made the argument that it was possible to predict presidential behaviour in office with active–positive characters being able to provide the best type of leadership. Needless to say, this argument is highly contentious and has not always been confirmed in practice. Despite these problems, Barber's approach still indicates that different kinds of leaders behave in different ways and illustrates that it is possible to generalise about particular behavioural styles.

The ability to generalise about leadership styles does not imply that there is a single style of leadership that is bound to be successful in any place at any time (Clarke, 1991, p. 331). For example, assertive leaders may mobilise followers at certain times and then alienate them at

---

**EXHIBIT 1.4**
**Barber's typology of the presidential character**

Barber proposed two baselines by which to classify Presidents:

1. Activity/passivity concerns the degree of energy which a person invests in the presidency. Active Presidents are more energetic than passive Presidents.
2. Positivity/negativity concerns how Presidents feel about their actions. Positive Presidents feel better about them than negative Presidents.

These two baselines combine to form four cells:

|  | *Active* | *Passive* |
|---|---|---|
| *Positive* | Active-positive | Passive-positive |
| *Negative* | Active-negative | Passive-negative |

To determine the cell in which a President should be placed, it is necessary to examine that person's character, world-view and style. Character is mainly developed in childhood, world-view in adolescence and style in early adulthood. So, the essential components of the presidential personality are fixed before coming to office. Consequently, it is possible to predict presidential behaviour by studying events in early life and by identifying the personality that is formed by them.

*Examples*:

| | |
|---|---|
| Active-positive: | Franklin D. Roosevelt, Harry Truman, John Kennedy, Gerald Ford and Jimmy Carter. |
| Active-negative: | Woodrow Wilson, Herbert Hoover, Lyndon Johnson and Richard Nixon. |
| Passive-positive: | William Taft, Warren Harding and Ronald Reagan. |
| Passive-negative: | Calvin Coolidge and Dwight D. Eisenhower. |

---

others. Responsive leaders may sometimes appear weak and lose support, but at other times they may be able to construct wide-ranging coalitions of support. Similarly, generalising about leadership styles does not imply that leaders exhibit a single leadership style across the many different arenas of political leadership. For instance, leaders may find it necessary to adopt a more uncompromising style in their relations with party activists than with Cabinet members. Instead, the ability to generalise about leadership styles simply implies that regular patterns of leadership behaviour are identifiable. In the chapters which follow, various such patterns will be identified. Again, in the final chapter, the extent to which these styles are determined by the nature of the leadership enviroment and by the structure of political resources will be examined.

## The leadership environment

Presidents and Prime Ministers operate within a framework of complex institutional structures, historical forces and societal demands. These institutions, forces and demands collectively comprise the leadership environment. This section briefly identifies the major elements of the leadership environment and examines the sorts of resources and constraints with which Presidents and Prime Ministers are faced. In so doing, it will introduce many of the themes and issues which will be encountered in the chapters to come. It will also set the scene for the theoretical discussion to be found in the final chapter in which the institutional foundations of leadership will be examined.

Although there are various ways to classify the different elements of the leadership environment (for previous examples, see, *inter alia*, Cole, 1994; Elgie, 1993b; King, 1993; Müller, 1993; Rockman, 1988; Rose, 1991; Vickers and Wright, 1988; and Weaver and Rockman, 1993), in this section the principal elements of the leadership environment will be grouped under two separate headings: institutional structures and the needs of the society. Let us look at each in turn.

### Institutional structures

As we shall see throughout the book, institutions play a major part in determining how political leadership is exercised. As Blondel notes, leadership is 'in part *the product* of office holding' (Blondel, 1987, p. 14). Indeed, in the final chapter, it will be argued that institutional structures are the most important aspect of the leadership process, partly determining the ambitions and styles of political leaders and mediating the impact of societal needs upon the decision-making process. At this point, though, in order to set the scene, we will simply identify which institutional aspects of the polity are important in determining the leadership process. In this context, it is useful to look at three aspects of institutional structures: the structure of resources within the executive branch of the central government; the structure of resources between this branch of government and the other branches and levels of government; and the structure of resources within and between political parties. Let us look at each aspect in turn.

• *The structure of resources within the executive branch of the central government*

The ways in which and the extent to which Presidents and Prime Ministers can influence the decision-making process is at least partly dependent upon the structure of resources within the executive branch of the central government. In the chapters which follow, this aspect of the leadership process will be a particular focus of attention. In order to introduce some of the main elements of enquiry in these chapters, it is useful to identify four elements which provide these leaders with potential resources and constraints.

**1.** The structure of resources within the executive is affected by the ways in which leaders both assume and leave office. In terms of how leaders assume office, the main distinction is between popular election and parliamentary approval. In presidential systems, where leaders are directly elected by universal suffrage, Presidents benefit from an undisputed popular authority, which helps to personalise the leadership process within the executive. By contrast, in parliamentary systems, where heads of government assume office by virtue of having the support of a parliamentary majority, the authority of the leader is dependent on the nature of this majority (see the party aspect below). It may be that in these systems the leadership process is as personalised as in presidential systems. However, it may also be that some leaders in parliamentary systems do not enjoy a personal authority and that they are less well-placed to exercise leadership. In terms of how leaders leave office, a distinction can again be made between presidential and parliamentary systems. Presidents enjoy a fixed term of office and can only be dismissed by impeachment. This security of tenure means that they can concentrate on the policy process and, where appropriate, on securing their re-election. By contrast, heads of government remain in office only for as long as they retain the support of a parliamentary majority. In some cases, because of constitutional or party reasons, their security of tenure may be relatively assured and they too may concentrate on the policy process. In other cases, though, because of similar reasons, their hold on power may be tenuous and their energies may be spent on manœuvring to remain in office, rather than on controlling the policy process. In the chapters which follow, the consequences of the ways in which leaders assume and leave office will be examined in particular detail.

**2.** The leadership process is affected by the distribution of constitutional and procedural powers. Constitutions establish disparities of power within political systems. They institutionalise formal sets of resources and constraints. In this respect, while they affect the structure of resources within the executive branch of government, they structure the leadership process outside this domain as well. Nevertheless, within the executive, leaders may be in a position to benefit from constitutional resources or they may be limited by constitutional constraints. In addition, executives develop formal sets of procedural rules. These rules permit the executive to develop an institutional memory. They ensure that there is a continuity to the governing process. A head of government's constitutional and procedural resources might include the right to appoint and dismiss Ministers, or to set the agenda of Cabinet. Constraints might include the provision for ministerial control of departmental decision-making, or for the Cabinet to have to ratify governmental decisions before they pass to the legislature. In these ways and many others, constitutional and procedural rules help to structure the relationship between the principal political leader, individual Ministers, and the government collectively. In some countries, formal leadership responsibilities will be personalised in the office of the President or Prime Minister. In others, they will be compartmentalised among the various Ministers. In yet others, they will collectivised in the Cabinet. It must be appreciated that neither constitutional nor procedural rules are always specific in their distribution of powers and that they are not always an accurate guide to political practice. As a general rule, though, the greater and more specific the constitutional and procedural powers that Presidents and Prime Ministers enjoy, the more likely it is that they will be able to control the decision-making process.

3. The distribution of power within the executive is partly affected by both the staff resources of Presidents and Prime Ministers and their relationship with the permanent administration. In terms of the former, there is no clear correlation between staff size and the ability to exercise leadership (King, 1993, p. 435). This is not to say, though, that staff size and organisation is unimportant. A leader who enjoys only a meagre administrative back-up may not be in a position to manage the decision-making process. Similarly, a leader who heads a large personal staff may have to spend time controlling its many members at the expense of wider governmental matters. In this way, staff size and its organisation are factors in the policy process, but the way that they matter needs to be investigated in each country.

In terms of the wider administration, it is necessary to consider the extent to which the bureaucracy has an input into the decision-making process. When the input of permanent administrators is high, it is usually at the expense of elected representatives. The degree of input varies across countries according to administrative cultures and the organisation of the bureaucracy. Again, where appropriate, both factors will be analysed in the chapters which follow.

4.  The structure of resources within the executive is partly dependent on the international position of the country in question. Presidents and Prime Ministers will be provided with certain resources and constraints on the basis of their country's military and economic power (Rockman, 1988, p. 56). This is because the nature of such power helps to determine the role that leaders play on the world stage, which, in turn, helps to determine the role that they play domestically. For example, Presidents and Prime Ministers whose countries possess nuclear weapons and who are themselves either the *de jure* or the *de facto* commander-in-chief are bound to enjoy a greater political stature than any other person in the executive. This point does not mean that the leaders of such countries are bound to be popular. It simply means that they are obliged to take strategic decisions which have profound domestic and international implications. Consequently, attention will be focused on them at the expense of other actors within the executive. It might be noted that all six countries in this book enjoy the status of being a considerable military and/or economic power. In this sense, their principal political leaders all enjoy a greater degree of status and prestige than any of their colleagues in the executive and than many of their counterparts in other countries. Nevertheless, as we shall see, there are variations across the six countries to be studied and these variations have implications for the ways in which they influence the policy-making process.

• *The structure of resources between the executive branch of the central government and other branches and levels of government*
Just as the structure of resources within the executive branch of the central government helps to determine the ways in which and the extent to which Presidents and Prime Ministers influence the decision-making process, so too does the structure of resources between this branch of government and the other branches and levels of government. In this respect, it is necessary to focus on three particular

elements: executive/legislative relations; the role of the courts; and the powers of subcentral units of government.

1. How Presidents and Prime Ministers exercise leadership is at least partly determined by the relationship between the executive and legislative branches of the central government. One aspect of this relationship has already been considered, namely, whether or not the legislature has the right to dismiss the principal political leader in a country. In some countries, there are constitutional provisions that make it comparatively difficult for the legislature to do so. In others, the task is rather easier. In any case, Anthony King has demonstrated that executive/legislative relations are often determined more by intra- and inter-party politics (see below), than by any formal arrangements (King, 1976). Still, the decision-making process will be affected by factors, such as the powers of legislative committees, or whether there is one working legislative chamber or two. Where appropriate, the country chapters will briefly outline the formal relationship between the executive and the legislature. One related matter of importance is the type of electoral system which is used for parliamentary elections. Although there is no causal link between the type of electoral system and the form of political leadership in a country, the electoral system may create incentives for political leaders to behave in certain ways. Again, in the chapters which follow, these incentives will be examined.

2. The role of the courts may impact upon the leadership process. In this respect, the role of the Supreme Court, or the equivalent institution, needs to be considered. In the situation where the Supreme Court is able to strike down legislation through a process of judicial review, then political leaders in the executive branch of government will not be free to shape the content of laws in any way that they may wish. In this sense, such courts may have an important role to play in the policy process and may act as an important constraint on political leaders. The reverse is also true. Where there is no process of judicial review, or where the process exists but has not yet developed into an institutionalised procedure of redress, then the Supreme Court will have a less important role to play in the policy process and political leaders will be less constrained. Consequently, amongst the factors which will be examined in the chapters which follow are the ways in which and the extent to which Supreme Courts are able to restrict the freedom of choice of political leaders.

3. It is necessary to examine the relationship between central and

subcentral units of government. In this respect, a basic distinction may be drawn between federal, regional and unitary systems (see Exhibit 1.5). In federal systems, where a considerable degree of autonomy is granted to subcentral units of government, political leaders at the central level are potentially restricted. For example, there may be certain policy areas in which they are not free to legislate. In such areas, policy-making may be the sole responsibility of representatives at the subcentral level. By contrast, in unitary systems, where sovereign subcentral units of government are absent, no such restrictions exist. In these systems, subcentral units of government only enjoy the powers which have granted to them by the central units of government. These powers may be rescinded at any time. In addition, there are also countries which have a system of regional government. In such systems, there are elected assemblies which sometimes have not considerable policy-making prerogatives over their territorial area. These preogatives may be constitutionally guaranteed, or they may be granted to the regional government by the central government. Whatever the case, in systems of regional government, subcentral decision-makers enjoy a degree of decision-making autonomy. Although there are different degrees and kinds of federal, regional and unitary systems, these points suggest that, as a general rule, the constraints faced by Presidents and Prime Ministers in federal systems are greater than those faced by equivalent leaders in regional systems and that the same is true for leaders in both federal and regional systems when compared with unitary systems.

---

**EXHIBIT 1.5**
**The distinction between federal, regional and unitary systems**

| | |
|---|---|
| *Federal systems* | The situation where legal sovereignty is constitutionally shared between the institutions of government at the central, or federal level, and the institutions of government at the subcentral level. |
| | Examples: Canada, Germany, Switzerland, United States. |
| *Regional systems* | These systems represent a mixed form of decentralised government, the existence of which is often constitutionally guaranteed, but the powers of which may be found either in the Constitution, or in an organic law. |
| | Examples: Italy, Portugal and Spain. |
| *Unitary systems* | The situation where legal sovereignty is constitutionally reserved for the political authorities at the central level. |
| | Examples: Britain, France, Greece, the Republic of Ireland. |

• *The structure of resources within and between political parties*
The impact of many of the different elements considered above
depends on the structure of resources within and between political
parties. For one observer at least, political parties provide the most
important resource that political leaders may potentially possess
(Jones, G. W., 1991, p. 164). Factors such as whether the Constitution presents an accurate picture of the distribution of power
within the executive, or whether the legislature acts as a general check
on the executive are all at least in part determined by the nature of
party competition. This point holds as true for countries where
parties are strongly institutionalised political actors as it does for
those countries where political parties are weak. In the former, parties
are a motive force in the operation of the political system whether for
good or for bad. In the latter, party activity is not absent, but its
comparative lack of salience means that the nature of political leadership is structured differently. As with the two previously mentioned
aspects of a country's institutional resources, the importance of
political parties will be considered in particular detail in the chapters
which follow. Its importance can be demonstrated in whether or not
the principal political leader is also a party leader; in the organisation of political parties; and in the level of party support in the
legislature.
   1.  How political leadership is exercised depends partly on
whether or not the principal political leader is also a party leader. In
the cases where Presidents or Prime Ministers are also the undisputed
leaders of their own political parties, then they will possess a key
leadership resource. In these cases, other party members, most cru-
cially those in the governmental and parliamentary arenas, are likely
to defer to their party leader and follow the direction that the leader
sets. In the most extreme case, if a President or Prime Minister is also
the historic leader of his or her own party, then the degree of deference is likely to be greater still. By contrast, in the cases where
Presidents or Prime Ministers are not party leaders, then they will face
a key constraint. In these cases, there are likely to be competing
centres of power in the system and political leadership will be a much
more complex process. Leaders may need to change their ambitions,
or manifest a different style. For these reasons, the relationship
between the principal political leader and his or her party will be a
common theme in the chapters which follow.
   2.  Whether or not the President or Prime Minister is also a party

leader, the nature of his or her leadership will depend on the organisational structure of that party. In this respect, the degree of both
party unity and cohesion are determining factors. Certain parties are
more unified than others. For example, some parties take the form of
unified 'rally' parties, which operate as electoral machines for the
benefit of the party leader. Other parties take the form of disunited,
factional parties, whose component parts are in little less than out-
right competition with each other. Although there are many variations between these two extremes, other things being equal, unified
'rally' parties act as a greater resource for political leaders than do
factional parties. Certain parties are also more cohesive than others.
For example, in the parliamentary arena, the total membership of
some party groups votes almost always *en bloc*, whereas the members
of other party groups vote more individually. Again, although there
are variations between these two extremes, the more cohesive parties
act as a greater resource for political leaders than do the more
individual parties.

3.    The level of party support in the legislature also determines
how leadership is exercised. In parliamentary systems, it is of fundamental importance whether the government enjoys majority or minority support in the legislature and whether the government consists
of a single party or a coalition of parties (Frognier, 1993). Leaders
who head majority governments are generally better placed than
leaders who head minority governments. In addition, leaders who
head single-party governments are generally better placed than leaders who head coalition governments. The latter tend to act more as a
board of management with party representatives conducting jointly
the affairs of state (Blondel and Müller-Rommel, 1993, p. 7). In
presidential systems, it is important whether or not the President's
party also controls the legislature. The likelihood of presidential
leadership is at least partly dependent on whether the presidential and
legislative majorities are congruent. In all these ways, the structure of
resources both within and between political parties helps to shape the
ambitions and behaviour of political leaders and to determine the
outcome of the decision-making process.

### The needs of the society

In the final chapter, it will be argued that institutional structures are
the key factor which determines the outcome of the leadership pro-

cess. Nevertheless, it will also be demonstrated that this process is inpart affected by the second aspect of the leadership environment, namely, the needs of the society. This term refers to a set of elements:

1. the historical baggage which leaders inherit;
2. the received social attitudes which they face;
3. the ever-changing set of popular desires to which they have to respond.

Needless to say, all three elements provide political leaders with potential resources and constraints. The general configuration of the first two elements may create an environment which is either relatively favourable or unfavourable for the exercise of leadership. The changing nature of the third element means that a political leader who holds office for a sufficiently long amount of time will be faced with circumstances which are both propitious and problematic for leadership. Let us briefly consider these three elements.

• *Historical legacy*
Political leaders operate within systems which have a history and a set of traditions that shape the outcomes of the decision-making process. For example, history feeds into the institutional environment which leaders face (King, 1994, pp. 159–61). In democracies that have recently experienced authoritarian regimes, political leaders are likely to face formal limits to their powers as a way of preventing such regimes from reoccurring. By contrast, in democracies which have recently experienced unstable governmental systems, political leaders may benefit from reforms that make governing easier. At a more general level, history also shapes both popular and élite behaviour. It opens up and closes off certain avenues of action by instilling behavioural norms amongst both the set of political leaders and the population as a whole. If a country has a tradition of 'great' leaders, there will be pressure for the current set of leaders to emulate the actions of their political predecessors. If a country has a 'revolutionary' tradition, popular attitudes may be more sceptical of political leaders and less amenable to personal rule. While it is undoubtedly the case that the strength of short-term popular desires may remove or at least temporarily shift the weight of history (see below) it remains the case that historical factors structure the outcomes of the decision-making process.

• *Societal attitudes*

There are two main ways in which societal attitudes impact upon the process of political leadership.

1. Societal attitudes are expressed through the partisan affiliation of the electorate. The leadership process is affected by the structure of such partisan affiliation. Needless to say, this aspect is closely linked to the points relating to political parties considered above. Nevertheless, it is useful to appreciate that the nature of party competition in the governmental arena flows at least partly from the distribution of partisan support in the country as a whole. For example, in certain countries partisan affiliation is divided on a class basis into two relatively impervious blocks of support: a bourgeois block and a socialist block. Such systems are likely to be reflected in an adversarial decision-making process. In other countries, partisan affiliation is more fragmented. In these systems, the decision-making process may result in a greater degree of consensual decision-making procedures. Moreover, to the extent that party identification is relatively unchanging (Lipset and Rokkan, 1967) these patterns of decision-making will also be relatively fixed. This is not to say that partisan identification is either immutable or totally inclusive of all the population. Partisan affiliation can change and there will always be floating voters whose support may be decisive in determining both the outcome of an election and the subsequent course of political leadership. It is simply to say that the structure of partisan affiliation is an important determinant of the leadership process and will be one focus of consideration in the chapters which follow.

2. Societal attitudes are also expressed through interest group activity. The leadership process may be affected by the nature of such activity in a country. For example, in some countries, interest groups may be formally included in the governmental decision-making process. They may be consulted by governmental representatives on a regular, ongoing basis. This integrative process means that political leaders will be obliged at least to listen to the demands of interest group representatives. At most, this process may mean that their room to manœuvre in certain areas of decision-making will be restricted. By contrast, in other countries, interest groups may operate outside the formal decision-making process. Their impact may be sectoral and sporadic. Political leaders may take notice of interest group demands only when the costs of not doing so become too high. In both sets of countries, interest groups may have a potentially

significant impact on the decision-making process. When this is the case in the six 'country' chapters which follow, then their role will be examined.

• *Popular desires*
One of the main tasks of political leaders is to respond to any short-term, popular desires which might arise within the system. It is impossible to give a full list of such desires as they may take many different forms. It is possible to state, though, that they may create a leadership environment which either helps or hinders leaders in their attempts to control the decision-making process. For example, short-term desires caused by a threat to the domestic polity from an external source may personalise the decision-making process. The threat of invasion and war creates a climate of collective fear to which leaders have to respond. Such a threat may create a window of opportunity for a particular political leader to propose a substantial package of constitutional, or policy reforms (Keeler, 1993a). By contrast, short-term problems caused by economic recession, or social unrest may disempower political leaders. They may be obliged to shelve reforms, or to abandon them altogether. Although there is no consistent pattern to such examples, the general point remains that popular desires provide the system with a dynamic which has the potential to alter the relatively fixed forms of leadership to be found in a country (Elgie, 1993b, pp. 185–9). In this respect, where such desires have influenced the decision-making process in the six countries to be considered, then their impact will be examined.

**Conclusion**

Political leadership is the product of the interaction between leaders and the leadership environment with which they are faced. On the one hand, political leaders are motivated by particular ambitions and their actions are guided by certain modes of behaviour. On the other hand, the leadership environment is comprised of many interlinked elements, which may be either mutually reinforcing or countervailing and which can be classified under two headings: institutional structures; and the needs of the society. Leaders are able to shape their environment, but the environment will also shape their ambitions and behaviour. The extent to which and the ways in which the one shapes the other is dependent on the precise nature of the interaction process. In particular, it is dependent upon the set of elements under the heading of institutional structures. The reasons as to why this should be the case will form the focus of the theoretical discussion in the final chapter. In the meantime, though, it is necessary to examine the process of political leadership in six liberal democracies. In the chapters which follow, the dominant leadership pattern in each country will be identified. Although each country's pattern of leadership is essentially unique, the reader will be able to identify similarities between three sets of countries: Britain and France; Germany and the United States, and Japan and Italy. Let us now turn to these countries and examine how political leadership is exercised in each.

# 2

# Britain:
# Prime Ministerial
# Leadership

In Britain, the leadership environment displaces leadership responsibilities upon the head of government, the Prime Minister. In part, this situation results from the distribution of institutional resources between the executive branch of the central government and the other branches and levels of British government and the partisan affiliation of the electorate. In a highly centralised state, with no provision for the judicial review of the constitutionality of legislation and where governments frequently enjoy a disciplined parliamentary majority, those in the executive branch are free from certain constraints and benefit from potentially significant resources. However, this situation also results from the distribution of institutional resources within the executive branch of the central government itself. Here, leadership responsibilities are concentrated upon the head of government. Although the British executive consists of 'a complex web' (Dunleavy and Rhodes, 1990, p. 3) of coordinating institutions, the Prime Minister occupies a key position within the overall structure. Again, the absence of certain constraints and the presence of certain potentially significant resources ensures that the Prime Minister has consistently been the central actor in the British political system. In this sense, Britain has tended to exhibit a form of prime ministerial leadership. (For a list of British Prime Ministers since 1945, see Exhibit 2.1.)

In this chapter, the nature of the British leadership environment will be examined. The first section identifies the major elements which combine to displace power onto the executive branch of government. It looks at the role of local government, the judiciary and the legis-

25

**EXHIBIT 2.1**
**British Prime Ministers and their parties since 1945**

| Prime Minister | Party | Office |
|---|---|---|
| Clement Attlee | Labour | 1945–51 |
| Winston Churchill | Conservative | 1951–55 |
| Anthony Eden | Conservative | 1955–57 |
| Harold Macmillan | Conservative | 1957–63 |
| Alec Douglas Home | Conservative | 1963–64 |
| Harold Wilson | Labour | 1964–70 |
| Edward Heath | Conservative | 1970–74 |
| Harold Wilson | Labour | 1974–76 |
| Jim Callaghan | Labour | 1976–79 |
| Margaret Thatcher | Conservative | 1979–90 |
| John Major | Conservative | 1990– |

lature. The second section examines the role of the Prime Minister within the executive. It will be demonstrated that the institutional structure of British politics have established a tendency towards prime ministerial government. However, it will also be demonstrated that the degree of prime ministerial power is never either absolute or constant. The tendency towards prime ministerial government is counterbalanced by the nature of the relationship which the Prime Minister enjoys with the Cabinet, individual Ministers and the party. The shifting nature of these relationships ensures that there is a dynamic element within the British system.

**The displacement of power onto the executive branch of government**

*A unitary and centralised state*

Britain is a unitary and highly centralised state. In contrast to federal systems, such as Germany and the United States, where there are subcentral units of government which have their own set of constitutionally guaranteed powers, in Britain, sovereignty resides in the Westminster Parliament at the central level. In Britain, there is an essentially asymmetrical constitutional relationship between central and subcentral units of government. The dominant feature of this relationship is the doctrine of *ultra vires*. According to this principle, subcentral governments can only exercise the powers which have been explicitly granted to them by an Act of Parliament. If they go beyond these powers, then their actions may be declared unlawful (or *ultra vires*) by the courts. The unitary nature of the British state and the doctrine of *ultra vires* creates a territorial distribution of power which is highly unequal. It means that the remit of political leaders at the central level is constitutionally unbounded by the prerogatives of leaders at the subcentral level.

In practice, the unitary British state is also highly centralised. Subcentral units of government have traditionally been granted few independent policy-making powers. Instead, they have largely been responsible for the administration of local services, such as education, health and public transport. Even then, their responsibilities have been further constrained by the regulatory and financial controls imposed upon them by the central government. The effect of this central/subcentral government relationship was to create a 'dual polity', or the 'state of affairs in which national and local polities were largely divorced from one another' (Bulpitt, 1983, p. 235). In the dual polity, the central government was responsible for matters of 'high' politics, such as foreign affairs, defence, taxation and the general framework of welfare policy. By contrast, subcentral government was responsible for matters of 'low' politics, such as the delivery of local welfare services. In this system, although local authorities still had a degree of control over how such services were delivered, strategic decision-making functions were incumbent on those at the central level. In this respect, leadership responsibilities were centralised.

Over time, the degree of centralisation in the British state has increased even further. The dual polity model of central/subcentral government relations has gradually broken down and the distinction between 'high' and 'low' politics has blurred. In order to control the conduct of 'high' politics, central government has found it increasingly necessary to control the conduct of 'low' politics as well. As early as 1979, Lagroye and Wright concluded that the degree of centralisation was so great that the powers of subcentral government belonged to a 'residual domain' of areas which local authorities had managed to preserve against 'marauding and malevolent' encroachments by the central government (Lagroye and Wright 1979, p. 5). Then, from 1979 to 1990, the Thatcher government linked local expenditure with national decisions (Rhodes, 1987, p. 34) even more explicitly that any of its predecessors. In particular, the independent revenue-raising powers of local authorities were decreased and public-sector functions were off-loaded onto the private sector. The net result was an increased politicisation of local politics, an increased nationalisation of the political process and an increased centralisation of leadership responsibilities.

### The absence of constitutional review of statute law

Within the British constitutional system, the principle of parliamentary sovereignty is dominant. Until recently, this principle was very explicit. It meant that Parliament had the right to make, amend or repeal any law whatsoever. No Parliament could bind its successors. There was no written Constitution, or list of inalienable human rights, which limited the law-making powers of the legislative branch of government. The British judiciary had no power to review the constitutionality of statute law. Partly as a consequence, there was (and still is) no British equivalent of the US Supreme Court, or the French, German, Japanese and Italian Constitutional Courts. However, this is not to imply that the judiciary has played an unimportant role in the British system (Drewry, 1992). In particular, judges have been called upon to make common law, to interpret statute law and to determine the legality of the discretionary powers of government Ministers. Indeed, it might be argued that, beginning in the 1970s, the judiciary was increasingly obliged to make controversial judgements on sensitive topics, such as race relations and industrial relations legislation (Hodder-Williams, 1986, p. 152). However, whatever the role of the judiciary and whatever its powers, judicial decisions could always be overturned by an Act of Parliament. The overriding principle of parliamentary sovereignty meant that the British judiciary traditionally placed little or no constraint upon those in the executive and legislative branches of government.

   More recently, though, the principle of parliamentary sovereignty has been challenged and the potential for judicial review has increased. Accession to the European Communities now European Union (EU) in 1973 meant that Britain is obliged to accept the principle that EU law takes precedence over domestic law. In the event of a conflict between the two, EU law is to prevail. This principle is inconsistent with the traditional notion of parliamentary sovereignty. It provides the potential for British judges to strike down domestic legislation on the grounds that it violates EU law. It also installed a supreme judicial authority, the Court of Justice, which acts as a final European court of appeal whose decisions are binding on domestic decision-makers. This was an important change in the constitutional distribution of power in Britain, not least because EU regulations, directives and decisions are often drafted on the basis of relatively broad principles. It created the opportunity for domestic judges to interpret EU legislation alongside existing or future parliamentary legislation and for the Court of Justice to issue binding judgements (Drewry, 1992, p. 13). To date, the impact of EU membership on the relationship between the three branches of British government has been relatively weak. As such, the judiciary still places only a comparatively minor constraint upon representatives in the other two branches of government. However, the potential for statutory review is now in place and the growing importance of the EU in European politics means that this potential is increasingly likely to be recognised.

*The decline of Parliament*

Although the principle of parliamentary sovereignty is central to the functioning of the British political system, leadership responsibilities are not incumbent upon either of the two Houses of Parliament – the House of Lords and the House of Commons. Members of the House of Lords are not directly elected. The majority are holders of either an hereditary peerage, which is granted by right of birth, or a life peerage, which is granted on the recommendation of, for example, the Prime Minister, or the Leader of the Opposition in Parliament. The nature of representation in the House of Lords meant that it was gradually sidelined from the political process as the British system democratised. For example, the 1911 and 1949 Parliament Acts greatly limited the power of the Lords to veto legislation passed by the Commons. The Lords can now only delay bills for two successive parliamentary sessions. Consequently, although its members include many senior political figures and although they have a degree of expertise in, for example, EU matters, the Lords now occupies only a marginal place in the political process.

It might appear, therefore, that the sovereignty of Parliament means the sovereignty of the House of Commons. In a formal sense, this is true. However, in practice, the House of Commons also plays only a residual role and the government has dominated the leadership process. There are three principal reasons as to why this should be the case: procedural rules; disciplined parties; and governmental majorities.

*Procedural rules*

The marginalisation of the House of Commons is partly due to certain procedural rules. For example, the government controls the parliamentary timetable, ensuring that priority is given to its own legislation. As a result, there are very few opportunities for Members of Parliament (MPs) to introduce their own legislation (Private Members Bills). In addition, the Commons has little control over the powers which have been delegated to the executive by virtue of previous Acts of Parliament. The extent of discretionary powers available to members of the government has increased over the years (Beloff and Peele, 1985, p. 141). Finally, the ability of MPs to scrutinise legislation and the activity of government departments is also limited. The scrutiny of government bills in parliamentary committees is subject to whipping (see below) and various procedures by which debate can be prematurely ended. The one area in which the authority of the legislature has increased in recent years concerns the parliamentary scrutiny of government departments. In 1979, fourteen special select committees were created. These were organised on departmental lines with the ability to hold hearings, call witnesses and issue reports. Although the creation of these select committees has not changed the fundamentally unequal pattern of executive/legislative relations, there is general agreement that the committees have achieved 'more systematic, comprehensive and rigorous scrutiny of executive actions than was the case either with the pre-1979 select committees or with present activity on the floor of the House' (Judge, 1992, p. 92).

• *Disciplined parties*

Party discipline has traditionally been strong within the House of Commons. By the end of the last century, intra-party cohesion had become a principal feature of parliamentary life (Norton, 1990, p. 14). This was mainly due to the growth of mass, national parties and to the development of a highly effective whipping system. In the government, there is a Chief Whip, who sits in the Cabinet and who may attend Cabinet committee meetings, as well as a Deputy Chief Whip and up to thirteen junior whips. The Opposition party has a similar system of whips. Once the official party line has been decided, it is up to the whips to ensure that discipline is maintained and a range of sanctions is available to them in order to discourage non-compliance. The development of cohesive party activity ensured that the control of legislation lay with political parties, rather than with shifting coalitions of loosely allied MPs. Consequently, with deviation from the party line being rare, governments with a Commons majority were all but assured of passing the totality of their legislative programme.

It was only after 1970 that the level of open intra-party dissent amongst the two main parties, the Conservative and Labour parties, began to increase significantly. Before 1970, there was dissent, but it was expressed to government Ministers more confidentially behind the scenes (Brand, 1992, p. 99). From 1970 to 1979, MPs proved to be increasingly willing to vote publicly against their own parties and with great effect (see Table 2.1). Indeed, even after 1983, when the Conservative party was returned to office with an exceptional majority, the degree of open dissent was more comparable with the 1970–79 period than with the 1945–70 period. For example, in the year following the general election in June 1983, there were 115 divisions (25.0 per cent of the total) in which either Conservative or Labour MPs dissented from the party line (Norton, 1985, p. 33). In 1986, the government was defeated at the second reading of a bill for the first time this century.

### TABLE 2.1

Divisions witnessing dissenting votes in the Commons, 1945–79

| Parliament | Number of divisions witnessing dissenting votes (Conservative and Labour parties) | Number of divisions witnessing dissenting votes as a percentage of all divisions |
|---|---|---|
| 1945–50 | 87 | 7.0 |
| 1950–51 | 6 | 2.5 |
| 1951–55 | 25 | 3.0 |
| 1955–59 | 19 | 2.0 |
| 1959–64 | 137 | 13.5 |
| 1964–66 | 2 | 0.5 |
| 1966–70 | 124 | 9.5 |
| 1970–74 | 221 | 20.0 |
| 1974 | 25 | 23.0 |
| 1974–79 | 423 | 28.0 |

*Source*: adapted from Norton, 1980, p. 248.

These attitudinal changes were primarily caused by the emergence on the political agenda of new issues, such as the EU, and by the rather uncompromising leadership styles of Edward Heath and Margaret Thatcher. Whatever their cause, they have ensured that Parliament is no longer marginalised in the policy cycle (Norton, 1990, p. 30), even if it cannot yet be classed as a legislature with a strong policy-making power.

• *Governmental majorities*
The growth of a mass electorate voting on party lines under a majoritarian electoral system has helped to ensure that a single party has often enjoyed the support of an absolute majority of seats in the House of Commons. (For elections results since 1945, see Table 2.2). The level of party identification amongst the British electorate has traditionally been high. Moreover, for much of the post-war period, party identification was split along class lines, with the Conservative party winning the support of middle-class voters and the Labour party winning the support of the working class. This distribution of electoral support encouraged political competition to take the form of a relatively balanced two-party system. Moreover, the electoral system reinforced this pattern of party competition. MPs are elected to the Commons in single-member constituencies under a plurality electoral system, whereby a candidate simply has to win more votes in the constituency than any other candidate in order to be elected. This majoritarian system reinforces the pattern of competition between the two large parties and penalises small parties, such as the Liberal Democrats, whose support is spread relatively evenly throughout the country.

Recently, though, the traditional patterns of post-war party identification have been declining. There has been the resurgence of third-party politics in the form of the Liberal Democratic party, as well as micro-nationalist politics in Scotland and Wales. Although single-party majorities have continued to be returned to the House of Commons, with the exception of the February 1974 election, the erosion of two-party politics has encouraged the likelihood that in the future there may well be both 'hung Parliaments', where no single party has an overall majority, and coalition governments, which have generally been confined to wartime in Britain. If either were to occur, the government's position would be more precarious than it has been to date under the British system and traditional leadership patterns would alter.

TABLE 2.2

Election results and majorities in the Commons, 1945–92

| Election | Conservative | Labour | Liberal | Others[1] | Majority |
|---|---|---|---|---|---|
| 1945 | 39.8 | 47.8 | 9.0 | 3.4 | L 146 |
| 1950 | 43.5 | 46.0 | 9.1 | 1.4 | L 5 |
| 1951 | 48.0 | 48.8 | 2.5 | 0.7 | C 17 |
| 1955 | 49.7 | 46.4 | 2.7 | 1.2 | C 58 |
| 1959 | 49.4 | 43.8 | 5.9 | 0.9 | C 100 |
| 1964 | 43.4 | 44.1 | 11.2 | 1.3 | L 4 |
| 1966 | 41.9 | 48.0 | 8.5 | 2.6 | L 96 |
| 1970 | 46.4 | 43.0 | 7.5 | 3.1 | C 30 |
| 1974 Feb. | 37.9 | 37.1 | 19.3 | 5.7 | (L 33 short) |
| 1974 Oct. | 35.9 | 39.2 | 18.5 | 6.4 | L 3 |
| 1979 | 43.9 | 36.9 | 13.8 | 5.4 | C 43 |
| 1983 | 42.4 | 27.6 | 25.4 | 4.6 | C 144 |
| 1987 | 42.3 | 30.8 | 22.6 | 4.3 | C 102 |
| 1992 | 41.9 | 34.4 | 17.8 | 5.9 | C 21 |

[1] 'Others' include Northern Irish parties, the Scottish Nationalist party and Plaid Cymru.

To date, though, most governments have consistently enjoyed the support of a disciplined, single-party majority in the House of Commons. They have been secure in office for the five year parliamentary term and they have been in a position to pass the majority if not all of their manifesto promises.

The effect of these factors has been to focus the public desire for leadership on the executive rather than the legislative branch of government. It remains the case that Parliament is a training ground for political leaders. The Opposition may embarrass the government in parliamentary debates. Select committees may periodically issue reports which the government may find inconvenient. Back-bench MPs may be increasingly willing to defy the official party line. In the main, though, key aspects of the leadership environment mean that the executive branch of government is at the heart of the machine. Indeed, members of the government increasingly consider their parliamentary appearances to be a secondary aspect of their role. For example, recent research has shown that, since 1916, Prime Ministers have appeared less and less frequently in the Commons (Dunleavy, Jones and O'Leary, 1990; Dunleavy and Jones *et al*, 1993). Indeed, the most successful post-war Prime Minister, Margaret Thatcher, was the most infrequent contributor to parliamentary debates, suggesting a highly detached style of leadership. To the extent that the decline of Parliament combines with the presence of a unitary and centralised state and with the absence of judicial review, then the leadership environment displaces leadership responsibilities upon the executive branch of the central government. It is now necessary to examine the nature of such responsibilities within the executive.

## Leadership in the executive branch of government

The British executive consists of a wide variety of political and administrative institutions. From amongst these institutions, it is possible to identify the 'core executive', or 'those organizations and structures which primarily serve to pull together and integrate central government policies, or act as arbiters within the executive of conflicts between different elements of the government machine' (Dunleavy and Rhodes, 1990, p. 4). Although there are various conflicting and mutually exclusive models of how the core executive operates in Britain (Dunleavy and Rhodes, 1990), it is useful to appreciate the potential for dynamism within the British leadership process. Although the structure of resources within the executive means that there is a tendency for some form of prime ministerial government to occur in the British system, the changing nature of the relationships within the core executive ensures that the intensity of prime ministerial government varies across and within administrations. In order to examine the nature of political leadership in Britain, it is necessary to examine the relationships which affect the workings of the core executive. In the rest of this chapter, these relationships will be considered under two separate headings: the Prime Minister and the Cabinet; and the Prime Minister and the party. The first of these subsections will deal with many of the formal aspects of the relationships which occur between the members of the core executive. The second will place these relationships in a wider popular and political context.

### The Prime Minister and the Cabinet

In 1963, Richard Crossman wrote: 'The post-war epoch has seen the final transformation of Cabinet Government into Prime Ministerial

Government' (Crossman, 1993, p. 52). In addition to the rise of disciplined parties (see above), Crossman identified three other institutional changes which reinforced the role of the Prime Minister in relation to the Cabinet (ibid, pp. 49–52). These involved the Cabinet Office; Cabinet committees; and the civil service.

• *The Cabinet Office*
The first change which Crossman identified involved the ending of Cabinet informality with the creation of a Cabinet Secretariat in 1916 during David Lloyd George's prime ministership. This reform had the effect of centralising the previously informal Cabinet decision-making process to the benefit of the Prime Minister. The Cabinet Office now consists of six units, which oversee the totality of government business (see Exhibit 2.2). Martin Burch describes the role of the staff in these units as follows: 'It is their job to ensure the flow of information through the Cabinet and its committees, to take minutes, to record Cabinet conclusions and to ensure they are circulated to those entitled to receive them – ministers, relevant officials and advisers' (Burch, 1988, p. 38). The units are headed by the Cabinet Secretary who is appointed by the Prime Minister and with whom the Prime Minister works very closely.

As its name suggests, the role of the Cabinet Office is to coordinate the activity of the Cabinet as a whole. However, the Prime Minister is best placed to benefit from the work of the different units and from the responsibilities of the Cabinet Secretary. One former Prime Minister, James Callaghan, has stressed the potential benefits

---

**EXHIBIT 2.2**
**The British Cabinet Office**

In 1994, the Cabinet Office consisted of six main organisations. These were:

1. Overseas and Defence Secretariat – dealing with foreign and defence policy.
2. Economic and Domestic Secretariat – treating all domestic policy, including economic policy.
3. European Secretariat – coordinating European Union business.
4. Telecommunications Secretariat – monitoring information.
5. Security and Intelligence Secretariat – coordinating the security and intelligence services.
6. Office of Public Services and Science – dealing with the civil service and other public management functions.

to be derived from the Cabinet Office: 'The conventional role of the Cabinet Office is to serve all members of the Cabinet, but if the Prime Minister chooses, as almost all of them do, to work closely with the Secretary of the Cabinet, then it becomes an instrument to serve him above the others' (quoted in James, 1992, p. 200). The Cabinet Office is not in a position to assume leadership responsibilities for itself. It has no political authority and its members have a neutral, managerial ethos, which eschews ideologically motivated behaviour. Nevertheless, to the extent that it can act as a resource for the Prime Minister, then its development has helped to shift the balance of power within the core executive to the advantage of the head of government.

• *Cabinet committees*
The second change concerned the creation of a network of Cabinet committees under the prime ministership of Sir Winston Churchill during the Second World War. Then, during the Attlee government (1945–51) procedures were codified and the committee system was institutionalised (Burch, 1988, p. 36). Now, permanent Cabinet committees oversee all areas of government responsibility (see Exhibit 2.3). In addition, there is a varying number of temporary, or *ad hoc*, committees, which meet occasionally to deal with specific issues. The permanent committees consist of a small number of senior Ministers appointed by the Prime Minister, who also personally chairs the most important of these committees. Temporary committees consist of a small number of both senior and junior Ministers, although appointments are still made by the Prime Minister who, again, will also chair the most important of them.

  Whereas previously policy discussions used to occur within the full Cabinet, they now take place almost exclusively between the Prime Minister and Ministers in these committees. By decentralising the Cabinet's work into discrete functional units, the Cabinet system was able to cope efficiently with the increased level of government activity during the Second World War and after. In this sense, the current Cabinet committee system is simply an extension of the traditional system of Cabinet government and does not damage the collective nature of the decision-making within the executive (Jones, George W., 1991, p. 128). All the same, the degree of secrecy which surrounds the committees places the Prime Minister in a privileged position. The power of appointment, the ability to chair committees and the

**EXHIBIT 2.3**
**Permanent British Cabinet committees in 1993**

| | |
|---|---|
| EPD | Economic and domestic policy. Chaired by the Prime Minister. |
| OPD | Overseas and defence policy. Chaired by the Prime Minister. |
| OPDG | Policy towards the Gulf states. Chaired by the Prime Minister. |
| OPDN | Nuclear and defence policy. Chaired by the Prime Minister. |
| OPDSE | European security policy. Chaired by the Prime Minister. |
| OPDK | Policy towards Hong Kong. Chaired by the Prime Minister. |
| NI | Northern Ireland. Chaired by the Prime Minister. |
| EDS | Science and technology policy. Chaired by the Prime Minister. |
| IS | Intelligence services. Chaired by the Prime Minister. |
| EDX | Public expenditure. Chaired by the Chancellor of the Exchequer. |
| EDI | Industrial, commercial and consumer policy. Chaired by the Lord Privy Seal. |
| EDE | Environmental policy. Chaired by the Lord Privy Seal. |
| EDH | Home and social affairs. Chaired by the Lord Privy Seal. |
| EDL | Local government. Chaired by the Lord Privy Seal. |
| EDR | Urban regeneration. Chaired by the Lord Privy Seal. |
| FLG | Queen's speech and future legislation. Chaired by the Lord President. |
| LG | Legislation in Parliament. Chaired by the Lord President. |
| EDC | Civil service pay. Chaired by the Lord President. |

strategic position of oversight mean that the Prime Minister possesses potentially key resources with which to coordinate and also to direct the flow of government business. For example, Mrs Thatcher had a very proactive approach to committee business, possessing 'the surest of grasps' (Seldon, 1990, p. 114) over appointments to the committees which dealt with her policy priorities. Therefore, although the Prime Minister's control of Cabinet committees is subject to certain constraints (see below), it is a source of power which was not available to pre-war heads of government.

• *The civil service*
The third change occurred as a result of the First World War with the unification and centralisation of the civil service. In 1919, the disparate departments of the civil service were brought together under the control of the Prime Minister who was also given the power to appoint departmental permanent secretaries and their deputies, the most senior civil service figures in these departments. These changes increased the power of the Prime Minister over the civil service itself. It is not that they allowed the Prime Minister to monitor personally

the work of the permanent administration and keep it in check. It is more that they allowed the Prime Minister to ensure that a particular leadership style would pervade throughout the wider set of administrative structures in the executive. Consequently, the Prime Minister 'is now at the apex not only of a highly centralised political machine, but also of an equally centralised and vastly more powerful administrative machine' (Crossman, 1993, p. 52).

It might also be noted, though, that there is still no official Prime Minister's Department in Britain. There is no equivalent of the Executive Office of the President in the United States, or the Federal Chancellor's Office in Germany. Nevertheless, the development of the institutions which collectively constitute the Prime Minister's Office has provided the Prime Minister with an additional set of administrative resources with which to exercise leadership (see Exhibit 2.4).

---

**EXHIBIT 2.4**
**The British Prime Minister's Office**

The Prime Minister's Office consists of six parts:

1. The private office – career civil servants providing administrative support.
2. The political office – linking the PM to party and Parliament and providing advice with a partisan slant.
3. The press office – dealing with media relations.
4. The policy unit – special appointees providing advice on policy matters.
5. Miscellaneous aides.
6. Junior officials, personal secretaries and support staff.

The total number of people in categories 1–4 is about twenty at any one time.

*Source*: Burnham and Jones, 1993, p. 301.

---

These resources do not guarantee that the Prime Minister will be able to impose a direction on the government. Yet the existence of the Prime Minister's Office does increase the potential for the Prime Minister's leadership style to prevail. The equivalent ministerial advisory structures are less-well-developed. Moreover, the organisation of the Prime Minister's Office reflects the individual preferences of each head of government to a much greater degree than that of the Cabinet Office (Burnham and Jones, 1993, p. 314). The Prime Minister's Office is a much more personal creation. It is part of the set of resources which empowers the head of government at the expense of the Cabinet collectively.

The structure of resources within the executive branch of government ensures that the Prime Minister enjoys an extensive set of formal powers (see Exhibit 2.5) and administrative support (see above). Together, these resources provide a framework within which there is the potential for support to be mobilised behind the particular direction that has been set. They combine to create the impression that there is a form of prime ministerial government in Britain. This impression is reinforced by two further factors. First, the Prime Minister's finger is on the nuclear trigger. Although formally the monarch is the Commander-in-Chief of the armed forces, in practice the Prime Minister is responsible for all military decisions including the decision to launch nuclear weapons. The mere fact that such an awesome charge is incumbent upon the head of government and no one else means that the Prime Minister is set apart. There is a gravity to the office that has no equivalent in any other office of state. In the realm of 'high' politics, the Prime Minister is responsible for that which is most 'high'. In the relationship with other members of the executive, such responsibility is a key resource for the Prime Minister in the decision-making process.

---

**EXHIBIT 2.5**
**The formal powers of the British Prime Minister**

1. The power of appointment to and dismissal from the Cabinet.
2. The power to allocate Cabinet portfolios.
3. The power to control Cabinet committees – the power to determine the structure of committees; to appoint the chair of the committees; and to choose committee members.
4. The power to control *ad hoc* meetings.
5. The power to control the flow of information.
6. The power to influence the press: the power of patronage: and the responsibility for the wider machinery of government.

*Source*: Adapted from James, 1992, pp. 99–113.

---

Second, the Prime Minister is the focus of a considerable degree of media and public attention. There are summit meetings of world leaders to attend; meetings of the European Council to go to; overseas visits to make; foreign visitors to receive; the Lord Mayor of London's banquet to address; visits to top sporting occasions to enjoy (or to endure, but to be seen to enjoy); the twice-weekly Prime Minister's Question Time in the Commons to undertake; and keynote party conference speeches to give. All such occasions serve to reinforce the sense of prime ministerial authority. They all help to institutionalise the impression that the Prime Minister is no ordinary political figure.

As a result, the Prime Minister is the pre-eminent figure within the British system of government. While in theory the Prime Minister is only *primus inter pares* (first among equals) within the Cabinet system, in practice the Prime Minister is more *primus* than *pares*. There is the collective expectation amongst Cabinet members that the Prime Minister *should* play a leadership role. James states that:

> ministers look to their premier to give purpose and direction to their collective efforts, to be a leader. They rely on him [*sic*] to oil the wheels of government, to solve problems and act as an honest broker between ministers in dispute. They look to him to encourage a common sense of purpose between them, to provide the cement that holds the Cabinet together (James, 1992, p. 125).

What is true for Ministers is true for the members of the Prime Minister's party and the public as well. The expectation that there should be prime ministerial leadership is entrenched within the British system. In contrast to the situation in much of post-war Italy and Japan, for example, direction-setting has been a fundamental part of the British Prime Minister's role. An unpurposeful Prime Minister who does not set a direction will be the subject of party and popular criticism. A purposeful Prime Minister who does set a direction will find that he or she has certain resources with which to encourage members of the Cabinet, the party and the public to follow.

In this way, the structure of resources within the British Cabinet system seems to facilitate the exercise of prime ministerial leadership. Given that all Prime Ministers work within this institutional framework, it might appear as if prime ministerial leadership is guaranteed. However, this is not necessarily the case. As Jones has argued: 'The prime minister is the leading figure in the cabinet whose voice carries most weight. But he is not the all-powerful individual which many have recently claimed him to be' (Jones, G. W., 1969, p. 216). In particular, while the presence of certain institutional resources renders prime ministerial leadership more likely, there are still other factors present in the functioning of the Cabinet system which limit the potential for prime ministerial leadership. Indeed, the extent to which the level of prime ministerial power varies is in part a function of these limiting factors. They are twofold: Cabinet collegiality and departmentalism.

• *Cabinet collegiality*
According to Patrick Weller, 'the language of government is collective' (Weller, 1985, p. 1). For Baylis, decision-making takes place within a relatively collegial context (Baylis, 1989) (see Exhibit 2.6). One of the main organising principles of the British system of government is that of collective Cabinet responsibility. That is to say, Cabinet members may disagree with each other in private, but in public they must all defend the decision that has been taken.

---

**EXHIBIT 2.6**
**National executives ranked according to collegiality**

| | |
|---|---|
| 5 (collegial) | Switzerland |
| 4 | Netherlands, Norway, Japan, Germany |
| 3 | Britain, Austria |
| 2 | Italy, Israel, Canada |
| 1 (monocratic) | United States, France |

*Source*: Adapted from Baylis, 1989, p. 147.

---

The principle of collective responsibility ensures that there must be some degree of discussion within the Cabinet system, either at full Cabinet level, or at the level of Cabinet committees. It ensures that there are mechanisms which force Cabinet Ministers, including the Prime Minister, to come together to discuss government policies (Jones, 1969, p. 216). Although the principle of collegiality does not preclude the pre-eminence of one or more senior figures (James, 1992, p. 6) and although Prime Ministers may adopt strategies to try to circumvent or minimise the impact of collective decision-making, nevertheless, there is still a residual collectivity to the British Cabinet system.

So, although the nature of the leadership environment within the Cabinet is such that its members look to the Prime Minister for leadership, the nature of the Cabinet is also such that the Prime Minister has to ensure a degree of collegiality. The Prime Minister is at once empowered and constrained. On the one hand, over-zealous

Prime Ministers will be limited in their attempt to exercise leadership by the principle of Cabinet collegiality. Those who refuse to acknowledge this constraint are likely to alienate the Cabinet. They will face disloyal Cabinet murmurings which may presage their own dismissal. On this count, Margaret Thatcher scores highly. On the other hand, unpurposeful Prime Ministers will be encouraged to exercise leadership by the Cabinet's collective need for guidance. Those who are unwilling or unable to do so will also face disloyal Cabinet murmurings. They will be considered as weak and unfit to govern. Here, the example of John Major springs to mind. Whichever scenario applies, prime ministerial leadership is at least in part a function of the personality of the office-holder and the relationship between the office-holder and the rest of his or her Cabinet.

• *Departmentalism*
The principle of departmentalism stands in direct contrast to that of collegiality, yet it affects the behaviour of all Cabinet members apart from the Prime Minister. Both legally and politically, there are centrifugal pressures within the Cabinet system, which drive Ministers apart from each other and which make the Prime Minister's co-ordinating role as well as his or her leading and guiding role more difficult. Legally, Ministers are responsible for the actions of their own departments. The principle of individual ministerial responsibility ensures that Ministers are responsible for departmental political mistakes. If any such mistakes are made, then, in theory at least, it is they who have to resign, rather than the administrators in their departments. In addition, Ministers have the power to appoint officials to various administrative posts in their departments and to agencies associated with their departments. In both respects, they are obliged to act with a certain degree of autonomy. Politically too, Ministers have the incentive to act individually rather than collectively. Political reputations are made and unmade on the basis of how well Ministers cope with the pressures that their departmental responsibilities place upon them. As a result, Ministers naturally seek to defend their own 'policy turfs' (Dunleavy and Rhodes, 1990, p. 12), as a way of safeguarding their Cabinet positions. Both legally and politically, therefore, there is a tendency for the Cabinet system to become compartmentalised.

In this event, the Prime Minister's ability to exercise leadership becomes more difficult. Although the non-departmental position of the Prime Minister ensures that Ministers look to the Prime Minister for a lead in the resolution of disputes and in the general direction of government policy, it is also the case that Ministers have to concern themselves with their own interests. Ministerial interests and the prime ministerial interest do not always coincide. Thus, on the one hand, the principle of departmentalism ensures that the non-departmental Prime Minister is empowered, but, on the other hand, it ensures that the level of prime ministerial empowerment is never absolute. Prime Ministers who do not take a lead will be taken advantage of by self-interested Ministers. Prime Ministers who do take a lead will find that they are likely to step on ministerial toes and make political enemies. Therefore, like the principle of collegiality, the principle of departmentalism ensures that prime ministerial leadership is subject to a twin tension, the resolution of which is at least in part a function of the relationship between the Prime Minister and individual Ministers.

*The Prime Minister and the party*

Prime ministerial leadership is also partly determined by the structure of resources within and between political parties. The Prime Minister and the party are closely linked. Exceptional circumstances aside, the prime ministership is awarded to the leader of the largest party in the House of Commons. Therefore, as King observes: 'the prime ministership is a party job before it is a governmental job' (King, 1991, p. 25). Such is the nature of the British prime ministership that the structure of resources within the executive branch of government, between the Prime Minister and the Cabinet collectively and between the Prime Minister and Ministers individually, is at least partly contingent upon the Prime Minister's own relationship with the party. In its most extreme manifestation, the Prime Minister only remains in power for as long as he or she has the confidence of the party. To the extent that disciplined party majorities render it unlikely that the government will be brought down between elections, the major threat to the Prime Minister's survival is if his or her own party decides some time before an election that a new leader is required. In 1990, Margaret Thatcher resigned not because her government had lost the confidence of the House of Commons, but because she had lost the confidence of the Conservative parliamentary party (see Exhibit 2.7 for the reasons why Prime Ministers have left office).

**EXHIBIT 2.7**
**Reasons why British Prime Ministers have left office**

| PM | Year | Reason |
|---|---|---|
| Attlee | 1951 | Lost the general election. |
| Churchill | 1955 | Ill-health. |
| Eden | 1957 | Ill-health, but was under severe party pressure. |
| Macmillan | 1963 | Ill-health, but was under severe party pressure. |
| Home | 1964 | Lost the general election. |
| Wilson | 1970 | Lost the general election. |
| Heath | 1974 | Lost the general election. |
| Wilson | 1976 | Retired voluntarily. |
| Callaghan | 1979 | Lost the general election. |
| Thatcher | 1990 | Resigned after doing badly in a party leadership contest. |

The prime motivation for the governing party wanting to dismiss its leader, the Prime Minister, is that the person in question is an electoral liability. In Britain, the ability to exercise leadership proceeds directly from the result of the last general election. The government has to win to retain power; the Opposition has to win to assume power; and the other parties have to do well to be given a share of power. Consequently, it is a primary role of all party leaders (including the Prime Minister) to ensure that their party is best-placed to do well at the next election. As such, the relationship between party leaders (again including the Prime Minister) and their party is to a great extent dependent upon whether or not they are successful in this role.

Moreover, this relationship is dependent not just upon whether or not they are successful, but also upon whether or not the party believes that they are likely to be successful in the future. Leaders who appear likely to succeed are empowered. Leaders who appear likely to fail may be dismissed. For example, in 1982, following the upturn in the economy and the victory in the Falklands war, Margaret Thatcher was in a particularly strong position within the Conservative party. This increased her ability to exercise leadership over the Cabinet and Parliament. In 1990, following the downturn in the economy and the poll-tax disaster, her relationship with the party was severely damaged. Consequently, her political authority was weakened and she eventually resigned.

It is apparent, therefore, that prime ministerial tenure is at least partly contingent upon the Prime Minister's relationship with the party. In addition, this relationship also helps to account for variations in the degree of prime ministerial leadership within individual administrations and across separate administrations. First, the degree of prime ministerial leadership varies within administrations. Prime ministerial authority is normally greatest immediately following a general election victory. Prime Ministers usually enjoy a 'honeymoon period' immediately after an election, during which time they can introduce substantial reforms. This period of euphoria then wears off and the passage of legislation becomes more complicated. Each of the three Thatcher administrations followed this pattern (Jones, George, 1990, p. 3). Second, the degree of prime ministerial leadership varies across administrations. Parties are institutions which exhibit (at least relatively) fixed patterns of authority relations within them. As a result, the degree of prime ministerial leadership is also contingent upon the differences between the organisational structures of the two main parties and which party is holding office. In particular, there are differences between the Conservative and Labour parties in terms of, first, the degree to which power is centralised in the hands of the party leader/Prime Minister and, secondly, the degree to which they are unified. Let us look at each in turn.

• *The degree to which power is centralised in the party leader/Prime Minister in Conservative and Labour parties*

The Conservative party is more centralised than its Labour counterpart. In this respect, it would appear as if Prime Ministers drawn from the Conservative party are likely to have an advantage over their Labour counterparts when it comes to exercising party leadership. In 1949, an official Conservative party report stated that the leader was 'the main fount and interpreter of policy' (quoted in Brand, 1992, p. 36). In a similar vein, Philip Norton has explained that:

> In keeping with its principles and perceptions of society, the Conservative Party is hierarchical. Great power is invested in the leader. The leader is the fount of all policy. All other bodies within the party serve in an advisory capacity (Norton, 1987, p. 23).

In his or her capacity as party leader, a Conservative Prime Minister has the power to appoint the party chairman; to restructure the party's organisation; and to determine the content of the party's election manifesto. These are resources which work to the advantage of Conservative Prime Ministers.

By contrast, in the Labour party, 'the lines of authority are more in doubt' (Weller, 1985, p. 31). Deference to the leader is not one of the Labour party's organising principles. The party has three rival power centres: the Cabinet (or Shadow Cabinet if Labour is in opposition), the Parliamentary Labour Party (PLP) and the party's National Executive Committee (NEC). The existence of these three bodies ensures that, at worst, there is open competition between them and that, at best, there is a conflict of loyalty in the case of overlapping membership, particularly with regard to members of the Cabinet who are also members of the NEC. In addition, a Prime Minister from the Labour party does not have the power to appoint the party chair; or to determine the composition of the NEC; or to select parliamentary candidates; or to determine the content of the party's election manifesto. Although there is no other figure within the party whose formal authority can rival that of the party leader, a Labour party leader/Prime Minister is still in a more complex position than his or her Conservative counterpart (Brand, 1992, p. 44).

There is one respect, though, in which the position of a Conservative Prime Minister is more fragile than that of a Labour Prime Minister. The Conservative party leader is now more susceptible to a leadership challenge than his or her Labour counterpart. Since 1965, Conservative party leaders have been elected by a vote of the members of the parliamentary party. Such an election may take place annually. The result is that the party leader needs continually to retain the support of the Conservative parliamentary party. In practice, this situation means that the Prime Minister may be destabilised by only a relatively small number of back-bench Conservative MPs. For example, in 1989, 85 per cent of the parliamentary party voted for Margaret Thatcher in the party leadership election. However, the fact that 15 per cent of the parliamentary party failed to support her meant that her previously unassailable authority within the party, the Cabinet and the country was weakened. A year later, she resigned after another leadership challenge. This example shows that Conservative Prime Ministers have to pay attention to the demands of relatively small cliques within the parliamentary party if they are to be assured of remaining in office.

By contrast, since 1981, Labour party leaders have been elected by an electoral college, made up in three equal parts, of (i) the votes of Labour MPs and Members of the European Parliament, (ii) the votes of members of Constituency Labour Parties, and (iii) the votes of members of trades' unions affiliated to the Labour party. Although an election may take place annually, potential rivals find it difficult to mount a challenge which has any chance of success. This is because candidates have to build a coalition of support from amongst the three different components of the electoral college. By contrast, once a candidate has been elected and the leadership coalition is in place, their position is relatively secure. Apart from John Smith's death in 1994, the two changes in the Labour party's leadership since 1981 have come about through resignation as a direct result of electoral failure. Michael Foot resigned after the 1983 election defeat and Neil Kinnock resigned after the 1992 defeat. Although there has yet to be a Labour government since the 1981 changes, it is reasonable to suggest that from now on a Labour Prime Minister will be more secure in office than a Conservative Prime Minister.

• *The degree of unification within Conservative and Labour parties*
The Conservative party is generally more unified than the Labour party. Again, this point would suggest that Conservative Prime Ministers have an advantage over their Labour counterparts. Traditionally, the Conservative party has been highly deferential to the policy preferences of its leader. It is true that the party's history has not been untroubled (Baker, Gamble and Ludlam, 1993, pp. 421–2). In 1846 and 1903, the party suffered damaging splits over the repeal of the Corn Laws and Tariff Reform respectively. In addition, the party was seriously divided over its electoral strategy in 1922 and its war strategy in 1940. Currently, there are groups within the party which exist to promote or oppose policy in particular areas. Such single-issue groups include the 'Bruges group', which is opposed to further European integration. At the same time, there are also groups which promote or oppose policy across a wider set of areas. Such multi-issue groups include the right-wing '92 group' and the more centrist 'Lollards'. These two groups have put up rival lists of approved candidates for elections to senior parliamentary positions. Indeed, the period since Mrs Thatcher's election as party leader in

1975 has generally seen an increase in ideological tensions within the Conservative party. To the extent that small groups of like-minded people may cause trouble for a Conservative Prime Minister if they try to launch a leadership election campaign, then they can act as a constraint on the Prime Minister. Moreover, to the extent that such groups can have an influence in the parliamentary process which far exceeds their numerical strength when the Conservative majority is small, then, again, they can act as a constraint on the Prime Minister. In this regard, John Major experienced considerable difficulty in ratifying the Maastricht Treaty in the Commons because of the resolute opposition of a comparatively small number of anti-European Conservative MPs. However, in the main and even including the Thatcher period of leadership, the Conservative party is an ideologically pragmatic party, which displays a high degree of loyalty to its leader. This high degree of unification is a resource which Conservative Prime Ministers can exploit in order to exercise political leadership.

By contrast, the Labour party has traditionally been a much less unified organisation. As Ingle states:

> Loyalty plays a great part in Labour party politics, but not loyalty to the leader. Loyalty is owed to a concept: the interests of the working class. But no statement exists of what precisely these interests are...What results is a permanent and growing tendency to sectarian division, with the leader finding his/her time and energy taken up by the attempt to keep all the faithful within the 'broad church' (Ingle, 1989, p. 130).

Sectarian division has a long history within the Labour party. In 1931, the Prime Minister, James Ramsay MacDonald, was expelled from the party as a result of his decision to form a national coalition government with the Conservative party. In the late 1950s, the Labour leader in opposition, Hugh Gaitskell, waged a bitter and ultimately unsuccessful war to try and end the party's constitutional commitment to economic nationalisation. Moreover, the internecine warfare of the 1970s and early 1980s resulted in the party splitting, with leading right-wingers leaving and forming the Social Democratic Party. These points represent crisis periods in the Labour party's history. Outside these periods, ideological differences have been slightly less intense. Indeed, the Labour party has recently become much more docile under the leadership of Neil Kinnock,

John Smith and Tony Blair respectively. Nevertheless, the Labour party still has a greater potential for disunity than the Conservative party and, as such, Labour leaders would again appear to be in a more complex position than their Conservative counterparts.

It would appear, therefore, that the structure of resources within the two main political parties means that Conservative leaders are likely to have an advantage over Labour leaders when it comes to exercising leadership. However, a few words of warning need to be sounded. First, even if this were the case, it would only be one aspect of the wider leadership environment within which leaders have to operate. All things being equal, Conservative Prime Ministers may have an advantage over their Labour counterparts in that they lead a generally more centralised and unified party. However, all things are not always equal. Consequently, certain Labour Prime Ministers, such as Attlee and Wilson, have a record of success which is greater than certain Conservative Prime Ministers, such as Eden, Home and Heath. Second (and more fundamentally) Conservative leaders are not necessarily in a better position to exercise leadership than Labour leaders, they are simply in a different position. Neither party's leader is necessarily stronger or weaker than the other. For example, it may be extremely difficult for Conservative leaders to meet the very high degree of expectations that exist within their own party. As a result, there may be a tendency for the relationship between the Prime Minister and the party to sour in the case of the Conservatives. Conversely, the need for Labour leaders to manage the complex situation within their own party means that they may be well-suited to dealing with the wider set of pressures that Prime Ministers have to face within the Cabinet system. Indeed, it is arguable that managerial Labour Prime Ministers, such as Clement Attlee and Harold Wilson, fared better than managerial Conservative Prime Ministers, such as Harold Macmillan, Alec Douglas Home and John Major. So, while the organisational differences between the two main parties create a different leadership environment for Prime Ministers, they do not necessarily create either a more favourable or a less favourable environment.

## Conclusion

In Britain, therefore, the leadership environment creates a general and well-established tendency towards executive leadership.

Moreover, the structure of resources within the executive branch of the central government creates an additional and equally well-established tendency towards prime ministerial leadership. The organisation of the British state and the nature of party politics means that power is displaced onto the executive branch of government in general and onto the prime ministership in particular. It remains, though, that the degree of prime ministerial leadership depends on the Prime Minister's relationship with both the Cabinet and the party. Although the Prime Minister is the focus of political attention in the country and although successive Prime Ministers have indicated a direction in which they wanted the country to go (neo-liberalism, Thatcher) or a theme by which they wanted to be remembered (the 'white heat' of the scientific revolution, Wilson; 'Back to Basics', Major), Prime Ministers have consistently found that they have been constrained by the nature of these two key relationships. Successful Prime Ministers have managed these relationships well (Attlee, Wilson and Thatcher for a time). Unsuccessful Prime Ministers have managed them badly (Eden, and Home). Therefore, despite the tendency towards prime ministerial government which exists with the system, the nature of the leadership environment is such that there is still a dynamic element to the exercise of executive leadership in Britain and to the power of the Prime Minister in particular.

# 3

# France:
# Presidential Leadership

There are certain similarities between the leadership process in both
Britain and France. For the most part, these similarities result from
the distribution of resources between the executive branch of the
central government and the other branches and levels of government.
Since the creation of the current French régime, the Fifth Republic, in
1958, the country's leadership environment has exhibited two institutional characteristics that have mirrored those of its British counterpart. In the first place, state institutions at the central level have
dominated those at the subcentral level. Second, at the central level,
the executive branch of government has dominated both the judicial
and legislative branches. Consequently, in France, as in Britain, the
system has encouraged a form of executive leadership.

However, the two countries differ in the type of executive leadership which they exhibit. In Britain, the structure of resources within
the executive has created a tendency towards prime ministerial leadership, whereas, in France, it has created a tendency towards presidential leadership. In France, the main restriction on presidential
leadership lies not in the organisation of the Cabinet system or in the
nature of political parties, as in Britain, but in the President's relationship with the head of government, the Prime Minister. In
France, there is a twin-headed, or bicephalous, executive. In contrast
to the British system, the French executive consists of a President and
a Prime Minister, both of whom are more than just figureheads and
both of whom have certain constitutional powers. The leadership
process in France is dependent on the relationship between the incumbents of these two institutions. For much of the period since
1958, the leadership environment has been such that the balance of
power has tilted towards the President and there has been presidential

leadership. However, on two occasions, it has been such that the balance of power has tilted towards the Prime Minister and there has been prime ministerial leadership (see Exhibit 3.1 for a list of Presidents and Prime Ministers since 1959).

---

**EXHIBIT 3.1**
**French Presidents and Prime Ministers since 1959**

| President | Prime Minister |
|---|---|
| Charles de Gaulle (1959–69) | Michel Debré (1959–62) |
| | Georges Pompidou (1962–68) |
| | Maurice Couve de Murville (1968–69) |
| Georges Pompidou (1969–74) | Jacques Chaban-Delmas (1969–72) |
| | Pierre Messmer (1972–74) |
| Valéry Giscard d'Estaing (1974–81) | Jacques Chirac (1974–76) |
| | Raymond Barre (1976–81) |
| François Mitterrand (1981– ) | Pierre Mauroy (1981–84) |
| | Laurent Fabius (1984–86) |
| | Jacques Chirac (1986–88) |
| | Michel Rocard (1988–91) |
| | Edith Cresson (1991–92) |
| | Pierre Bérégovoy (1992–93) |
| | Edouard Balladur (1993– ) |

---

This chapter examines the foundations of presidential and prime ministerial leadership since 1958. It begins by examining the structure of resources between the executive branch of the central government and the other branches and levels of government. In so doing, it analyses the powers of local government, the role of judicial review and the organisation of the legislature. It then goes on to examine the reasons why the system was presidentialised after 1959 and why presidential leadership has twice been replaced by prime ministerial leadership.

## The displacement of power onto the executive branch of government

### *The system of local government*

Like Britain, France has a unitary and centralised state. According to Article 2 of the 1958 Constitution, the French Republic is 'indivisible'. Unlike the situation in the USA and Germany, in France there is no constitutional separation of powers between central and subcentral units of government. As in Britain, the absence of any provision for federalism ensures that there are no formal limits placed on the law-making powers of the central state institutions by units of government at the local level. Local governmental authorities in France cannot act as a formal check on the decision-making powers of the authorities at the central level. As in Britain, the principle of *ultra vires* applies. Moreover, the presence of representatives of the central state in the localities (ministerial field services and prefects) ensures that decisions taken at the local level are supervised and coordinated. Overall, the leadership capacities of the central state institutions are not formally restricted by the powers of the local governmental authorities (for the structure of local government, see Exhibit 3.2).

---

**EXHIBIT 3.2**
**The structure of local government in France**

| *Level* | *Local political institutions* | *Representatives of central institutions* |
|---------|-------------------------------|--------------------------------------------|
| Region (22) | Regional Council headed by a President | Regional ministerial services. Regional prefect |
| Department (96) | General Council headed by a President | Departmental ministerial services. Prefect |
| Commune (+ 36,000) | Municipal Council headed by a mayor | Local ministerial services |

---

Moreover, the ordinary French person looks towards the central state for guidance and for the resolution of the country's problems. The myth of the all-powerful central state (or 'State') is ingrained in the national political culture. In the French political tradition, the state does not represent divisive, sectional interests, but the common good. It represents the will of the French people, legislating on its behalf and implementing legislation in a way which is rational and impartial. The state defends the individual against potentially harmful private interests. It protects the system from centrifugal tendencies, which would otherwise threaten to tear the country apart. It allows a long-term perspective to prevail over short-term expediency. For all these reasons, there is a widespread belief that political leadership can only be exercised from the centre. Only political leaders at the central level have the authority to take the initiative and to exercise leadership. Therefore, both constitutionally and psychologically, the remit of political leaders at the central level is both legitimised and unbounded by territorial constraints.

At the same time, while in a formal sense centre–periphery relations in France are similar to those found in Britain, in practice the role of French local government is more influential than its feeble British counterpart. France has a highly developed local political culture. Local identities are strong and the informal powers of political élites at the local level (*notables*) are well-entrenched. In particular, mayors in France are much more influential than their British counterparts whose functions are purely ceremonial. In France, mayors are the chief executives of municipal councils. As such, they are the principal representative of the commune and the source of political patronage. This power gives them a position of status in the local community; a privileged position with which to negotiate with the state's local representative, the prefect; and, in the case of mayors of large towns, a political base from which to take part in national politics. Consequently, despite their formal powers, the central state institutions cannot simply ignore and ride roughshod over the wishes of those in the localities. Representatives of the central state institutions must negotiate with their counterparts at the local level. Dupuy describes this situation:

> centralization does not mean the unilateral and arbitrary domination of the centre over the periphery, the state over local bodies, Paris over the provinces. Centralization is rather part of a complex ensemble which forms a French model of equilibrium between central and local government (Dupuy, 1985, p. 102).

Moreover, unlike the situation in Britain, the formal powers of local authorities in France have increased over the last decade. A new equilibrium has been reached at a point which is more favourable to local authorities than before. The arrival in power of the socialist government in 1981 was followed by a series of reforms guided through the legislature by the Minister for Decentralisation, Gaston Defferre. These reforms were designed to extend the rights and freedoms of the local authorities. Amongst other reforms, the powers of oversight enjoyed by the state-appointed prefects over local councils were reduced; a new tier of elected local authorities at the regional level was introduced; and more powers were given to the mayors of municipal councils. Overall, these reforms have served to increase the role played by local authorities in the political system. The central state is still the dominant partner in the relationship with the localities, but a new and more equitable distribution of power has been established between the two levels of government.

## The Constitutional Council

Unlike Britain, France has a codified Constitution. Also unlike Britain, in France there is the provision for constitutional judicial review of statute law. There is a supreme judicial authority in France, the Constitutional Council, whose role is to interpret the Constitution and whose decisions are binding upon all concerned. The Constitutional Council represents the highest court of appeal for constitutional matters and is the equivalent of the US Supreme Court (see Chapter 5). However, for much of the period since 1958, the Constitutional Council has been limited in the extent to which it has been able to practise judicial review. For example, the Council has no power to determine for itself which bills it wishes to examine. It may only consider bills which are placed before it for consideration. Even then, there is no provision for the public to petition the Council. Submissions may only be made by the President of the Republic, the Prime Minister, the Presidents of the two houses of the legislature and, since 1974, sixty deputies or senators. Moreover, unlike the US Supreme Court, the Council cannot make retrospective judgements. Bills may be sent to the Council only in the period immediately after they have been passed by the legislature and before they become law. The Council has no power to strike laws down after they have been formally promulgated. All these factors have served to limit the Council's role in the decision-making process.

By its decisions, from 1959 to 1971, the Council favoured the executive (Keeler and Stone, 1987, p. 162). For example, the Council refused to strike down the November 1962 referendum, which was held at de Gaulle's request in highly dubious constitutional circumstances (see below). However, in 1971, the Council invalidated a piece of government-sponsored legislation for the first time. In its way, this decision was the French equivalent of the US Supreme Court's 1803 *Marbury* v. *Madison* decision (see Chapter 5). Then, in 1974, a constitutional amendment was passed which allowed sixty deputies or senators to refer bills to the Council. This amendment opened the way for opposition parties in the legislature to petition the Council in the hope that government legislation would be struck down. Since 1974, the Constitutional Council has played an increasingly important role in the political system. For example, the number of bills which have been placed before it and the number of texts it has censured have both increased (see Table 3.1). On occasions, major

**TABLE 3.1**

**The increasing role of the French Constitutional Council, 1959–90**

|                                                  | 1959–73 | 1974–80 | 1981–90 |
|--------------------------------------------------|---------|---------|---------|
| Number of referrals:                             | 9       | 66*     | 183*    |
| Number of decisions censuring referred text:     | 7       | 14      | 66      |
| Number of decisions favourable to referred text: | 2       | 32      | 57      |

* Due to multiple referrals, the number of referrals is larger than the number of decisions.
*Source*: Adapted from Stone, 1992a, p. 35.

pieces of government legislation have been struck down. For example, in 1982, the socialist government was obliged to alter a major part of its nationalisation programme because of an unfavourable Council ruling. Similarly, in 1986, the right-wing coalition government was forced to pass a new law after the Council had censured part of the original version of its controversial broadcasting bill.

In addition, as in Germany (see Chapter 4), the influence of the Council has also expanded as a result of the fact that governments have engaged in the practice of 'self-limitation'. Self-limitation may be defined as 'the government's exercise of legislative self-restraint resulting from anticipation of a referral to and an eventual negative decision of the Council' (Keeler and Stone, 1987, p. 175). Fearful of bills being censured by the Council, governments now regularly amend their own pieces of legislation before they have even been introduced to parliament. The practice of self-limitation is built into the governmental stage of the legislative process and the indirect influence of the Council in the policy-making process has increased. From 1981 to 1986, self-limitation 'served as a subtle yet significant obstacle to Socialist reform' (Keeler and Stone, 1987, p. 176). Laws as diverse as the government's nationalisation programme, the decentralisation reforms and restrictions on the concentration of press ownership were all prepared in the knowledge that they had to be as Council-friendly as possible in order to minimise political embarrassment and avoid a delay in the government's reform programme. Even then, the degree of self-limitation is never necessarily enough to prevent a negative Council ruling.

All the same, whilst the Council's role as a check on the government has become more important over the years, its influence should still not be overestimated. The traditional limitations to the exercise of judicial review by the Council still apply. There are also distinct limits to the extent to which governments are willing to engage in the practice of self-limitation (Stone, 1989, pp. 24–5). In all, while the government has become increasingly aware of the Council's potential to frustrate attempts to pass legislation in the form that it wants and while, as in the British case, the Council will increasingly have to take into account the content of EU law, still the increasing influence of the Council has failed to overturn the potential for executive leadership.

## The legislature

As in Britain, leadership responsibilities are not incumbent upon either of the two Chambers of the French legislature. The absence of parliamentary leadership since 1958 is at least partly deliberate. The Fourth Republic (1946–58) was criticised for being a parliamentary régime. The government was subordinate to parliament. It had few constitutional powers at its disposal with which to arm itself against a hostile legislature where no single party had an absolute majority. Governments were frequently brought down. There were twenty-four governments in the twelve year history of the Fourth Republic. Legislation was passed not as a result of disciplined parties voting for government-sponsored legislation, but as a result of the interaction of 'fluid parliamentary cliques' (Reif, 1987, p. 33) often amending bills so as to suit their own partisan or local interests. Of the ten party groups present in the last Assembly of the Fourth Republic, only two voted in a disciplined manner (Criddle, 1987, p. 138). The result was a discredited régime, whose politicians were unable to provide strategic leadership and which lurched from one crisis to the next.

To avoid any repetition of the débâcle of the Fourth Republic, the

---

**EXHIBIT 3.3**
**Constitutional restrictions on parliamentary powers since 1958**

| | |
|---|---|
| Article 16: | In a national emergency, the President may assume emergency powers and issue decrees which have the force of law. |
| Article 23: | On their appointment to government, Ministers have to resign their parliamentary seats. |
| Article 28: | Parliamentary sessions last a maximum of 170 days a year. |
| Article 34: | The areas in which parliament may legislate are limited. In all other areas, the PM issues decrees which have the force of law. |
| Article 38: | The parliament may authorise the government to legislate by decree. |
| Article 40: | Any parliamentary amendment reducing public income or increasing public spending is unconstitutional. |
| Article 42: | Parliament must begin the discussion of a bill by first examining the text proposed by the government. |
| Article 43: | The number of parliamentary committees is limited to six. |
| Article 44: | The government may refuse to consider any parliamentary amendment which has not been examined in a parliamentary committee. The government may call for a package vote on a bill containing the amendments that it selects (*vote bloqué*). |
| Article 45: | The government may declare a bill to be urgent so as to accelerate its passage through parliament. |
| Article 47: | The time in which parliament may discuss the budget is limited to seventy days, after which time, if the budget has not been passed, the PM issues decrees which have the force of law. |
| Article 48: | The government fixes the parliamentary timetable. |
| Article 49: | There are severe restrictions on the ability of the National Assembly to dismiss the government from office. |

---

constitutional framers of the Fifth Republic agreed that severe limits had to be placed on the powers of parliament (see Exhibit 3.3). The executive would have to be able to impose its will on the legislature. This is what has happened. In the words of Philip Williams: 'Under the new régime the Parliament of France, once among the most powerful in the world, became one of the weakest' (Williams, 1968, p. 21). For example, as with the House of Lords in Britain, the Upper Chamber of the French parliament, the Senate, has been sidelined from the law-making process. Its assent is no longer needed for the passage of legislation. Moreover, the policy-making role of the Lower Chamber, the National Assembly, now borders on the marginal. There is little opportunity for the opposition to scrutinise the government – the role of parliamentary committees has declined; the percentage of private members' bills (*propositions de loi*) passed has decreased – 29.7 per cent of all legislation passed in the Fourth Republic was initiated by parliament, whereas in the Fifth Republic the figure is 11.5 per cent (Keeler, 1993b, p. 522); and it is now more difficult for the National Assembly to dismiss the government – even governments which enjoy only a relative majority in the National Assembly may use the constitutional powers at their disposal not only to avoid being dismissed from office, but also to pass legislation at the same time (Elgie, 1993a). As Frears has argued: 'The procedures for controlling executive power, for scrutinising or debating or questioning executive acts, are completely inadequate' (Frears, 1990, p. 50).

Despite its constitutional weaknesses, though, the Fifth Republic's legislature is not totally impotent. Apart from presidential elections, parliament still remains the principal arena where the main political, economic and social issues of the day are debated. Its members retain the potential to embarrass the government, for example, during the questions to the government in the National Assembly on Wednesday afternoons. Moreover, senators and deputies still retain certain powers to obstruct the passage of government legislation. If the degree of obstruction is sufficiently determined, then the government may have to give in to the demands of the parliamentarians. Nevertheless, although these points mean that members of the executive branch of government cannot simply ignore the wishes of those in the legislative branch, the 1958 Constitution presents them with a raft of constitutional resources with which to exercise leadership.

### Leadership within the executive

It is apparent, therefore, that the French leadership environment and, particularly, the distribution of resources between the executive branch of the central government and the other branches and levels of government contrives to create the expectation that there should be executive leadership. The architecture of the French state creates an institutional framework which favours such leadership. As in Britain, then, the question arises as to what form of executive leadership there is likely to be. What is the structure of resources within the executive branch of government? Who is able to exercise leadership there? One part of the answer to these questions is that leadership is certainly not exercised by the members of the government collectively. In France, the Council of Ministers, the equivalent of the British Cabinet, is not a decision-making body. Moreover, neither is it a deliberative nor an advisory body (Suleiman, 1980, p. 113). Meetings of the Council of Ministers are short; votes are rarely taken; Ministers tend to confine their comments to their own policy areas; and substantive decisions are taken prior to the meetings in informal interministerial committees and councils. In no sense is there any form of collective leadership in France, which is reflected in Baylis's index of collegiality (see Chapter 2, Exhibit 2.6), where France is ranked as a monocratic system alongside the United States.

Instead, in France, there is a form of personal leadership. In this case, the most pertinent question is whether such leadership is exercised by either the President or the Prime Minister? Unfortunately, the structure of resources as set out in the 1958 Constitution does not provide an accurate answer to this question. A literal reading of the Constitution would give the impression that there should be prime ministerial leadership (see Exhibit 3.4). For example, apart from a national emergency, when the President may assume extraordinary powers to issue decrees which have the force of law (Article 16), the President's policy-making powers are few and ambiguous (Article 5) and tend to be confined to foreign and defence matters (Articles 15 and 52). By contrast, the Prime Minister's policy-making powers are great and specific and cover the whole range of government policy-making responsibilities including domestic policy-making (Articles 20 and 21). However, despite this constitutional distribution of power, with the exception of two brief periods of 'cohabitation' (see below), there has been presidential leadership in France since 1958. There has been a presidentialisation of the policy-making process.

How is it that, in the absence of a set of explicit constitutional policy-making powers, successive Presidents have been able to exercise leadership across a full range of policy areas? The answer to this question is not to be found in the structure of administrative resources at the President's disposal. Indeed, the French presidency is extremely lightly staffed when compared with, for example, its US counterpart (see Chapter 5). Indeed, the French equivalent of the British Cabinet Office is to be found under the direction of the Prime Minister (see below). Instead, Presidents have exercised leadership for two other reasons: the precedent set by de Gaulle and the subsequent presidentialisation of the political system as a whole; and the direct election of the President. Let us look at each of these reasons.

**EXHIBIT 3.4**

**The constitutional powers of the French President and Prime Minister**

| *President* | *Prime Minister* |
|---|---|
| Art. 5: Sees that the Constitution is respected. Ensures by his arbitration the regular functioning of the public authorities. Guarantees national independence and territorial integrity. | Art. 8: Proposes the names of government Ministers to the President. |
| | Art. 20: The government determines and conducts the nation's policies. |
| Art. 8: Appoints the Prime Minister. | Art. 21: The Prime Minister is head of government. |
| Art. 9: Chairs the Council of Ministers. | Responsible for national defence. |
| Art. 10: Can request that Parliament re-examines a bill. | Ensures that laws are implemented. In areas where Parliament cannot legislate, s/he issues regulations which have the force of law. |
| Art. 11: Can call for a referendum on certain issues. | |
| Art. 12: Can dissolve the National Assembly. | |
| Art. 13: Has power to appoint military and non-military personnel. | Art. 29: Can demand an extraordinary parliamentary session. |
| | Art. 33: May ask Parliament to sit in a closed session. |
| Art. 15: Commander-in-chief of the armed forces. | Art. 34–51: Government's powers over Parliament (see Exhibit 3.3). |
| Art. 16: Can assume emergency powers if the nation is threatened. | |
| Art. 52: Negotiates and ratifies treaties. | Art. 39: Has the right to initiate legislation. |
| Art. 56: Appoints three members of the Constitutional Council | Art. 61: Can refer a bill to the Constitutional Council. |
| Art. 61: Can refer a bill to the Constitutional Council. | Art. 89: Can propose that a referendum be held. |
| Art. 89: Can propose that a referendum be held. | |

**Presidential leadership**

*De Gaulle's precedent and the presidentialisation of the system*

By the spring of 1958 the Fourth Republic was dead on its feet. The régime was discredited. On the domestic front, there was an ever-increasing demand for change. The country lurched from one crisis to the next. Governments were headed by weak, ineffectual figures whose energies were devoted to keeping fragile coalitions together. The government enjoyed only a limited party base in the legislature. Over 40 per cent of the seats in the lower house were held by representatives of parties which were opposed to the political system of the Fourth Republic. Moreover, on the colonial front, the situation was deteriorating rapidly. The war in Algeria was escalating and threatened to spill over onto mainland France. The government appeared to be ready to make concessions to representatives of those fighting for Algerian independence. However, those who remained loyal to French Algeria reacted violently to the threat of any such concessions. The prospect of a military takeover by those loyal to the cause of French Algeria became a very real prospect.

On 13 May 1958, military leaders loyal to this cause seized power in Algiers. On 24 May, paratroopers loyal to the same cause landed in Corsica and appeared to be preparing for a future landing in Paris. The threat of a military takeover was imminent. It was in this context that the President of the Fourth Republic asked Charles de Gaulle to return from his self-imposed political exile in order to try to bring stability to the political system. De Gaulle was called upon because he was a reassuring figure. Although he came from a military background, de Gaulle's democratic credentials were impeccable. He was the leader of the Free French forces during the war, coordinating the resistance to the German occupation of the country. He also had governmental experience, having led the provisional government in the period immediately following the liberation of France in 1944. Finally, he was not associated with the discredited Fourth Republic. In 1946, he resigned as head of the provisional government as a protest against the way in which the Constitution of the new Republic was being drawn up. In the context of the events of May 1958, he was the one person who could calm the fears of a military takeover. He agreed to assume political office once again on condition that he would be the last head of government of the Fourth Republic and that a Constitution for a new Republic would be drawn up. On 1

June, de Gaulle's government won a vote of confidence in parliament and two days later a Constitutional Law was passed, beginning the process by which the Fifth Republic was established. The wording of 1958 Constitution was largely inspired by de Gaulle's vision of executive leadership. He believed that there was a need for leadership; that leadership should be exercised by the head of state; that in order to exercise leadership the head of state needed important constitutional powers; and that the head of state should express the will of the people (Carcassonne, 1988, p. 243). In all but this last respect, de Gaulle's vision of executive leadership prevailed in the new Constitution. Once the new régime was in place, de Gaulle started to intervene personally in the policy-making process. From 1958 to 1962, he largely confined himself to the constitutionally prescribed areas of foreign and defence policy, dealing with the Algerian war and building up the Franco-German alliance. However, after 1962 and the granting of independence to Algeria, de Gaulle turned his attentions to domestic policy as well, intervening closely in the areas of economic, cultural and local government policy amongst others. Moreover, from 1958 onwards, de Gaulle used his power of appointment to the full. Loyal Prime Ministers and Ministers were appointed and loyal advisers were placed in strategic public-sector posts. At the same time, the Gaullists grew in strength, providing him with a key party political resource and allowing him to consolidate his exercise of political leadership.

In all these respects, de Gaulle's exercise of power after 1958 created the expectation that there should be presidential leadership in France. Moreover, it created the expectation that there should be presidential leadership not just in the areas of foreign and defence policy-making, but more generally in all areas of domestic policy-making as well. In this respect, de Gaulle set a precedent for presidential leadership which went beyond the bounds of the 1958 Constitution. *De facto* presidential powers were grafted on to the *de jure* provision for prime ministerial leadership in domestic matters. As a result, presidential leadership was not simply tolerated, it became the norm. Political figures who threatened to weaken or eliminate the exercise of presidential leadership were rejected by the electorate – Mitterrand at the 1965 presidential election and Poher in 1969. De Gaulle's leadership style became the model which other politicians were and still are obliged to follow. Indeed, so entrenched did this style of personal leadership become that following his election as

President in 1981 and in contrast to the attitude he adopted in the mid-1960s, Mitterrand was left to declare that: 'the institutions were not made with me in mind, but they suit me very well'. Partly because of the precedent set by de Gaulle, the structure of resources within the executive tilted towards the President. The system was presidentialised. For example, the structure of resources within political parties came to reflect this system. Political parties are now dominated by the activity and interests of their prospective presidential candidate (*présidentiable*). Party organisation is highly centralised on the activity of the party's *présidentiable*, leaving little room for input from rank-and-file party members. Presidential candidates determine their own election manifestos, rather than campaigning on their party's own programme. In addition, in their role as head of state and the primary representative of France abroad, Presidents receive a greater degree of media and public attention than any other public figures. Presidents are not just figureheads whose role is simply to open flower shows (*pour inaugurer les chrysanthèmes*). Instead, they negotiate with foreign governments on France's behalf. They represent France at EU summit meetings and at meetings of the Group of Seven leading industrial countries. It has been estimated, for example, that Mitterrand spent nearly half of 1990 attending international meetings and taking decisions on France's behalf (Massot, 1991, p. 22). Presidents also have the power of patronage not just over the government, but over a range of posts in the public and para-public sector. They have the power of pardon. They have to arbitrate impartially between all the sectional interests which are expressed during times of economic, political and social crisis. In sum, they are the nation's principal pedagogue (Wright, 1989, p. 28).

Most importantly of all, as with British Prime Ministers, Presidents have their finger on the nuclear trigger. The Constitution states that the Prime Minister is responsible for national defence (Article 21), while the President is designated as Commander-in-Chief of the armed forces (Article 15). Over the years, though, the President's formal and practical authority in defence matters has expanded far beyond this purely honorific title (remember that the monarch holds the same title in Britain). For example, the governmental decree of 18 July 1962 states that the President chairs meetings of the Defence Council, the main interministerial defence policy-making forum; the decree of 14 January 1964 gives the President the sole responsibility for engaging France's nuclear weapons; and the decree of

10 December 1971 placed the Joint Chief of Staff under the President's command (Howorth, 1993, pp. 152–3). These powers gave the presidency a status and the President a responsibility which far exceeds that of any other institution or person in the country. They enhanced the President's authority. As in the case of the British Prime Minister, they ensured that the President is always more than just the first among equals.

## The direct election of the President

In the 1958 Constitution, the only aspect of de Gaulle's vision of executive leadership not to be realised was that the President should express the will of the people. In December 1958, de Gaulle was elected indirectly by an electoral college consisting largely of local *notables*. Although the college was made up of a wide-ranging set of political figures and although he established a personal link with the people in the early years of the Republic by holding frequent referendums at which he placed his mandate on the line (see Wright, 1978, and Table 3.2), de Gaulle was aware that, as it stood, the presidency

TABLE 3.2

**De Gaulle's use of referendums, 1958–62**

| Date | Topic | For (%) |
|------|-------|---------|
| September 1958 | Constitution of the Fifth Republic | 79.3 |
| January 1961 | Self-determination for Algeria | 75.3 |
| April 1962 | Independence for Algeria | 90.7 |
| October 1962 | Constitutional amendment: Direct election of the President | 61.8 |

lacked a popular legitimacy. Without such legitimacy, the exercise of presidential leadership was unlikely to outlast the first incumbent of the office and there was the likelihood that the parliamentary régime would take hold again. Consequently, following an assassination attempt on his life in August 1962, de Gaulle took advantage of a wave of public sympathy to put forward a constitutional amendment proposing the direct election of the President by universal suffrage. In November 1962, the amendment was approved in a referendum. Ever since, although the direct election of the President places certain constraints upon the head of state, it has also been the key institutional factor which has encouraged presidential leadership. It has done so in four ways.

• *Personalisation of political leadership*
First, the direct election of the President personalises the exercise of political leadership. Although presidential candidates need the support of political parties and although they campaign upon selected policy issues, the personality of candidates is still the most important criterion which structures the vote (see Table 3.3). This is not to say

**TABLE 3.3**

**Motivations of French voters at the first ballot of the 1988 presidential election**

| Candidate | Personality | Past acts | Issues | Party | Other reasons | Don't know |
|---|---|---|---|---|---|---|
| All | 29 | 16 | 23 | 17 | 14 | 1 |
| *Voting for*: | | | | | | |
| Mitterrand (socialist) | 32 | 22 | 8 | 24 | 13 | 1 |
| Chirac (Gaullist) | 42 | 22 | 12 | 16 | 7 | 1 |
| Barre (centrist) | 45 | 17 | 19 | 8 | 10 | 1 |
| Le Pen (extreme right) | 7 | 3 | 61 | 7 | 20 | 2 |
| Lajoinie (communist) | 8 | 8 | 39 | 36 | 8 | 1 |
| Waechter (ecologist) | 6 | 2 | 48 | 16 | 27 | 1 |

*Source*: Adapted from Charlot and Charlot, 1992, p. 142.

that all successful presidential candidates will be larger-than-life charismatic figures. For example, in contrast to the very personal relationship which de Gaulle established with the French people, neither the avuncular Pompidou, nor the technocratic Giscard d'Estaing, nor the machiavellian Mitterrand can truly be described as charismatic. Indeed, in the case of Pompidou and Mitterrand (at least in 1988), the successful candidates owed their election at least in part to their lack of charisma, to the fact that they reassured the electorate and to the belief that they would scarcely disturb the equilibrium of the system. Still, personal qualities are important. Giscard's youth and vigour were particular assets which accounted for his success at the 1974 election and both Mitterrand and Pompidou were elected because the leadership style that they projected in the election campaign matched the mood of the country better than any of their rivals at the time.

Moreover, the personalisation of the political process extends beyond the period of the presidential election campaign (Parodi, 1988, p. 31). Presidents are expected to impose and do impose their own imprint on the political system. The most visible manifestation of this point can be found in the monuments that Presidents have left to the nation to commemorate their term in office – the Pompidou Centre, the Musée d'Orsay (Giscard), the Pyramid in the Louvre and the National Library (Mitterrand). A consequence of this expectation, though, is that Presidents who are not up to the job, who lose their way, who allow the country to drift, who fail to make an impression, who are unable to follow in de Gaulle's footsteps are liable to be sanctioned. For example, Giscard's defeat at the 1981 presidential election was partly a result of his personal weaknesses, such as his lack of personal courage:

his love of the symbol and the political gadget, his occasional superficiality, perhaps due to his preference for clarity over exactitude, his monarchical habits or "anti-Republican" mannerisms, his misuse of his family for political ends, his quiet arrogance, his vanity and occasional cynicism (Machin and Wright, 1982, p. 14).

Similarly, Mitterrand's vacillation during his second seven-year term (*septennat*) at the time of the Moscow *coup* in 1991, for example, partly accounts for the disastrous performance of the Socialist party at the 1993 legislative elections. In all, as in the USA, the direct election of the French President personalises the leadership process. In so doing, it provides both a resource which the President may utilise in order to leave a mark on the system, but also an exaggerated emphasis on personal qualities which may leave the President a hostage to fortune.

• *Statement of personal vision for the future*
Second, the direct election of the President provides presidential candidates with the opportunity to map out the direction in which they wish the country to proceed. Presidential candidates have to make promises, in the form of manifesto policy proposals, which they undertake to introduce if elected. These promises may be vague or specific. The most detailed manifesto to have been presented to date was Mitterrand's 1981 list of reforms, the so-called 'One Hundred and Ten Proposals for France'. By contrast, his 1988 election manifesto, the 'Letter to all the French', was relatively free of policy promises. Candidates also have to present an image of the type of

leadership that they will exercise if elected. They may present themselves as reassuring figures, or as being task-oriented. They may tour the country, meeting ordinary people, or, if their aim is to be re-elected, they may play upon their presidential status, emphasising their difference. Their discourse may be triumphalist and transcendental (Gaffney, 1988, p. 45) or it may be conservative and defensive. Successful presidential candidates win office with both a programme which is ready to be put into effect and an image of the type of leadership that they wish to exercise implanted in the public psyche. In this sense, the presidential election campaign helps to set the political agenda and to determine the successful candidate's leadership style.

At the same time, though, the visionary aspect of presidential campaigns creates a climate of expectations which it is sometimes very difficult for reformist Presidents to meet once in office. It is not that Presidents, such as Giscard after 1974 and Mitterrand from 1981 to 1986 and 1988 to 1993, were unable to bring about any change whatsoever. It is more that they were unable to bring about all the changes to which they committed themselves in their election campaigns. In this way, they disappointed many of the people whose support they were initially able to obtain. This factor provides another reason why Giscard was not re-elected in 1981 and why the socialists were defeated in both the 1986 and 1993 legislative elections. Indeed, the failure to live up to expectations applies not just to reformist Presidents, but to all presidential incumbents. Presidents have a tendency to draw up grand plans, or *projets de société*, in order to create the impression that they are initiators and not just political caretakers. However, grand plans have a tendency simply to be grand exercises in rhetoric, rather than practical blueprints for reform. Again, the result is the disappointment of expectations. As Hoffmann notes: 'a gap persists between the pragmatic and illusionless great bulk of the electorate, and a party-political culture that feeds on inflated rhetoric and *projets de société* even when the ideology behind them is obsolete or sterile' (Hoffmann, 1987, p. 350). The likelihood that Presidents will disappoint expectations leaves them vulnerable to public sanction.

• *Empowerment to implement a programme*
Third, direct election provides Presidents with at least an initial mandate which empowers them to implement their programme and

adopt their preferred leadership style. The mandate which French Presidents receive is more direct than British, German, Italian or Japanese heads of government as it is not mediated through party support in the legislature. Moreover, the popular mandate which French Presidents receive can be greater than their directly elected counterparts in the USA. Unlike US presidential elections, the French President is elected according to a two-ballot system, whereby only two candidates are allowed to stand at the second ballot. Consequently, whereas Bill Clinton won just 43 per cent of the popular vote in the USA, successful presidential candidates in France will always win more than 50 per cent of the votes cast and the mandate to which they can lay claim is, therefore, founded on the certainty of a majority rather than the possibility of one (see Table 3.4). At least at the beginning of their seven-year term in office, therefore, Presidents are assured of widespread backing for their leadership.

**TABLE 3.4**

**Results of French presidential elections, 1965–88**

| Year | Candidates (party) | (%) |
|------|--------------------|-----|
| 1965 | de Gaulle (Gaullist) | 54.5 |
|      | Mitterrand (socialist) | 45.5 |
| 1969 | Pompidou (Gaullist) | 57.6 |
|      | Poher (centrist) | 42.4 |
| 1974 | Giscard d'Estaing (centre-right) | 50.7 |
|      | Mitterrand (socialist) | 49.3 |
| 1981 | Mitterrand (socialist) | 51.8 |
|      | Giscard d'Estaing (centre-right) | 48.2 |
| 1988 | Mitterrand (socialist) | 54.0 |
|      | Chirac (Gaullist) | 46.0 |

The problem facing Presidents is that the mandate which they initially receive, however great it might be, is not necessarily sufficient to see them through their full seven-year term in office. Just as Presidents derive their authority from the people, so they may be deprived of it in the same way. For example, the defeat of de Gaulle's reform proposals in the April 1969 referendum was taken by the General as a popular disavowal and he immediately resigned. Similarly, Pompidou's authority was weakened after the disappointing turnout in the April 1972 referendum to confirm the enlargement of

European Community and Mitterrand failed to restore his authority with the referendum on the Maastricht Treaty on European Union in September 1992.

It is also the case that other elections which take place between presidential elections can be taken as a direct vote of confidence or no-confidence in the President's authority. In 1983, the third devaluation of the franc and the socialist government's embrace of budgetary rigour coincided with heavy defeats at the municipal elections in March of that year. The ultimate disavowal in this respect is when the President's party loses the legislative election and a period of 'cohabitation' ensues, as in 1986 and 1993, in which case leadership responsibilities shift to the Prime Minister (see below).

The potential for Presidents to be deprived of their popular authority causes a cycle of presidential decision-making to occur (Avril, 1986, p. 243). Immediately after their election, there is a presidentialisation of all aspects of the decision-making process, be it discreet as in the case of Pompidou, or ostentatious as in the case of Giscard. However, as the popular authority of Presidents declines, so they withdraw from intervening so personally in the decision-making process. In particular, just as US Presidents tend to concentrate increasingly on foreign policy during their term in office (see Chapter 5), so do French Presidents. If de Gaulle is an exception to this rule, it applies very clearly to both Giscard and Mitterrand and to a lesser degree to Pompidou. Moreover, this cycle of decision-making also reflects on the nature of presidential/prime ministerial relations. The first Prime Minister whom a President appoints tends to be a political figure whose role is to implement the President's election programme. However, the second Prime Minister, usually appointed after three years, tends to be a more technocratic figure whose role is to manage the system as efficiently as possible in the face of forthcoming electoral challenges (see Exhibit 3.5). (Again, the exception of 'cohabitation' should be noted, where the President has to appoint a political opponent.)

• *Party basis for presidential government*
Finally, the introduction of the direct election of the President has altered the structure of resources between political parties. In particular, it has helped to bipolarise the French party system and provide a party basis for presidential government. As in Britain, party support is essential in allowing the President to exercise leadership. The

**EXHIBIT 3.5**
**The cycle of prime ministerial appointments in France**

| First PM: 'political' | Second PM: 'technocratic' | Exceptions |
|---|---|---|
| Debré, Chaban-Delmas, Chirac (1974), Mauroy, Rocard | Pompidou, Couve de Murville, Messmer, Barre, Fabius, Bérégovoy | Cresson and, during 'cohabitation', Chirac (1986) and Balladur |

need to win 50 per cent of the votes cast has ensured that presidential candidates have had to construct wide-ranging coalitions of support in order to be elected. In particular, they have sought to build electoral alliances between parties of the same political family in order to maximise their chances of success. On the right, Gaullist and centre-right candidates have consistently been obliged to seek each other's support or risk defeat. On the left, the socialist candidate has sought the support of the communists. The strength of these alliances has meant that they have continued beyond simply the period of election campaigns. Once elected, Presidents have rewarded their allies in other parties by appointing their representatives to government. From 1958 to 1981, the Gaullists and the non-Gaullist centre-right were allied together in office. In 1981, Mitterrand appointed four communists to government. As a result, Presidents have come to office not just as the undisputed leader of a single party, but also as the leader of a relatively stable coalition with a broad range of support in the country.

At the same time, though, the nature of the relationship between the head of state and the governing coalition has also provided a potential constraint to the exercise of presidential leadership. On occasions, Presidents have also been constrained by the presence of coalition partners in the government. Such constraints were most acute during the Giscard d'Estaing presidency, when the coalition brought together the Giscardians and the Gaullists. From 1974 to 1981, the President's party was not the dominant force within the government. In contrast to the postion occupied by the Gaullists for much of the period 1959–74 and the socialists after 1981, the President's party was simply a co-equal partner in the government. Moreover, during the latter period of Giscard presidency (1976–81), the competition between the governing parties was intense as the preparation for the 1981 presidential election began. As a result, the

Gaullists became increasingly hostile to the President and actively frustrated the implementation of the presidential policy agenda.

### Presidential/prime ministerial relations

The French leadership environment, therefore, consists of institutional and societal factors which indicate a tendency towards presidential leadership. However, these factors also indicate that such leadership is not guaranteed. Ultimately, Presidents are only able to exercise leadership when they can rely on the support of both a loyal Prime Minister and a loyal parliamentary majority. It must be remembered that the Constitution of the Fifth Republic gives the President specific policy-making powers in only a few areas. Presidential leadership has occurred because successive Presidents have taken advantage of Article 8 of the Constitution and appointed acquiescent Prime Ministers who have undertaken to implement the President's policy programme. This is not to say that all Prime Ministers since 1958 have been politically impotent. The structure of resources within the executive means that the Prime Minister is a key political and policy actor (Wright, 1993, p. 104). He or she is in charge of the governmental machine. For example, the administrative resources which oil the machinery of government are under the Prime Minister's control (see Exhibit 3.6). The Prime Minister has a hand-picked personal advisory staff (*cabinet*) consisting of upwards of forty people. In addition, he or she is in charge of around 5000 career bureaucrats who provide administrative services to the government as a whole. Both the members of the Prime Minister's *cabinet* and representatives of the central administrative services (particularly the General Secretariat of the Government, the equivalent of the British Cabinet Office) ensure that the head of government is at the heart of the decision-making process. Many of the meetings which take substantive policy decisions are chaired either by the Prime Minister personally, or by a representative of the Prime Minister's staff. The Prime Minister is not only kept fully informed of the decision-making process, but is also an active participant in it.

However, for most of the time since 1958, Prime Ministers have been unable or unwilling to use the strategic position that they occupy in the decision-making process to impose an overall strategy on government policy. Instead, there has been a strict division of labour

```
                          EXHIBIT 3.6
      Administrative resources under the French Prime Minister's control

Logistical staff:
           Cabinet

Central services:
           The General Secretariat of the Government
           The General Secretariat of National Defence
           The General Secretariat of the Interministerial Committee on
           European Economic Cooperation

Services relating to the permanent administration:
           The General Direction for the Administration and Civil Service
           National School of Administration
           Legal and Technical Information Service
           High Council of Broadcasting

Interministerial services:
           Official Journal
           Interministerial Centre for Administrative Information
           Mediator

Organisations for economic and social development:
           General Planning Commissariat
           Territorial Development
           Economic and Social Council
```

*Source*: Adapted from Massot, 1993, p. 155.

between the President and the Prime Minister. Presidents have managed the nation's destiny, dealing with France's long-term problems and setting the major defining options for the country (Duhamel, 1987, p. 144). Prime Ministers have looked after the basic details of policy-making, organising the day-to-day activity of the governmental machine and ensuring the smooth running of the administration (see Exhibit 3.7). The President has been the country's political leader, while the Prime Minister has been the chief manager (Avril, 1986, p. 244).

Presidents, though, cannot always appoint loyal Prime Ministers. The Prime Minister and the government as a whole are constitutionally responsible to the National Assembly (Article 20). Consequently, in order for Presidents to appoint a loyal Prime Minister, they must also have the support of a loyal parliamentary majority. In this sense, the opportunity for presidential leadership is to be found not just in the results of the last presidential election, but also in the

---

**EXHIBIT 3.7**
**De Gaulle's conception of presidential/prime ministerial relations**

In view of the importance and the extent of the duties of the Prime Minister, he could not but be 'my man'. So he was, chosen expressly, maintained for a long time in office, collaborating closely and constantly with me ... Just as, on board a ship, the time-honoured experience of mariners demands that the chief officer should have his part to play alongside the captain, so in our new Republic the executive comprised, after the President who was dedicated to all that was basic and permanent, a Prime Minister concerned with day-to-day matters (de Gaulle, 1971, pp. 274–5).

---

results of the last general election (Wright, 1993, p. 105). On the occasions when legislative elections have returned absolute, or even relative parliamentary majorities which have supported the President, then the political conditions have facilitated presidential leadership. However, on the occasions when legislative elections have returned parliamentary majorities which have been opposed to the President and in favour of the Prime Minister, then the conditions have facilitated prime ministerial leadership (see Table 3.5).

**TABLE 3.5**

**Support for the President in the French National Assembly, 1958–93**

|  | Absolute majority (presidential leadership) | Relative majority (presidential leadership) | Majority opposed (prime ministerial leadership) |
|---|---|---|---|
| de Gaulle | 1962–69 | 1958–62 |  |
| Pompidou | 1969–74 |  |  |
| Giscard d'Estaing | 1974–81 |  |  |
| Mitterrand | 1981–86 | 1988–93 | 1986–88, 1993– |

*Prime ministerial leadership*

The 1986–88 period marked a turning-point in the history of the Fifth Republic. Prior to 1986, the parliamentary majority was loyal to the President (or at least relatively loyal in the case of the Giscard presidency). However, the 1986 legislative elections returned a majority to the National Assembly which was clearly opposed to the President. Consequently, the socialist President, François Mitterrand, had to appoint a Prime Minister who was acceptable to the newly elected right-wing majority in National Assembly. With minimal constitutional fuss, the President appointed the leader of the Gaullist party, Jacques Chirac, as Prime Minister and the period known as 'cohabitation' began. 'Cohabitation' may be defined as the situation where a President representing one political party (or coalition of parties) is faced with a parliamentary majority representing an opposing political party (or coalition of parties) and where, consequently, the President is obliged to appoint a Prime Minister who belongs to that majority.

From 1986 to 1988, there was prime ministerial leadership. The Prime Minister assumed control of the policy-making process. Chirac decided which parts of the governing coalition's legislative election manifesto were to become law. For example, although the government's manifesto included the promise to reform the telecommunications industry, the Prime Minister decided that any such reform had to be delayed (Elgie, 1993b, p. 50). Similarly, when it was decided to undertake a reform in a particular area, the Prime Minister acted much as Presidents had done previously. Chirac took a more long-term, strategic view of the policy-making process, leaving policy details to be thrashed out amongst the members of his government and intervening only to arbitrate between conflicting Ministers where necessary. It was Chirac who decided that the first television channel, TF1, should be privatised, rather than the second or third channels, each of which had their supporters amongst government Ministers and advisers (Elgie, 1993b, pp. 49–59). Even in the areas of foreign and defence policy, where the President has certain explicit constitutional prerogatives (Articles 15 and 52; see Exhibit 3.4), Chirac still influenced the course of events. It was his decision to restore diplomatic links with Iran, to reappoint an Ambassador to South Africa and to negotiate with hostage-takers in the Lebanon. In many respects, the exercise of leadership prior to 1986 was similar to the exercise of leadership from 1986 to 1988, with the exception that in the former period it was the President who was steering the ship of state, whereas in the latter period it was the Prime Minister whose hands were at the tiller.

The first period of 'cohabitation' ended in 1988 when Mitterrand, following his re-election as President in May of that year, invoked Article 12 of the Constitution (see Exhibit 3.4) and dissolved the National Assembly. In the ensuing election, the right-wing parliamentary majority was overturned and the socialists were returned to power albeit with only a relative majority. Once again, the majority in the National Assembly was drawn from the same political persuasion as that of the President and presidential leadership was reasserted. In this sense, the inherent presidential logic of the Fifth Republic was reconfirmed. However, events since 1988 have confirmed that the potential for prime ministerial leadership is also inherent in the political system. Presidential and parliamentary elections are not synchronised. The President is elected for a seven-year term, yet elections to the National Assembly take place every five years. Assuming that the two sets of elections take place simultaneously, or at least immediately after each other, as in 1981 and 1988, then after five years of the President's term in office, there will have to be another set of legislative elections. These legislative elections (the equivalent of mid-term elections in the USA) provide the opportunity for prime ministerial leadership to occur. In 1986, a right-wing majority was returned to the National Assembly and the first period of 'cohabitation' was ushered in. In 1993, during Mitterrand's second term of office, another right-wing majority was returned to the National Assembly and the second period of 'cohabitation' began.

After the 1993 legislative elections, Mitterrand appointed another Gaullist, Edouard Balladur, as Prime Minister. Once again there was prime ministerial leadership. For example, the Prime Minister assumed responsibility for France's negotiations in the GATT world trade talks in December 1993. The deal which France was able to negotiate was considered to be a personal success for Balladur. By contrast, the President was only able to exercise a certain influence in the areas of foreign and defence policy. For example, he still received a copy of the telegrams which are sent to the Foreign Affairs Ministry by French Embassies abroad. Also, he had weekly meetings with both the Minister for Foreign Affairs, Alain Juppé, and the Defence Minister, François Léotard. In both respects, the President was at least kept up to date with the major developments in foreign and defence policy. In all other areas, though, the Prime Minister was unequivocally in charge. Like Chirac before him, Balladur controlled the policy process.

**Conclusion**

It is apparent, therefore, that in France, as in Britain, the leadership environment ensures that there is a well-established tendency towards executive leadership. The presence of a strong central state, the limitations placed on judicial review and the weakness of the legislature all combine to displace power onto the executive branch of government. Although the remit of the executive branch is not absolute, because of the entrenched local political culture, the increased judicial activism of the Constitutional Council and the threat of a bill being defeated in the National Assembly, still political competition is centred upon winning executive office. Only by occupying positions of power in the executive branch of government is it possible to exercise political leadership.

Within the executive, the structure of resources both within the executive and within and between political parties has presidentialised party competition and the decision-making process as a whole. There has been presidential leadership. However, the foundations of presidential leadership are insecure. The President is dependent upon the support of a loyal Prime Minister and a loyal parliamentary majority. Such has been the extent of presidentialisation since 1958 that, for much of the time, the loyalty of both has been largely a formality. However, in 1986 and again in 1993, President Mitterrand was disempowered following the legislative election. He had to appoint Prime Ministers who themselves were able to impose their vision upon the decision-making process. In this sense, the two periods of 'cohabitation' have highlighted the dynamism of executive politics in France. Even if the result of the 1995 presidential elections were to reassert the exercise of presidential leadership, the threat of such leadership being overturned once again would remain inherent in the system.

# 4

# Germany:
# Dispersed Leadership

In Germany, as elsewhere, historical factors weigh heavily upon the current exercise of political leadership. Just as the weakness of government in the French Fourth Republic instilled the need for executive leadership in the Fifth Republic, so the weakness of government in the German Weimar Republic (1919–33) instilled a similar need in the Federal Republic (1949– ). Similarly, just as the experience of Mussolini's dictatorship created the desire to limit executive power in post-war Italy (see Chapter 7), so the experience of Hitler's Third Reich created a similar desire in Germany. As a consequence of these historical factors, political leadership in the Federal Republic is marked by conflicting tensions. On the one hand, unlike the situation in Japan and Italy, there is a personalisation of political leadership within the political system. Yet, on the other, unlike the situation in Britain and France, there are strongly entrenched, formal limitations to the extent to which such leadership is personalised. As such, similar to the USA where there is a form of divided leadership, in Germany there is a form of dispersed leadership (Müller-Rommel, 1988b, p. 152).

In Germany, as elsewhere, historical factors have fed into the institutional structures of the country. In the Federal Republic, the structure of resources within the executive branch of the central, or federal, government is such that leadership responsiblities are incumbent upon the head of government, the Chancellor. In this way, there is a personalisation of political power reminiscent of the situation in both Britain and France. Even so, within the central executive, there are also institutional limits on Chancellor leadership, resulting from the role of individual Ministers, the Cabinet and the structure of resources within and between political parties. More

fundamentally, the structure of resources between the central executive and the other branches and levels of government further limits
the potential for Chancellor leadership. In particular, the Chancellor
is constrained by the role of the legislature, the judiciary, para-public
institutions and subcentral, or *Land*, government. As a result,
whereas in Britain and France leadership responsibilities are concentrated in the executive branch of the central government, in Germany, as in the United States, they are diluted and a system of
dispersed leadership occurs. Using a form of words which, as we shall
see in Chapter 5, would not be out of place if applied to the United
States, Kommers has stated that the German system 'takes the form
of representative institutions enframed by a complex scheme of
divided and separated powers undergirded by a tangled web of
checks and balances' (1994, p. 471).

This chapter will identify the main features of the complex and
tangled system of the Federal Republic. It will demonstrate the ways
in which they combine to form a system of dispersed leadership. We
will begin by examining both the structure of resources within the
executive branch of the central government and the structure of
resources within and between political parties. Under the heading
'Leadership in the federal executive', we will focus on the role of the
Federal Chancellor. We will then turn to the wider context of political
leadership and examine the structure of resources between the executive branch of the central government and the other branches and
levels of government. Here, we will focus on the role of legislature, the
judiciary, para-public institutions and the system of federalism.

## Leadership in the federal executive

In Germany, as in Italy, the head of state, the Federal President, is not
a key political actor. Unlike the French and US Presidents, the
German President is not directly elected (for a list of Federal Presidents since 1949, see Exhibit 4.1). Instead, the President is elected for
a five-year term by a 'Federal Assembly', consisting of members of
the lower house of the federal legislature, the Bundestag, and an
equal number of representatives from *Land* legislatures at the subcentral level (Article 54). As a result, the President has no direct popular
authority. Choosing the President is a party affair and those chosen
have been respected, but secondary figures. For example, the current

```
                        EXHIBIT 4.1
        German Federal Presidents and their parties since 1949

        President               Party           Office

        Theodor Heuss           FDP             1949–59
        Heinrich Lübke          CDU             1959–69
        Gustav Heinemann        SPD             1969–74
        Walter Scheel           FDP             1974–79
        Karl Carstens           CDU             1979–84
        Richard von Weizsäcker  CDU             1984–94
        Roman Herzog            CDU             1994–

   Key: CDU: Christian Democratic Union. Centre-right.
        FDP: Free Democratic party. Centre/liberal.
        SPD: Social Democratic party. Centre-left.
```

President, Roman Herzog, was previously the head of the Federal Constitutional Court.

The German President has few constitutional powers. Although he or she has formal powers to conclude treaties with foreign governments (Article 59) and to appoint certain federal civil servants and government officers (Article 60), these powers have, in effect, been transferred to the federal government. Also, although the President is involved in the nomination of the Chancellor and government Ministers (Articles 63 and 64), he or she has little influence over actual appointments. More importantly, the President may have some latitude in the decision to dissolve the Bundestag (Articles 63 and 68). In 1982, President Carstens decided to dissolve the Bundestag at the request of the newly-elected Chancellor, Helmut Kohl. For the most part, though, the President is little more than a symbolic figurehead with no active role to play in the governmental decision-making process. In this sense, there are few expectations that the head of state should exercise political leadership.

By contrast, there are considerable expectations that the Federal Chancellor should exercise leadership (for a list of Chancellors since 1949, see Exhibit 4.2). The Chancellor is the single most powerful individual within the German political system. Indeed, Chancellors have been so influential that the German system of government has been called a 'Chancellor democracy' (Padgett, 1994, pp. 18–19; Sturm, 1994, pp. 99–102). Some observers have argued that the system of Chancellor democracy is institutionalised within the

---

**EXHIBIT 4.2**

**Federal Chancellors and their parties since 1949**

| Chancellor | Party | Office |
|---|---|---|
| Konrad Adenauer | CDU | 1949–63 |
| Ludwig Erhard | CDU | 1963–66 |
| Kurt-Georg Kiesinger | CDU | 1966–69 |
| Willy Brandt | SPD | 1969–74 |
| Helmut Schmidt | SPD | 1974–82 |
| Helmut Kohl | CDU | 1982– |

---

German system (see Ridley, 1966). Others have suggested that such a system operated only during the early years of the Federal Republic under Konrad Adenauer (Smith, 1991, pp. 56–57). It is certainly the case that Adenauer's time in office was exceptional. He took decisions which shaped the general policy orientations of the country, such as German membership of NATO and the formation of the EC; he enjoyed an unparalleled degree of control over his own party, the CDU; and, from 1957 to 1961, the CDU and its Bavarian sister party, the CSU, were supported by an absolute majority in the Bundestag. Whatever approach is adopted, it is undoubtedly the case that there is a personalisation of leadership (albeit subject to certain limits) within the executive branch. In this respect, therefore, there are similarities between the German system of government and the British and French systems. Where the German system differs from the British and French systems is in the wider relationship between the executive and other forces in the political system. It is this relationship that produces the German system of dispersed leadership. Before we go on to examine this wider relationship, it is necessary to outline the Chancellor's position within the executive branch of government and the relationship between the Chancellor and political parties. To this end, four factors which impinge on the Chancellor's leadership capacity will be considered: constitutional powers; administrative resources; popular legitimacy; and party competition.

*Constitutional powers*

According to Ridley, the system of Chancellor government is firmly anchored in the German Constitution, the Basic Law (Ridley, 1966, p. 447). Article 65 sets out the so-called 'Chancellor principle'. It states:

The Chancellor determines and bears responsibility for the guidelines of policy. Within these guidelines each Federal Minister conducts his department independently and under his own responsibility. The Federal Cabinet decides on differences of opinion between ministers. The Chancellor conducts the business of government in accordance with the rules of procedure adopted by it and approved by the Federal President.

This Article gives the Chancellor three powers:

1. There is the power to determine 'the guidelines of [government] policy'. This means that there is a natural tendency for both the government and the public to look towards the Chancellor for policy leadership.
2. Ministers are not individually responsible to the legislature, as in Britain, rather it is the Chancellor who 'bears responsibility' for government policy to the Bundestag. In this sense, responsibility for the affairs of the federal government is embodied in the institution of the Chancellor.
3. The Chancellor 'conducts the business of government in accordance with the rules of procedure adopted by [the government]. . .'. These rules include the provision that the Chancellor should be kept informed of departmental activities. In this way, the Chancellor is not excluded from the policy-making process.

In all three respects, the Chancellor is the focus for leadership in the system.

In addition, the Chancellor benefits from a number of more specific powers, such as the power to nominate government Ministers, to determine the number and attribution of government Ministries and to supervise the work of the Press Office and the Federal Intelligence Service. It must be noted, though, that in the area of defence there is a constitutional ban on actions which would 'disturb the peaceful relations between nations' (Article 26). Consequently, in Germany, as in Japan, heads of government have not enjoyed the same status in defence matters as either British Prime Ministers or French and US Presidents. As the unified Germany's military and diplomatic role evolves, it is possible that the Chancellor will also obtain more authority in this area as well. For the most part, though, these specific powers have allowed Chancellors to shape the general composition and activity of the federal government. The number of Ministries has varied over the years from fifteen under Adenauer in 1949 to twenty-four under Kohl in 1987 (Müller-Rommel, 1988a, p. 173). In general and mainly for reasons associated with party competition, the Adenauer and Schmidt governments were more hierarchically organised than the Erhard, Kiesinger, Brandt and Kohl governments (Müller-Rommel, 1988a, p. 175). For example, Adenauer himself assumed the post of Foreign Minister after the creation of the Foreign Affairs Ministry in 1951. The more hierarchical the government, the more likely it is that the Chancellor will be able to exercise leadership.

Finally, unlike their Japanese and Italian counterparts, German Chancellors enjoy a certain security of tenure (see Exhibit 4.3 for the reasons why they have left office). The Chancellor may be dismissed from office only if the Bundestag passes a 'constructive vote of no confidence'. Article 67 of the Basic Law states: 'The Bundestag can only pass a vote of no-confidence in the Chancellor by the election with an absolute majority of his or her successor.' That is to say, if the Bundestag wishes to dismiss the Chancellor, an absolute majority of its members has to propose someone else as a replacement. Given the difficulty that opposition parties are likely to have in agreeing on a replacement and given that it is unlikely that large numbers of the Chancellor's own party will openly rebel and vote with opposition parties against their leader, then a Chancellor is relatively free from the threat of dismissal. Unlike Conservative Prime Ministers in Britain, the Chancellor's future is not dependent on keeping the support of small party cliques. As we shall see, the Chancellor's party may apply informal, behind-the-scenes pressure for the Chancellor to step down, but, for the most part, a Chancellor can survive from one election to the next without the fear of being dismissed by a formal

---

**EXHIBIT 4.3**
**Reasons why Federal Chancellors have left office since 1949**

| Chancellor | Year | Reason |
|---|---|---|
| Adenauer | 1963 | Retired, aged 85, but under pressure from party and coalition partner |
| Erhard | 1966 | Resigned under pressure from party and coalition partner |
| Kiesinger | 1969 | After election, FDP allied with SPD |
| Brandt | 1974 | Resigned following Guillaume spy affair |
| Schmidt | 1982 | Lost a constructive vote of no-confidence as the FDP allied with CDU |

parliamentary vote. Only twice since 1949 has Article 67 been invoked in an attempt to remove an incumbent Chancellor and only once has it been successful. On 24 April 1972, a constructive motion of no-confidence nominated Rainer Barzel as the CDU's replacement for the incumbent SPD Chancellor, Willy Brandt. The motion gained 247 votes, two short of an absolute majority, and Brandt remained in office. On 1 October 1982, a similar motion nominated Helmut Kohl as the CDU's replacement for Helmut Schmidt. On this occasion, the motion gained 256 votes, seven more than were needed, and Kohl replaced Schmidt as Chancellor.

Therefore, it is apparent that the Basic Law provides the Federal Chancellor with certain constitutional resources with which to exercise leadership. Consequently, it would be tempting to conclude that the system of Chancellor democracy is constitutionally guaranteed. However, it is important to appreciate that the Basic Law also places certain limitations on individual leadership within the executive branch. In particular, there are two constitutional principles which restrict the Chancellor's powers: the Minister principle and the Cabinet principle. These are equivalent to the British principles of departmentalism and Cabinet collegiality.

• *The Minister principle*
In addition to the 'Chancellor principle', Article 65 of the Basic Law also sets out the so-called 'Minister principle'. This principle is to be found in the statement that, within the guidelines of policy laid down by the Chancellor, Federal Ministers conduct and are responsible for the business of their own departments. The Chancellor is not allowed to issue Ministers with specific orders, nor can he bypass the Minister and issue orders to departmental civil servants (Ridley, 1966, p. 457). The Minister is placed at the head of the department and is subordinate to no one for the work of that department. The result is that the policy-making process is compartmentalised. Ministers are encouraged to operate autonomously of each other. As Mayntz notes:

> German federal ministers are constitutionally defined as sectoral leaders who exercise executive authority in their own right and not merely in the Chancellor's name (Mayntz, 1980, p. 150).

They expect to control policy-making over the areas in their departmental remit and they will jealously guard any attempts to reduce this remit (Müller-Rommel, 1988b, p. 166).

The Minister principle forces the Chancellor to play a co-ordinating role. With each Minister being constitutionally obliged to promote his or her own policy interests, Chancellors have to try to bring some order to this potentially chaotic situation. There is a need for a conciliator and Chancellors have to respond to this need. In so doing, they may liaise informally between conflicting Ministers; they may instruct representatives in the Chancellor's office to contact administrators in the conflicting departments; or more rarely they may use Cabinet committees as a forum for different departmental interests to be expressed (Müller-Rommel, 1988a, pp. 179–80). Chancellors may have a preferred method and they may take an active interest themselves in certain policy areas, such as Adenauer and Brandt in foreign policy, Schmidt in monetary and economic policy and Kohl in German unification. Whatever the preferred method and whatever their personal interests, the Minister principle obliges Chancellors to play a mediating role, which detracts from their ability to impose a strategic direction upon the policy-making process.

• *The Cabinet principle*
The third principle contained in Article 65 is the 'Cabinet principle'. The relevant section here states that: 'The Federal Cabinet decides on differences of opinion between ministers.' In practice, this is the least important of the three principles. The rules of procedure dictate that Cabinet approval is needed for a bill before it is sent to parliament, but the approval process rarely consists of anything more than the formal ratification of decisions taken elsewhere. The Cabinet does not have adequate administrative resources in order to act as a coordinating body in its own right (Paterson and Southern, 1991, p. 101). In Cabinet meetings, Ministers often desist from commenting on matters outside their own departmental policy remit and many proposals simply go through on the nod (Müller-Rommel, 1988b, pp. 165–6). As a result, although Germany is ranked high on Baylis's index of collegiality (see Chapter 2, Exhibit 2.6), this ranking is mainly a consequence of the wider aspects of the German political system outlined in this chapter, rather than being a result of any entrenched collective Cabinet decision-making culture.

Nevertheless, the Cabinet principle is not inconsequential. The potential for discussion is at least present in the system. Moreover, given that there have been coalition governments since 1949 (see below), Chancellors have always been aware of the threat that disputes between coalition partners may be raised in the Cabinet. Any such Cabinet-level disagreement would receive widespread public attention and would be damaging for the Chancellor's image and for that of both the Chancellor's party and the government as a whole. Therefore, the Cabinet principle reinforces the need for pre-Cabinet conciliation procedures to exist. Paradoxically, it reinforces the Chancellor's role as chief co-ordinator and conciliator within the governmental system.

*Administrative resources*

The Chancellor's constitutional powers are bolstered by an important set of administrative resources. Chief amongst these is the Chancellor's Office (*Kanzleramt*). As Smith notes: 'the *Kanzleramt* provides [the Chancellor] with the essential reins of government co-ordination' (Smith, 1991, p. 50). As Müller-Rommel notes: 'It is ... inconceivable that a chief executive would be able to fulfil the multiplicity of complex tasks associated with governmental leadership without the administrative (and often political) support of the Chancellor's Office' (Müller-Rommel, 1994, p. 105). The size of the Chancellor's Office has increased over the years from around 300 to nearly 500 members (Mayntz, 1987, p. 10). Its role is to advise the Chancellor about policy matters; to organise the Chancellor's press statements and television appearances; and to provide secretarial services to the Cabinet as a whole. It is headed by a Cabinet level figure and the internal structure of the Chancellor's Office mirrors the wider organisation of the government departments, although there are cross-sectional units which exist to facilitate inter-departmental policy co-ordination (see Exhibit 4.4).

Overall, the Chancellor's Office serves as a watchdog, aiding the detection of areas of policy conflict within the governmental structure and allowing the Chancellor to respond effectively to them (Mayntz, 1987, p. 10). In part, the manner in which it operates depends on the Chancellor's own leadership style. For example, during Erhard's term in office, the Office's role was weakened and Ministers developed a greater personal responsibility for their own policy affairs. By contrast, during Schmidt's term, the Office became 'the hub of executive management' (Müller-Rommel, 1994, p. 121) as the Chancellor played a more active role in the decision-making process. In fact, these two examples neatly illustrate the Office's

---

**EXHIBIT 4.4**
**The Federal Chancellor's Office**

Head of the Chancellor's Office (Federal Minister)

Six divisions (*Abteilungen*):

1. Central division, responsible for Chancellor's Office personnel, budget and organisation and the planning of governmental work.
2. Foreign policy, external security, development aid.
3. Internal, social and environmental affairs.
4. Economic and financial affairs.
5. Social and political analysis, communication and publicity.
6. Federal intelligence and the coordination of the intelligence services.

These divisions are split into fifteen subdivisions (*Gruppen*), which are further split into forty-one units (*Referat*).

*Source*: Adapted from Müller-Rommel, 1994, pp. 108–10.

---

general role in the political system. The mere existence of the Chancellor's Office is no guarantee that the Chancellor will be able to lead the government. It is simply a support unit. At the same time, though, without the support of the Office, the Chancellor would be a more marginalised figure within the governmental system. In this way, the Chancellor's Office may simply be regarded as 'an instrument of executive leadership' (Müller-Rommel, 1994, p. 126).

*Popular legitimacy*

The structure of resources within the federal government also means that the Chancellor enjoys a popular legitimacy which, although less than that of the directly elected French and US Presidents, is at least as great as that of the British Prime Minister and is certainly greater than that of both the Japanese and Italian heads of government. The Chancellor's popular authority is derived from the personalisation of the German electoral process. According to Article 63 of the Basic Law, the Chancellor is chosen by the Bundestag in the period immediately following a general election. However, each party nominates its Chancellor candidate before the election. At the election, therefore, voters choose not only on the basis of their established party identification, as in Britain, but also on the basis of the personal qualities of their preferred Chancellor candidate. In this way, similar to French and US presidential elections, German elections serve to concentrate public attention on the personality and 'fitness for office' of prospective Chancellors just as much as they reaffirm party loyalties and endorse party programmes. This personalisation of the electoral process has the consequence of detaching successful Chancellors from their own parties. As Mayntz argues:

> A candidate who wins elections for his party finds his dependence on the party organisation is attenuated. By achieving the popular image of a national leader, a Chancellor secures a certain autonomy for himself (Mayntz, 1980, p. 149).

Clearly, the more the victory is seen as a personal one for the Chancellor, then the greater the autonomy that the Chancellor subsequently enjoys. Whatever the degree of victory, though, the Chancellor has an initial basis of support which is separate from that of the party and the government as a whole. This is not say that the Chancellor's political fortunes are totally independent of these other actors, nor that this basis of support will persist indefinitely. It is simply to say that the Chancellor's enjoys a personal legitimacy which may at least temporarily increase his hold over the decision-making process. In this respect, Adenauer and Kohl stand out. Adenauer deliberately personalised electoral contests in the 1950s so that they became referendums on his style of leadership. When his party won, he took the credit. Similarly, in the 1990 election, Kohl's role in negotiating the speedy process of German unification rendered the CDU's victory a highly personal one for the incumbent Chancellor. As Chandler notes: 'After victory in the Bundestag elections, the *Kanzler der Einheit* immediately found himself in a dominant and advantageous position' (Chandler, 1993, p. 138).

However, in Germany as elsewhere, leaders who derive their support from the people are empowered for only as long as they retain that support. In Germany, the Chancellor's honeymoon period is generally just as limited as that of British Prime Ministers and French and US Presidents. For example, the economic and social difficulties brought about by the speedy unification of Germany in 1990 had profound political consequences for Kohl's popularity as Chancellor and for the popularity of the government as a whole (Niclauss, 1993, pp. 106–7). In particular, Kohl's position within the CDU came under threat. In October 1992, the Defence Minister, Volker Rühe, tried to assume the post of Vice-President of the party. From this position, he might have been able to challenge Kohl's position as the CDU's natural Chancellor candidate at the 1994 federal elections. Although Rühe was unsuccessful in his attempt, the Chancellor's popular standing was temporarily weakened as was his authority over the government. Similar problems were faced by previous Chancellors. Adenauer's popularity declined from 1959 onwards. Although he led the CDU-dominated government to victory in 1961, it was much less of a personal triumph than previous elections. Indeed, he was obliged to give a written undertaking that he would resign before the 1965 election, which he did (Dönhoff, 1982, p. 104). In this way, German Chancellors are in a similar position to their British, French and US counterparts. They depend upon their special public standing to bolster their authority over the government, but when their standing declines so too does their ability to exercise leadership.

*Party competition*

In these ways, it can be seen that the leadership capacity of the German Chancellor is dependent on the structure of resources within the executive branch of the federal government. In addition, it is also partly dependent on the structure of resources within and between political parties. In Germany, as in Britain and France, political parties play a central role in the leadership process. Much of the Chancellor's effective power is derived from the relationship between both the Chancellor and his or her own party and between the Chancellor and the other parties in the governmental coalition (Padgett, 1994, p. 7). However, as in Britain and France, there is no fixed pattern to either of these relationships. As such, the party dimension serves as a variable factor in the Chancellor's attempt to exercise leadership. Nevertheless, it is possible to make certain generalisations about both sets of relationships and to indicate the opportunities and the constraints that Chancellors face in this respect. In terms of intra-party politics, it is useful to distinguish between the CDU and SPD. In terms of inter-party politics, it is necessary to look at the dynamics of coalition government.

• *The Christian Democratic Union (CDU) and the Social Democratic Party (SDP)*
The CDU is a catch-all party (or *Volkspartei*). That is to say, rather than being a party which appeals only to a specific part of the

electorate (such as the working class or big business), it is a party which is organised highly professionally and whose 'electoral appeal, programme and personnel are based on ... "non-ideological" values' (Padgett and Burkett, 1986, p. 106). This is hardly coincidental. In the late 1940s, the pragmatism associated with a non-ideological approach was very appealing to the CDU's founding fathers as a way of uniting the disparate regional, religious and social interests within the Christian democratic movement. Since then, although the CDU has consistently been associated with certain policies, such as anti-communism and the 'social market' economy, it remains the case that the party has been committed to maintaining the economic and social *status quo*, or at least to promoting only incremental change. In one sense, of course, far from being 'non-ideological', this is itself a highly ideological approach, being based on the fundamental principles of conservatism. Officially, though, the role of ideology has been downplayed. The party has aimed to win support from all sections of society and has tailored its programme to that end. In this sense, ideology in the CDU has taken a back seat to winning and retaining power.

This emphasis on winning and retaining power, though, has had profound consequences for party leaders. In particular, as Smith notes: 'the question of party leadership assumes a pivotal importance' (Smith, 1986, p. 94). As with Conservative party leaders in Britain, CDU leaders are judged primarily in terms of their vote-winning potential. When a leader is successful in this respect, then the party is loyal. Here, Adenauer's leadership (at least until 1959) is exceptional in terms of both the CDU's electoral success and the loyalty that the party showed to him. However, when the leader is (or appears likely to be) unsuccessful, then the party is less docile. For example, neither of Adenauer's immediate successors, Erhard and Kiesinger, was able to consolidate his hold over either the electorate or the party. Similarly, Kohl was able to maintain his position within the party after 1982 only because he balanced the various interests and factions within the CDU with great skill (Chandler, 1993, p. 133). So, although CDU leaders are not as susceptible as their Conservative counterparts in Britain to being dismissed by small cliques of disgruntled party supporters, their relationship with the party is still contingent. The CDU will defer to its leader for as long as its leader is likely to return the party to power.

In contrast to the CDU, the SPD only assumed the mantle of a catch-all party at its Bad Godesberg Conference in 1959. Here, a new 'Basic Programme' was adopted, which stripped the party of its Marxist baggage. In government from 1966 to 1982, the SPD was a model of pragmatism. As Padgett and Burkett note:

> The Grand Coalition [1966–9] showed clearly the sort of party the SPD had become. Pragmatic and managerial in style, it stood for economic growth and stability, and security in the social order (Padgett and Burkett, 1986, p. 58).

Despite the party's commitment to a catch-all strategy and its similarity with the CDU in this respect, ideology has always remained more important to the SPD than to the CDU. SPD leaders have had to fulfil the dual tasks of winning power *and* appealing to the more ideologically preoccupied elements within the party. By the late 1970s, this circle became more and more difficult to square. At this time, Schmidt ran into particular problems with his party, most particularly over the questions of taxation and defence policy. Growing levels of dissent within the SPD encouraged the FDP to shift its allegiances to the CDU. The later years of Schmidt's time in office demonstrate that, although SPD leaders are chosen partly on the basis of their electoral appeal, the inoffensive Rudolf Scharping being a recent example, the party still has a slightly more ambiguous attitude towards leadership than the CDU. In this respect, the SPD resembles the British Labour party and the CDU the Conservative party. Leadership is not necessarily more difficult for SPD leaders than CDU leaders; the former simply have a different internal party agenda to address.

• *The dynamics of coalition government*
There are certain majoritarian aspects to the otherwise proportional German electoral system (Duhamel, 1993, p. 93). On the one hand, one half of the Bundestag's members are elected directly in single-member constituencies under a British-style plurality system. On the other hand, the actual distribution of parliamentary seats is calculated proportionally subject to a party having crossed the '5 per cent threshold' necessary for representation. As in Britain, the majoritarian aspect of the electoral system encourages competition between the two main parties. However, as in Italy, the proportional aspect of the system encourages coalition government. Indeed, since the establishment of the Federal Republic in 1949, coalition government has

been the norm and Chancellors have had to manage an often complex set of inter-party relations within the governmental arena (for election results since 1949, see Table 4.1). For the most part, the FDP has

TABLE 4.1

The results of Bundestag elections since 1949 (in %)

| Year | CDU/CSU | SPD | FDP | Greens | Others |
|------|---------|-----|-----|--------|--------|
| 1949 | 31.0 | 29.2 | 11.9 | — | 27.8 |
| 1953 | 45.2 | 28.8 | 9.5 | — | 16.5 |
| 1957 | 50.2 | 31.8 | 7.7 | — | 10.3 |
| 1961 | 45.3 | 36.2 | 12.8 | — | 5.7 |
| 1965 | 47.6 | 39.3 | 9.5 | — | 3.5 |
| 1969 | 46.1 | 42.7 | 5.8 | — | 5.5 |
| 1972 | 44.9 | 45.8 | 8.4 | — | 0.9 |
| 1976 | 48.6 | 42.6 | 7.9 | — | 0.9 |
| 1980 | 44.5 | 42.9 | 10.6 | 1.5 | 0.5 |
| 1983 | 48.8 | 38.2 | 7.0 | 5.6 | 0.5 |
| 1987 | 44.3 | 37.0 | 9.1 | 8.3 | 1.2 |
| 1990[1] | 43.8 | 33.5 | 11.0 | 3.9[2] | 7.8[3] |
| 1994[1] | 41.5 | 36.4 | 6.9 | 7.3 | 7.9[3] |

*Notes*:
[1] Figures include votes cast in what was the German Democratic Republic (GDR).
[2] A Greens/Alliance 1990 list in the former GDR did win seats in the Bundestag.
[3] The PDS, the ex-ruling party in the former GDR, also won seats in the Bundestag.

been the pivotal partner in coalition governments either with the CDU/CSU for most of the period before 1966 and after 1982, or with the SPD from 1969 to 1982. From 1966 to 1969 there was a 'grand coalition' between the CDU/CSU and the SPD. Whatever the composition of the coalition, the presence of inter-party competition within the governmental arena has had a significant impact on the Chancellor's exercise of leadership.

Coalition governments generally constrain the activities of national political leaders. They oblige leaders to broker the interests of the different coalition parties. They force them to act as managers forging compromises in order to keep the coalition together. Germany is no exception. Since 1961, the Chancellor's capacity to impose a general direction on the political system has been constrained by having to act within the confines of a restrictive coalition government (Saalfeld, 1990, p. 71). One of the unwritten rules of German coalition politics has been that Chancellors have had to accept the ministerial nominations of their coalition partners (Niclauss, 1993, pp. 103–4). In this sense, their power of appointment has been limited. In addition, the FDP has colonised the Ministry of Foreign Affairs since 1969. Since this time, therefore, in the realm of 'high' politics Chancellors have had to share leadership responsibilities with a political opponent. In 1990, this situation meant that the electoral benefits of German unification were also felt by the FDP. Moreover, in contrast to Italian coalitions (see Chapter 7), German coalitions assume office with the coalition partners having already agreed a programme of government. This programme defines the limits within which the government (including the Chancellor) may act. It must still be appreciated, though, that the extent to which coalition imperatives limit the Chancellor's authority varies as a function of the relative strength of the Chancellor's party in the government (see Table 4.2). For example, Adenauer, Schmidt and Brandt all had relatively comfortable majorities in the Cabinet. By contrast, Kiesinger and Kohl enjoyed a comparatively low degree of party strength in the Cabinet. Consequently, the former leaders were less

TABLE 4.2

The strength of the Chancellor's party in the governing coalition, 1949–94

| Period | Chancellor | Chancellor's party (% of Ministers) | Other parties (% of Ministers) |
|---|---|---|---|
| 1949–53 | Adenauer (CDU) | 36 | 64 |
| 1953–57 | | 55 | 45 |
| 1957–61 | | 88 | 12 |
| 1961–63 | | 65 | 35 |
| 1963–65 | Erhard (CDU) | 59 | 41 |
| 1965–66 | | 62 | 38 |
| 1966–69 | Kiesinger (CDU) | 42 | 58 |
| 1969–72 | Brandt (SPD) | 80 | 20 |
| 1972–74 | | 71 | 29 |
| 1974–76 | Schmidt (SPD) | 73 | 27 |
| 1976–80 | | 73 | 27 |
| 1980–82 | | 75 | 25 |
| 1982–83 | Kohl (CDU) | 50 | 50 |
| 1983–87 | | 53 | 47 |
| 1987–90 | | 55 | 45 |
| 1990–94 | | 60 | 40 |

*Source*: Adapted from Müller-Rommel, 1988a, p. 174, and updated by the author.

constrained in this respect than the latter and were better placed to exercise leadership.

So, institutional and societal factors within the German leadership environment mean that leadership responsibilities are incumbent upon the Chancellor. In this respect, there are similarities between the potential for Chancellor leadership in Germany and both prime ministerial leadership in Britain and presidential leadership in France. In each case, the chief executive is the focus of political leadership in the system. However, other institutional and societal factors mean that there are greater limits to the leadership responsibilities of the German Chancellor than to those of either the British Prime Minister or the French President. Moreover, in order to understand fully the dynamics of leadership within the German system, it is necessary to place the federal executive within the context of the wider political system (Smith, 1992, pp. 46–7). In Germany, as in the USA, the executive is only one part of a more general system of dispersed, or divided, leadership. We will now turn to the other salient aspects of the German leadership environment. We will identify the structure of resources between the executive branch of the federal government and the other branches and levels of government. In so doing, we will examine four key elements: the Bundestag, the Constitutional Court, para-public institutions and federalism.

**The wider context of political leadership**

*The Bundestag*

In Britain and France, the government has generally enjoyed the support of a workable parliamentary majority, backing an agreed programme and exhibiting a high degree of intra-party discipline. This situation has resulted in the executive dominating the legislature. In Germany, a similar situation has occurred, but with different results. The lower house of the German legislature, the Bundestag, has not simply been a 'debating' chamber or a 'rubber-stamp' chamber. Instead, it has been a 'working' chamber and an important element within the system of dispersed leadership. One element of this system is that there is a degree of cooperation between the executive and legislative branches of the federal government. The federal executive does not simply railroad its policy proposals through the legislature. In part, this is because such activity would undermine the cohesion of the governmental coalition by causing resentment both within and between the parliamentary representatives of the coalition partners. It is also because the upper house of the legislature, the Bundesrat, represents the interests of the subcentral units of government whose consent is needed to pass legislation which affects them (see below). If their views were ignored, government legislation would run a greater risk of being defeated there. For whatever reason, party representatives in the executive branch accept that they are obliged to negotiate with their colleagues in the legislative branch. In this way, bargaining and compromise are essential elements of the German legislative process.

In the Bundestag, the key representatives with whom the government negotiates are the leaders of the parliamentary party *(Fraktion)*. During the period of the 'grand coalition' (1966–9), the relationship between the SPD's *Fraktion* leader, Helmut Schmidt, and the CDU/CSU's *Fraktion* leader, Rainer Barzel, was instrumental in allowing the government to survive and operate efficiently. During Brandt's time in office, the SPD's *Fraktion* leader, Herbert Wehner, saw his role in terms of ensuring that the party's parliamentary group supported government policy (Paterson, 1981, p. 6). In the main, though, *Fraktion* leaders tend to reflect rather than shape the demands of the *Fraktion* members. For example, *Fraktion* leaders enjoy a close relationship with their parties' working groups in the Bundestag (*Arbeitskreise*). Members of these groups develop a policy expertise, which ensures that they resist attempts to exclude them from the policy-making process. As a result, governments accept (willingly or otherwise) that their proposals will be amended by *Fraktion* representatives. The relatively high degree of intra-party cohesion within the German system (Saalfeld, 1990, pp. 74–5) is at least partly brought about by successful negotiations between the government and *Fraktion* members.

In addition, there is also a high degree of cross-party cooperation within the German system. For the most part, such cooperation takes place in parliamentary committees. The Bundestag's committees are heavily policy-oriented. They shadow Federal Ministries and all bills introduced to the Bundestag are automatically referred to the relevant committee. The committees are the arena for negotiation and compromise and their meetings are closed to the public. They are staffed by parliamentarians, but Ministers will regularly participate in committee meetings as will civil servants. In the past at least, the result of cross-party cooperation in these committees was that upwards of 60 per cent of all bills were amended in committee and that up to 70 per cent of all legislation was unanimously approved at its final reading (Saalfeld, 1990, pp. 77–82). It would be misleading to suggest either that compromises were always easy to reach, or that a government which was unwilling to compromise had no option but to cede. The later years of Schmidt's period in office demonstrated that executive/legislative relations are not necessarily always harmonious. Nevertheless, the general point remains that executive/legislative relations in Germany differ from those in both Britain and France. Similar to their US counterparts, German Chancellors operate within a situation in which they are aware that they will have to negotiate, bargain and compromise. In this respect, the Bundestag takes its place in a system of dispersed leadership.

*The Constitutional Court*

As in France, so also in Germany, the Constitutional Court has the power of judicial review. The Constitutional Court is the guarantor of the Basic Law and, as such, it has the power to strike down any piece of legislation which it considers to be in violation of it. The jurisdiction of the Court is laid out primarily in Articles 21, 93 and 100 of the Basic Law, although its organisational structure and operational procedures were not established until a federal law was passed in 1951. Since this time, its role has gradually increased. As early as 1952 the Court was active, banning the neo-Nazi Socialist Reich Party. In 1956, the Communist party (KPD) was banned. When the SPD came to power in 1966, the Court's activism increased and it engendered greater political controversy than before (Stone, 1994, p. 452). Overall, from 1951 to 1990, the Court declared 198 federal laws to be wholly or partly unconstitutional out of 4298 bills passed, a total of 4.6 per cent (Landfried, 1992, pp. 50–1). In the same period, the Court ruled on 2529 occasions when lower-level courts filed federal and state laws which they considered to be unconstitutional. Similarly, 78 449 constitutional complaints were made to the Court by individuals, 2.25 per cent of which were upheld. What is more, it has been closely associated with more recent events. For example, it was called upon to adjudicate a number of problems arising from unification. In a decision on 29 September 1990, the Court declared that the proposed electoral law for the first set of post-unification elections to the Bundestag was unconstitutional and, in consequence, a new law had to be drafted. These examples illustrate that, as with the French Constitutional Council and the US Supreme Court, the German Constitutional Court has played a significant role in the policy-making process. As Stone notes: 'One important macropolitical effect of evolving judicialization in France and Germany has been to close off reform routes that would otherwise be open to reform-minded governments' (Stone, 1994, p. 446). As in France, the German Constitutional Court limits the sovereignty of political leaders.

The influence of the Court, though, is greater even than the above figures and cases might suggest. First, as with the case of the French Constitutional Council, both the Federal government and the Bundestag exercise 'self-limitation' and take account of a potentially negative Court ruling before bills are even passed. Stone notes: 'policymakers in both countries have institutionalised a range of practices to insulate bills from constitutional censure' (Stone, 1992b, p. 237). For example, Bundestag hearings are held with legal experts prior to a bill being passed in order to arrive at a form of wording which will avoid censure. Second, the Court's influence in the policy process is not simply negative. In its rulings, the Court often specifies how a bill would need to be worded for it to be declared constitutional. Needless to say, this encourages policy-makers to adopt this form of wording when the bill is rewritten or when a new bill in the same area is passed. Finally, it is necessary to place the Court in the wider context of the German *Rechtsstaat* (Stone, 1994, p. 464). The relationship between the Court and the other federal institutions is not essentially conflictual. The Court is part of the general commitment to a state ruled by law. One aspect of this commitment is that there is a tolerance for judicial solutions to be found for problems of an essentially political nature (Stone, 1992b, p. 235). When negotiation fails to produce a compromise between parties in the Bundestag, or between the federal and *Land* governments, for example, then the Court may be called upon to impose a legal solution. Judicial review is treated by political leaders as a legitimate and necessary part of the policy process. It is an expression of the *Rechtsstaat*. Political leaders accept the primacy of law and the role that the judicial authorities have in upholding it. As the highest judicial authority, the Constitutional Court is the most important political actor in this respect and is part of the dispersion of power.

*Para-public institutions*

Para-public institutions are organisations regulated by law, which carry out important policy-making, implementing and regulatory functions in particular policy fields. They operate in specific policy areas under the auspices of the wider state administration and consist largely of representatives of social actors, such as business and labour organisations, professional bodies, foundations and institutes. Unlike their counterpart institutions in Italy, their primary function is not to act as a repository of posts, which parties and their factions colonise. As in Italy, though, they operate with a great degree of autonomy from federal departments, although they still exhibit a degree of formal subordination to the central state. Para-public institutions include the Bundesbank, the Council of Economic Experts, Chambers of Industry and Commerce, the Conference of University Presidents, the Science Council and Labour Courts.

The most important of these institutions is the Bundesbank (see Exhibit 4.5). Although the federal government is constitutionally responsible for the direction of macroeconomic policy, the Bundesbank is legally responsible for the management of monetary policy. Given the dependence of the former on the latter, the role of the Bundesbank in the process of economic policy-making is great indeed. Moreover, given that the Bundesbank operates quasi-

---

**EXHIBIT 4.5**
**The 1957 Bundesbank Law**

1. The Bundesbank is obliged to 'support the general economic policy of the Federal Government'. At the same time, it 'shall be independent of instructions from the Federal Government'.
2. The key function of the Bundesbank is to regulate 'the amount of money in circulation and of credit supplied to the economy . . . with the aim of safeguarding the currency'.
3. The Bundesbank has various instruments of monetary policy at its disposal, including two key interest rates and currency reserves.
4. The Bundesbank is obliged to advise the government of matters of monetary policy and to supply it with information where required.
5. The Bundesbank has the right to be consulted on proposed economic legislation.
6. Directors of the Bundesbank are appointed by the Federal President on the recommendation of the Federal Government.

*Source*: Kennedy, 1991.

autonomously from the federal government, one of the major reins of economic policy is at least partly out of the grasp of the Chancellor and the Federal Finance Minister. In their desire to impose an overall strategy on the German economy, Chancellors have found themselves in conflict with the President of the Bundesbank. Moreover, it is a conflict in which they have been by no means guaranteed of success.

The presence of para-public institutions in the German political system has several consequences for the exercise of political leadership. Firstly, they serve to reinforce the sectoral nature of policymaking as they are responsible for relatively specific policy areas. This is not to say that the Chancellor or the federal government is disempowered in the policy areas covered by the para-public institutions. For example, in 1990, Chancellor Kohl imposed the decision on a very reluctant Bundesbank President, Karl Otto Pöhl, that in the process of monetary unification the conversion rate between the East and West German Marks would be one to one. However, the role of para-public institutions is such that the ability of political leaders to impose an overall strategy on governmental policy-making is rendered ever more difficult. Secondly, because the policy process is compartmentalised in this way, para-public institutions reinforce a tendency towards incrementalism in the policy-making process. By limiting policy conflict to a more technical level, they 'promote policy continuity and serve as obstacles to dramatic change' (Bulmer, 1989a, p. 27).

*Federalism*

Like the USA, Germany is a federal state. Article 20 of the Basic Law states that federalism is one of the fundamental principles of the German system. Although German federalism takes a different form from that of US federalism, the basic organisational principle is the same. Subcentral units of government enjoy certain constitutionally guaranteed powers, which cannot be taken away from them by the central government. In contrast to Britain and France, therefore, in Germany, the sovereignty of the central state institutions is formally limited. The territorial remit of political leaders at the national level is not absolute. Instead, they are obliged to work within a system in which political leaders at the subcentral (or *Land*) level have certain powers and responsibilities. Each *Land* (and there are currently 16

*Länder*) has its own Constitution, its own parliament, government, head of government and bureaucracy. The powers of the *Land* institutions are laid down in the Basic Law. Essentially they are threefold: legislative powers; participation in the Bundesrat; and administrative responsibilities. Let us look at each in turn in order to see how leadership is territorially dispersed.

• *Legislative powers*
The *Länder* have three main legislative powers (see Exhibit 4.6). Although there are certain policy areas over which the federal government has exclusive responsibility, such as foreign and defence policy-making, there are other areas, such as broadcasting, education, health and law and order, in which *Land* governments have the exclusive right to legislate (Articles 72–82). In other policy areas, framework laws are passed at the federal level, the main principles of which *Land* authorities must then incorporate into any legislation that they might wish to pass in these areas. Finally, in yet other policy areas, the powers of the federal and *Land* levels are concurrent. That is to say, the *Land* may legislate in these areas if the federal

---

**EXHIBIT 4.6**
**Legislative powers of the Federation and the *Länder***

*Exclusive powers*

| *Federation* | *Länder* |
|---|---|
| Foreign affairs | Cultural affairs (inc. broadcasting) |
| Defence | Education |
| Citizenship | Health service |
| Passports, immigration | Police |
| Currency matters | |
| Customs and free movement of goods | |
| Post and telecommunications | |

| *Framework conditions* | *Concurrent powers* |
|---|---|
| Principles of higher education | Civil and criminal law and sentencing |
| Hunting and conservation | Registration of births, deaths and |
| Press and film industry | marriages |
| Land distribution and regional | The law of association and assembly |
| planning | Residence and establishment of aliens |
| | Production and use of nuclear energy |

*Source*: Adapted from Bulmer, 1989b, p. 43.

government has not already done so. Overall, while the key tasks of any government, such as the defence of national sovereignty and the promotion of national economic well-being, are the preserve of the Federation, political leaders at the *Land* level have their own (albeit limited) areas of legislative competence.

It has been argued, though, that the legislative competence of *Land* governments relative to that of the Federation has dwindled since the 1950s. There has been a process of 'creeping centralisation' (Bulmer, 1991). In the 1950s new policy concerns, such as nuclear energy, appeared on the political agenda and were dealt with by the Federation. In the late 1960s, the fiscal crisis at the *Land* level provoked a set of constitutional reforms allowing for 'Joint Tasks' to occur between the federal and *Land* governments in certain areas (Articles 91 a and b). These areas include the construction of university buildings, agricultural policy and regional economic policy. Although these joint tasks involve formal cooperation procedures between both federal and *Land* governments, they represented an encroachment by the Federation in areas where previously it did not intervene. Finally, in the 1990s, the economic and social problems arising from German unification have resulted in a more active role for the Federation, particularly in the affairs of the *Länder* in the former GDR. For example, although the Unification Treaty states that policy-making in areas such as culture, broadcasting and education are the responsibility of the new Länder (consistent with the Basic Law), the federal government is bound to co-finance initiatives in these areas at least on a transitional basis (Klatt, 1992, p. 10). Overall, the territorial remit of political leaders at the federal level has gradually increased at the expense of the powers of those at the *Land* level.

• *Participation in the Bundesrat*

This creeping centralisation has partly been offset by an increased role for the *Länder* in their second area of responsibility, namely, their participation in the Bundesrat. The Bundesrat plays an important role in the legislative process at the federal level. It is composed purely of representatives from the *Land* governments and, as such, it is the equivalent of the US Senate. There are certain important differences, though, between the two institutions. For example, the members of the Bundesrat are not elected. Instead, they are appointed by *Land* governments (Article 51). The level of representation from each *Land* is not equal. Instead, it varies between the

*Länder*, ranging from six seats for the *Länder* with the greatest population, such as Bavaria and Lower Saxony, down to three seats for Hamburg, Hessen and the Saarland. Similarly, in the Bundesrat, rather than each delegate voting individually, each *Länder*'s delegation votes *en bloc* according to instructions received from the *Land* government. Finally, the assent of the Bundesrat is not needed for every piece of federal legislation. The Bundesrat has the right to veto only that legislation which strongly affects *Land* affairs (consent laws).

The Bundesrat is no ordinary upper chamber of parliament. Its primary role is neither to act as a check on the Bundestag, nor purely as an arena for competition between opposing political parties. Instead, the Bundesrat provides the opportunity for representatives from the *Land* level to consider bills which affect them before they become law. In this sense, it is an expression of Germany's federal structure. It is certainly the case that, when the governing majority in the Bundestag has been different from the majority in the Bundesrat, most notably from 1972 to 1982, the level of conflict between the two chambers has increased. However, on these occasions, the level of conflict has still remained very low. For example, the number of bills passed by the Bundestag but vetoed by the Bundesrat increased from 0.4 per cent in the 1965–9 parliament to only 3.1 per cent in the 1976–80 parliament (Wehling, 1989, p. 57). Rather, these periods have been marked by an increased level of consultation between the Bundestag and the Bundesrat. Negotiations between them have ensured that legislation agreeable to both chambers has been passed.

Overall, while the legislative competence of the *Länder* has decreased over the years, the role of the Bundesrat as an instrument of territorial representation has increased. As the prerogatives of the Federal government have expanded, so the number of federal laws which impinge upon the responsibilities of the *Länder* has risen. The number of consent laws rose from 41.8 per cent of all legislation in the 1949–53 parliament to 60.6 per cent in the 1983–7 parliament (Wehling, 1989, p. 57). In this respect, although the powers of the Bundesrat are less than those of the US Senate, the right of representatives from *Land* governments to consider and to veto legislation if they so desire still ensures that the Bundesrat is the most important practical expression of German federalism.

• *Administrative responsibilities*
Finally, the *Länder* play an important role in implementing federal legislation. Article 83 of the Basic Law states that the *Länder* are charged with implementing most federal legislation as well as their own laws. Indeed, only three federal departments, Foreign Affairs, Defence and Labour, have a fully developed set of administrative agencies at the subcentral level. For all other departments, the administration of federal legislation is carried out by bureaucrats working in the *Länder*. In the implementation of legislation, the *Land* authorities have a certain degree of discretion. Although less important than the other two powers, the effect of this responsibility is to increase the role of the *Länder* in the policy process.

The main consequence of this territorial dispersion of power is to limit the sovereignty of the governing institutions at the federal level. In certain policy areas, the influence of national political leaders is virtually non-existent. In other areas, where framework laws apply or where there are concurrent powers, then it is restricted. One result of the formal powers of the *Länder* is that political leadership at the federal level is necessarily sectoral. For example, Federal Chancellors, such as Adenauer and Schmidt, have been encouraged to adopt foreign and defence policy as their main concerns because these are two policy areas over which they have an unambiguous jurisdiction. Political leaders in the *Länder* cannot intervene.

A further consequence is that the central governing institutions have difficulty in imposing an overall political direction on the subcentral units of government (Katzenstein, 1987, p. 50). If they so wish, *Land* governments can combine to resist centrally inspired reform initiatives (ibid, p. 45). In normal circumstances, though, there is no need for them to do so. The German system is one of 'cooperative federalism'. Relations between the central and subcentral levels are based on negotiation and compromise. This process is structurally determined through a series of inter-linking institutional mechanisms. Such mechanisms include the set of permanent joint committees which bring together *Land* and Federal Ministers. The most notable of these mechanisms is the Standing Conference of Minister-Presidents, which is also attended by the Federal Chancellor and now generally meets every two months. There are eleven other such ministerial committees, such as finance, justice and education, which meet more frequently and have a more specialised remit in specific policy areas. In addition, there are hundreds of other permanent intergovernmental committees, bringing together, for example, officials at the *Land* and federal levels. In the Bundesrat, there is the 'conference committee', which meets to iron out any differences that might arise with the Bundestag. The conference committee consists of an equal number of representatives from the Bundesrat and the Bundestag. On the committee, the Bundesrat members are not bound by the wishes of their home *Land* government and may vote individually. Moreover, the Bundesrat committee members usually consist of officials who have an administrative, rather than a party political mentality (Paterson and Southern, 1991, p. 133). These factors facilitate the conciliation process. Rarely does the conference committee fail to reach agreement.

In all respects, German federalism limits the sovereignty of national political leaders by a system of interlocking political structures, rather than by a system of divisive and confrontational politics. Political leaders at the federal level are not disempowered, except in a few specific policy areas. Instead, they are encouraged to bargain with their counterparts at the *Land* level. Indeed, they have little option but to do so. As Katzenstein argues: 'The federal government has no choice but to negotiate and cooperate with centres of state power over which it has no control' (Katzenstein, 1987, p. 16). In this sense, Germany has a system of 'cooperative federalism'.

**Conclusion**

It is apparent, therefore, that there are both similarities and differences between the leadership environments in Germany, Britain and France. In Germany, as in Britain and France, institutional structures ensure that executive leadership is personalised in the Chancellorship. However, there are also greater constitutional and political limitations to the degree of personalisation in Germany than in either Britain or France. In particular, the nature of party competition and the constraints of coalition politics affect the Chancellor's leadership role. Moreover, within the wider political system, the executive is only one part of a more diluted system of leadership. The dispersion of political power across the set of institutions in the country creates a leadership style based upon negotiation, compromise and incrementalism. Moreover, this style is not simply adopted in an *ad hoc* fashion by political leaders, but institutionalised in a whole series of procedures which draws together representatives from different institutions and parties in a process of mutual recognition.

What is perhaps remarkable about the German leadership style is that it does not foster immobilism in the policy process. As will be seen in the next chapter, the dispersion of power in the American system can sometimes lead to inaction, because of an absence of political will. In Germany, inaction is not a feature of the leadership process. In exceptional circumstances, such as those enjoyed by Adenauer and Kohl in 1990, the Federal Chancellor may be able to impose a coherent leadership strategy upon the system as a whole. More often than not, though, political leadership is exercised both territorially and sectorally. Away from the huff and bluff of the most visible of the country's political leaders, the Federal Chancellor and the Federal government, the dispersion of power creates an institutional structure, which produces a complex mosaic of leadership responsibilities.

# 5

# The United States: Divided Leadership

In 1787, the Founding Fathers of the United States created a political system in which power was dispersed among the various levels of government and among the various branches of the central government. Rather than being concentrated in one level, power was divided between the federal government at the central level and state governments at the subcentral level. Moreover, at the federal level, power was divided among the three branches of government, executive, legislature and judiciary, according to the twin principles of the separation of powers and checks and balances. That is to say, each of the three branches of the federal government was given both its own set of constitutional powers and powers to limit the actions of each of the other two branches of government as well. In a seminal book, Richard Neustadt characterised this system as one of 'a government of separated institutions *sharing* powers' (Neustadt, 1965, p. 33). More recently, Charles O. Jones has classified the system as 'a government of separated institutions competing for shared power' (Jones, C. O., 1990, p. 3). Whatever the classification, in the American system of government leadership responsibilities are divided between representatives in the various, separated institutions. In this respect, the US leadership environment more closely resembles its German counterpart than either its British or French equivalent.

As in Germany, though, the distribution of resources between the executive branch of the federal government and the other branches and levels of government does not mean that it is impossible to exercise individual leadership. In particular, the President is a focus for leadership in the US system. The recent history of the country includes Presidents who have left their mark on the political system and not just in a negative way. For example, Franklin D. Roosevelt and Harry S. Truman are now regularly classed as having been amongst the greatest chief executives in the country's history. Others, such as John F. Kennedy, Lyndon B. Johnson and Dwight D. Eisenhower, rank above average (Murphy, 1984). In this sense, in the United States, as in Britain, France and Germany, there is a personalisation of leadership responsibilities in the executive branch of the central (or federal) government. However, in the United States, as in Germany, but in contrast to Britain and France, the leadership capacity of the chief executive is fundamentally constrained by the wider distribution of power within the political system. In particular, the US leadership style is framed by the President's relationship with the legislature, the judiciary and state governments. The interplay of these elements produces a system of divided leadership similar to the German system of dispersed leadership.

This chapter examines the US system of divided leadership. To begin with, we will focus on the structure of resources within the executive branch of the federal government by analysing the role of the President. We will then examine the relationship between the federal executive and the other branches and levels of government by identifying the role of the Congress, the Supreme Court and the system of federalism.

**Presidential leadership**

The one person who is seemingly well-placed to exercise political leadership within the US system is the President (for a list of Presidents since 1933, see Exhibit 5.1). As with the Chancellor in Germany, the US President is the central focus for leadership within an otherwise divided system of government. Unlike the German Chancellor, though, the US President has few party resources on which to draw. Political parties act only as weak and largely unreliable support mechanisms for US Presidents (see below). However, in the USA, as in Germany, there are three dimensions of presidential leadership: constitutional powers, administrative resources and popular legitimacy. Although the various elements of these three dimensions serve as the basis for presidential leadership, they also present the President with certain challenges and constraints. In this way, although the presidency represents the fulcrum of leadership in the country, the system is such that the President's ability to set and realise the leadership agenda is never guaranteed.

| EXHIBIT 5.1 US Presidents since 1933 | | | |
|---|---|---|---|
| *President* | *Party* | *Office* | *Reason for leaving office* |
| Franklin D. Roosevelt | Democrat | 1933–45 | Died in office. |
| Harry S. Truman | Democrat | 1945–53 | Decided not to run again. |
| Dwight D. Eisenhower | Republican | 1953–61 | Completed two full terms. |
| John F. Kennedy | Democrat | 1961–63 | Assassinated. |
| Lyndon B. Johnson | Democrat | 1963–69 | Decided not to run again. |
| Richard M. Nixon | Republican | 1969–74 | Resigned following scandal. |
| Gerald Ford | Republican | 1974–77 | Defeated at election. |
| Jimmy Carter | Democrat | 1977–81 | Defeated at election. |
| Ronald Reagan | Republican | 1981–89 | Completed two full terms. |
| George Bush | Republican | 1989–93 | Defeated at election. |
| Bill Clinton | Democrat | 1993– | |

*Constitutional powers*

Consistent with the twin notions of the separation of powers and checks and balances, the constitutional prerogatives of the President are considerable, but qualified. One of the overriding concerns of the Founding Fathers was to avoid creating a presidency whose incumbent would resort to the 'tyranny of the one'. So, while Hamilton could write in *The Federalist Papers*, no 70, that 'energy in the executive is a leading character in the definition of good government', at the same time strict limitations were placed on the President's powers, so as to ensure that not too much energy could be expended at any one time. For example, on the one hand, Congress may not dismiss the President from office except by the exceptional procedure of impeachment. This gives the President a security of tenure and means that, unlike heads of government in parliamentary systems, they do not have to worry about losing office between elections. On the other hand, US Presidents are limited to a four-year term of office (and, since 1955, a constitutional maximum of two terms in office); their actions are subject to judicial review; and senatorial approval is required for many presidential appointments. Overall, the Constitution legitimises, encourages and empowers presidential leadership, but at the same time it sets certain parameters within which such leadership may be exercised.

Aside from enjoying a security of tenure, another of the President's main constitutional resources is derived from the fact that the US executive is monocratic. Article 2, section 1 of the Constitution states: 'The executive Power shall be vested in a President of the United States of America.' Unlike the situation in Britain, France and Germany, the US President is both head of state and (effectively) the head of government. Moreover and, again, unlike the British and German cases, for example, the Cabinet does not act as a check on presidential power. Bessette and Tulis note:

> The architects of the presidential office consciously rejected a plural executive or one checked by an executive council in order to ensure that the presidency would possess those capacities which, they believed, characterised every well-constructed executive branch: decision, activity, secrecy, and dispatch (Bessselte and Tulis, 1981, p. 17).

There is no formal mention of the Cabinet in the Constitution and, while there is a Cabinet in practice, it is not a decision-making body. The USA is the most monocratic and the least collegial of the democracies in Baylis's index of collegiality (see Chapter 2, Exhibit 2.6). Paradoxically, though, this lack of collegiality is also a source of presidential weakness. The personal and political fates of the President and Cabinet members are not closely tied together (Heclo, 1983, p. 27). Cabinet members tend to feel only a contingent loyalty to the President. They are likely to look to their departments for initiatives. They depend on the Congress for funds to finance these initiatives. They respond to the client groups with which their departments have to do business. In general, the Cabinet cannot overrule the President, but nor can it act as unified team promoting the President's policy agenda.

Other executive powers may also be found in the Constitution. These powers serve to delineate further the scope for presidential leadership. In particular, the Constitution sanctions leadership more explicitly in the fields of foreign and defence policy than in domestic policy. In terms of foreign and defence policy, the President is at once the Commander-in-Chief of the armed forces and the country's chief diplomat. By virtue of the former, the President has the power of appointment to and dismissal from the top ranks of the military. President Truman, for example, took the controversial decision to relieve General Douglas MacArthur of all his commands in 1951. More fundamentally, Presidents have the power to send troops into battle. There are constitutional limitations to this power. Most notably, it is Congress which declares war and which appropriates the money to fight them. However, in practice, successive Presidents have waged war without it having been officially declared. Since 1789, Congress has declared war eight times, but troops have been deployed on more than 200 further occasions (Pious, 1991, pp. 195–6). Reasons of expediency and secrecy have ensured that Presidents have exploited their constitutional prerogatives in the field of defence to the full.

In foreign policy-making, the President has a similar set of powers. Most importantly, Presidents have the power to negotiate treaties with foreign governments. However, such treaties have to be ratified by a two-thirds majority in the Upper House of Congress, the Senate. This stipulation ensures that, while some treaties are swiftly ratified, others take much longer, such as President Carter's Panama Canal treaty, or fail altogether. As a result, Presidents are tempted to use another of their powers, the right to conclude executive agreements with foreign governments, as a means of conducting foreign policy. In contrast to treaties, executive agreements do not have to be ratified by the Senate. Over the years, Presidents have frequently and consistently resorted to concluding executive agreements, rather than signing treaties. Indeed, the use and possibly the abuse of executive agreements reached its peak under the Reagan presidency (see Table 5.1). For example, many of the key deals made under the auspices of the Iran–Contra affair during the Reagan administration were concluded by executive agreement.

While there are certain constitutional restrictions to presidential leadership in the fields of foreign and defence policy, these restrictions are comparatively minor when compared with the problems that Presidents face in domestic policy-making. One consequence of this situation, it has been argued, is that, as their term in office develops, Presidents are encouraged to concentrate on foreign and defence issues, rather than on domestic issues, as the chances of success would seem to be higher (Wildavsky, 1975). In fact, the chances of success are at best even and Presidents are often obliged to address such issues, rather than having any choice in the matter. The Cold War, European security, strategic questions in the Middle East and the nuclear threat are all issues which on occasions have left Presidents with no option but to act. US Presidents in the post-war period have been and continue to be faced with responsibilities of such global importance that there is no escape from them. Chief

TABLE 5.1

Treaties and executive agreements in the United States, 1933–93

| President | Number of treaties | Number of executive agreements |
|---|---|---|
| Roosevelt | 131 | 369 |
| Truman | 132 | 1324 |
| Eisenhower | 89 | 1834 |
| Kennedy | 36 | 813 |
| Johnson | 67 | 1083 |
| Nixon | 93 | 1317 |
| Ford | 26 | 666 |
| Carter | 79 | 1476 |
| Reagan | 125 | 2840 |
| Bush | 67 | 1371 |

*Note*: Figures for executive agreements are approximate.
*Source*: Stanley and Niemi, 1994, p. 280.

executives in other countries, such as Japan and Italy, have never had to take decisions of similar import during the same period. In Britain, France and Germany, only sporadically have any decisions even approaching such a level of importance had to be taken. In this respect, the exigencies of national, foreign and defence policy making set US Presidents apart from their international counterparts. This situation increases the President's status and prestige both at home and abroad, but it also renders the exercise of leadership more difficult. It is because the issues with which the President has to deal are so important that the chances of success are limited.

In terms of domestic policy making, the President's constitutional powers are relatively weak. As we shall see, the Congress is specifically empowered in this domain. However, Presidents still have both a positive and a negative power. On the positive side, they have both the power and the duty to place policy recommendations before Congress. Presidents are the country's chief political agenda setter. They are the 'Great Initiators' (Neustadt, 1965, p. 6). Since the beginning of what may be termed the 'modern presidency' under Franklin D. Roosevelt, it has been incumbent upon chief executives to give Congress and the public a lead in policy-making. At his inauguration in 1933, Roosevelt stated: 'I am prepared under my constitutional duty to recommend the measures that a stricken nation in the midst of a stricken world may require.' With Roosevelt's 'New Deal' measures being so popular, presidential agenda-setting became the norm. Now, the main forum for Presidents to present their agenda is the annual 'State of the Union' address to Congress. As will be seen, the nature of Congress is such that Presidents are by no means guaranteed that the measures they present will be adopted. (For presidential success rates, see Table 5.2). Nevertheless, there is the expectation amongst both the public and the political élite alike that Presidents have a role to play upstream in the legislative process.

**TABLE 5.2**

**Presidential success rates in Congress, 1953–93**

| President | Average success rate (%) | |
| | House | Senate |
|---|---|---|
| Eisenhower | 68.4 | 70.7 |
| Kennedy | 83.7 | 85.2 |
| Johnson | 85.9 | 79.7 |
| Nixon | 68.2 | 61.5 |
| Ford | 51.0 | 65.0 |
| Carter | 73.1 | 79.7 |
| Reagan | 45.6 | 77.9 |
| Bush | 40.2 | 65.6 |

*Note*: 'Presidential success rate' refers to the number of congressional votes support-
    ing the President divided by the total number of votes where the President
    adopted a clear position.
*Source*: Stanley and Niemi, 1994, pp. 274–5.

On the negative side, Presidents have a role to play downstream in the legislative process as well. They have a qualified power to veto bills after they have been passed by Congress (see Table 5.3). In normal circumstances, the veto may still be overridden if two-thirds of the members in both the House of Representatives and the Senate vote to do so. It is also an essentially negative power, because, as its name suggests, the veto is simply an attempt to defeat the bill in question. When Congress cannot expect to muster a two-thirds ma-jority capable of overriding the veto, then the mere threat of a veto may be enough to encourage Congress to amend a bill in a way which suits the President. For example, it has been estimated that from the time he took office through to September 1990 George Bush issued 120 veto threats. In most of these cases, the 'purpose in threatening a

TABLE 5.3

Presidential vetoes in the United States, 1933–93

| President | Regular vetoes | Vetoes overridden | Pocket vetoes | Total vetoes |
|-----------|------|------|------|------|
| Roosevelt | 372 | 9 | 263 | 635 |
| Truman | 180 | 12 | 70 | 250 |
| Eisenhower | 73 | 2 | 108 | 181 |
| Kennedy | 12 | 0 | 9 | 21 |
| Johnson | 16 | 0 | 14 | 30 |
| Nixon | 24 | 7 | 17 | 41 |
| Ford | 48 | 12 | 18 | 66 |
| Carter | 13 | 2 | 18 | 31 |
| Reagan | 39 | 9 | 39 | 78 |
| Bush | 29 | 1 | 17 | 46 |

*Note*: Unlike regular vetoes, pocket vetoes cannot be overridden by Congress.
*Source*: Stanley and Niemi, 1994, p. 278.

veto was to force substantive concessions from congressional supporters of the legislation' (Sinclair, 1991, p. 168). Nevertheless, the decision to veto remains an essentially negative if frequent way in which the President may influence the legislative process.

The result of presidential involvement in the legislative process, but also of Presidents' inability to guarantee success for their measures, is that a bargaining process occurs between Presidents and members of Congress on Capitol Hill. Presidents have the authority of their office with which to bargain, but bargain they must. This situation is similar to that faced by any of the political leaders considered in this book. Neither British Prime Ministers nor French Presidents can simply issue orders and expect them to be carried out. However, as in the German Chancellship, the formal division of power within the American system serves to institutionalise leadership as a bargaining process. Moreover, and unlike the situation in Germany, the distinctiveness of the American system, to be found mainly in the weakness of party identification and the atomised nature of Congress, renders the bargaining process which US Presidents have to undertake a highly difficult one. Before examining these issues, it is necessary to look briefly at the advantages and constraints inherent in the President's other major powers, beginning with the President's administrative resources.

*Administrative resources*

In 1936, President Roosevelt appointed a Committee on Administrative Management to report on how Presidents could best be provided with the means to handle the ever-expanding responsibilities of the office. The subsequent report recommended that the number of presidential advisers should be increased and, more controversially, that the organisation of the executive branch should be thoroughly overhauled. The basic recommendations of the report were accepted by Congress and, in 1939, the President issued an executive order which brought into being a new advisory unit, the White House Office (WHO), under the general auspices of the Executive Office of the President (EOP). (For a list of the major units in the EOP, see Exhibit 5.2). Since this time, the President's closest advisers have generally been found in the WHO and the EOP has expanded as further units

---

**EXHIBIT 5.2**
**The Executive Office of the US President in 1993**

1. Office of Management and Budget.
   Created in 1970 (known as Bureau of the Budget from 1921 to 1970). Staff: 600. Prepares and executes budget, evaluates federal programmes and prepares executive orders.
2. White House Office.
   Created in 1939. Staff: 388. Gives general policy advice.
3. Council of Economic Advisers.
   Created in 1946. Staff: 34. Analyses and appraises the national economy.
4. National Security Council.
   Created in 1947. Staff: 66. Advises on all domestic, foreign and military policies relating to national security.
5. Special Representative for Trade Negotiations.
   Created in 1963. Staff: 193. Directs trade negotiations and formulates trade policy.
6. Office of Policy Development.
   Created in 1970. Staff: 24. Advises on long-range domestic and economic policy.
7. Office of Science and Technology.
   Created in 1976. Staff: 43. Is the source of scientific, engineering and technical analysis.
8. Office of Administration.
   Created in 1978. Staff: 252. Provides administrative support services to the EOP.

*Source:* Stanley and Niemi, 1994, p. 269.

have been added to it. While it has fluctuated in size over the years, the EOP now employs approximately 1800 people, covering all aspects of foreign and domestic policy.

The creation of the EOP and the addition under the Truman presidency of major units, such as the Council of Economic Advisers and the National Security Council, resulted in what has become known as the 'institutionalised presidency'. There is now no major policy area which is not covered by the EOP. Any number of advisers are constantly at hand to help Presidents in all aspects of their work, from liaising with Congress, through to drawing up the budget and running covert military actions. (The Iran–Contra scandal under the Reagan presidency was perpetrated through the National Security Council.) In its legitimate business, those working within the EOP ensure that Presidents are much better placed to exercise leadership than they would be if they were without their assistance. As Hart notes:

> the presidential staff have enabled the President to do things he would otherwise be unable to do on his own. Without such assistance the modern presidency would be a perilously weak institution (Hart, 1987, p. 203).

In this respect, the various institutions of the EOP represent a major resource at the President's disposal.

However, it is also the case that the creation and subsequent expansion of the EOP has brought with it other problems to which Presidents have had to respond and which have complicated the nature of presidential leadership. In particular, Presidents have a tendency to become dependent on their staff for advice. Presidents turn inwards to a small coterie of trusted advisers, rather than outwards to the public as a whole. When the advisory structures are good and the advisers competent, then the President benefits. For example, much of Reagan's success during his first term in office may be attributed to the advice he received from the *troika* of James Baker as Chief of Staff, Ed Meese as Counsellor to the President and Michael Deaver as Deputy Chief of Staff. According to one observer, this triumvirate provided everything that a President needed: 'namely someone who knew the town and how to make trains run on time there, an ideological conscience and a political operative with a sense for how to get and maintain media attention' (Campbell, 1992, p. 96). However, when the advisory structures are bad and/or the advisers are incompetent, then the President is weakened. For example, Donald Regan, Chief of Staff during Reagan's second term in office, assumed what Kernell claimed was 'a faulty model of organisation and control' (Kernell, 1991, p. 341). Similarly, Carter suffered from failing to appoint Washington insiders who knew how the system worked. In this way, Presidents benefit from the support of a large staff, but they also have to learn how to manage the staff members efficiently.

A further hindrance to presidential leadership may be found in the size of the EOP. Rather than being surrounded simply by a small number of loyal aides working collectively towards a common goal, the members of the President's advisory staff are dispersed both geographically throughout the White House and adjoining buildings and institutionally throughout the various units of the EOP each with their own separate remits. The net result is that Presidents have to persuade their own staff to follow their lead (Neustadt, 1965, p. 41). So while the EOP provides the necessary logistical support which is needed for the exercise of presidential leadership, it also complicates the exercise of such leadership. On the one hand, it empowers Presidents in their task of drawing up, seeing through and implementing a coherent set of policy proposals. On the other, it also acts as a barrier to the successful completion of each of these tasks. It is a source of presidential power and an element in the division of power within the system as a whole.

The same is true for the relationship between Presidents and the federal bureaucracy. Presidents would appear to be well-placed to control the federal bureaucracy. Each incoming President appoints around 12 000 bureaucrats to some of the most senior positions in the administration. Presidents use this power of patronage to reward campaign workers and to introduce an element of loyalty into the administration. In practice, though, this 'spoils system' does not ensure presidential control of the bureaucracy. Most of the appointments are often largely, if not wholly, unknown to the President and the degree of loyalty is not great. Moreover, presidential appointments represent only the tip of the administrative iceberg. There are approximately three million people in the federal civil service as a whole. In addition, many civil servants operate in semi-independent agencies over whose work Presidents have little influence. For all these reasons, Presidents are separated from the wider bureaucracy.

Heclo has characterised the relationship between Presidents and the bureaucracy as being one of 'institutional estrangement' (Heclo, 1983). It is not that there is an antagonistic relationship between the two, rather there is 'a diminishing set of mutual needs' between them (Heclo, 1983, p. 38). For example, rather than looking towards transient Presidents, people in administrative agencies look first and foremost towards their clients with whom they have to do business over a long period of time. In particular, as administrators of federal programmes, they look both towards interest groups, which benefit from the programmes they administer and which seek to keep them running, and towards congressional committees, which appropriate the monies to fund the programmes. By contrast, Presidents have little to give the administration. As Hodgson notes: 'the point is that the public officials involved look not upwards to a hierarchy of power with the President at its apex but sideways, to their constituency in the world outside government, and to their opposite numbers in Congress' (Hodgson, 1984, p. 83). In this sense, power is not just divided constitutionally between the different branches of the federal government, there is also an element of division within the executive branch of government itself in terms of the President's relationship with both the EOP and the federal bureaucracy.

*Popular legitimacy*

As in the case of the French President, the US President is the only democratically elected person in the system whose constituency is the country itself (see Table 5.4 for election results since 1932). This situation gives the President a popular legitimacy which far exceeds that of any other elected official. Unlike members of Congress, for example, the President can justifiably claim to represent the will of the people and can use this claim (at least in the short term) as a means by which to bring about innovative policy change. Presidents who benefit from a landslide victory (Roosevelt in 1932, Johnson in 1964) will find that they are especially well-placed to make such a claim. However, all newly-elected Presidents benefit from a 'honeymoon' period immediately following their election, during which time the various elements of the divided system defer (albeit temporarily) to their demands (Rockman, 1984, pp. 115–16). The most dramatic expression of such a period came with the first 100 days of Roosevelt's presidency in 1933 when a series of key reforms was passed. In

TABLE 5.4

US presidential election results since 1932

| Year | Democrat | (%) | Republican | (%) | Other | (%) |
|------|----------|-----|------------|-----|-------|-----|
| 1932 | Roosevelt | 57.4 | Hoover | 39.6 | Thomas (Soc) | 2.2 |
| 1936 | Roosevelt | 60.8 | Landon | 36.5 | Lemke (Union) | 1.9 |
| 1940 | Roosevelt | 54.7 | Wilkie | 44.8 | Thomas (Soc) | 0.2 |
| 1944 | Roosevelt | 53.4 | Dewey | 45.9 | Thomas (Soc) | 0.2 |
| 1948 | Truman | 49.6 | Dewey | 45.1 | Thurmond (SR) | 2.4 |
| 1952 | Stevenson | 44.4 | Eisenhower | 55.1 | Hallinan (Prog) | 0.2 |
| 1956 | Stevenson | 42.0 | Eisenhower | 57.4 | Andrews (SR) | 0.2 |
| 1960 | Kennedy | 49.7 | Nixon | 49.5 | Hass (SL) | 0.1 |
| 1964 | Johnson | 61.1 | Goldwater | 38.5 | Hass (SL) | 0.1 |
| 1968 | Humphrey | 42.7 | Nixon | 43.4 | Wallace (Ind) | 13.5 |
| 1972 | McGovern | 37.5 | Nixon | 60.7 | Schmitz (Am) | 1.4 |
| 1976 | Carter | 50.1 | Ford | 48.0 | McCarthy (Ind) | 0.9 |
| 1980 | Carter | 41.0 | Reagan | 50.7 | Anderson (Ind) | 6.6 |
| 1984 | Mondale | 40.6 | Reagan | 58.8 | Bergland (Lib) | 0.2 |
| 1988 | Dukakis | 45.6 | Bush | 53.4 | Paul (Lib) | 0.5 |
| 1992 | Clinton | 43.0 | Bush | 37.4 | Perot (Ind) | 18.9 |

*Key*:
Soc – Socialist; SR – States' Rights; Prog – Progressive; SL – Socialist Labor; Am –
American; Ind – Independent; Lib – Libertarian.

the context of a system in which power is divided between many
political actors and in which party ties may be weak, status and
prestige are intangible but precious presidential resources.

As in France, though, the degree of status and prestige that is
afforded to the US President is partly offset by the concomitantly
high level of responsibility which is incumbent on the officeholder.
The greater the legitimacy that Presidents enjoy, the greater the
expectations they face and the greater the expectations they face, the
greater the difficulty they will have in exercising leadership. Presidents who use the authority of the office to their own ends will only be
successful for as long as that authority remains intact. In this respect,
despite the sight of Air Force One and the sound of 'Hail to the
Chief', Presidents soon find that their honeymoon period wears off.
(Indeed, Clinton hardly benefited from one at all.) The awareness that
problems are intractable sets in and early enthusiasms are sobered
(Rockman, 1984, p. 116). Consequently, lame-duck Presidents
(Reagan after 1984), disgraced Presidents (Nixon during the

Watergate scandal), unpopular Presidents (Bush in 1992) and Presidents whose parties suffer losses in mid-term congressional elections (Reagan in 1982, Clinton in 1994) will find that some of their initial source of power deserts them. Their power to persuade is diminished.

## The wider context of political leadership

It is apparent, therefore, that there is a personalisation of leadership within the executive branch of government. Although party ties are weak and although the organisation of the EOP and the federal bureaucracy divides power within the executive branch, the President remains the key political actor. Only the President is in a position to set and realise the leadership agenda within the executive branch. However, neither the essential uniqueness of the presidency, nor the upswings and downswings of presidential popularity should mask the point that at all times the President has to bargain with the other elements in the US political system. It is in this respect that the role of the US President resembles that of the German Chancellor. In both systems, there is a personalisation of leadership responsibilities, but institutional structures ensure that there are also formal limits to the extent to which such responsibilities are personalised. When the presidency is viewed in a wider context, then the system of divided leadership becomes apparent. In the rest of this chapter, the other essential elements of this system will be examined. We will begin by looking at the Congress before turning to the Supreme Court and then the system of federalism.

## Congressional leadership

Congressional leadership is an oxymoron – a contradiction in terms. Congress is now essentially a reactive institution. It may be able to provide specific, policy-oriented leadership in certain areas at certain times. However, it is incapable of providing coherent, programmatic leadership across all areas at any time. Only in times of crisis does it tend to act speedily and decisively and then only with the help of the President. The legislative records of the 'New Deal' (1933–7), wartime (1941–5) and 'Great Society' (1964–8) Congresses stand out as periods of exceptional activity guided by an interventionist President

(Polsby, 1990, p. 32). As with the presidency, though, the inability of Congress to provide effective leadership may at first seem somewhat surprising. After all, like the presidency, the Congress enjoys a seemingly formidable set of constitutional powers. Once again, though, we find that both the division of power between the different branches of government and within the legislature itself renders the exercise of congressional leadership an extremely difficult task. In this section, we will examine the division of power from the congressional point of view by briefly sketching the constitutional powers of Congress and by looking at the effect of so-called 'divided government' on the system. We will then examine the division of power within Congress by looking at the absence of party discipline in the system.

*The dispersion of power between institutions*

Article 1, Section 1 of the Constitution states: 'All legislative Powers herein granted shall be vested in a Congress of the United States which shall consist of a Senate and House of Representatives.' Many of these powers are set out in Article 1, Section 8 of the Constitution. They include the right to lay and collect taxes, to regulate commerce with foreign countries, to establish laws of naturalisation, to declare war and to pass any law 'which shall be necessary and proper' for the good government of the USA. In addition, Article 1, Section 9 explicitly states that no money will be drawn from the federal Treasury without it having been appropriated by law. In this sense, Congress and, in particular, the House of Representatives, was given the 'power of the purse'. Moreover, Congress is also empowered by virtue of what other institutions were constitutionally prescribed from doing. For example, Article 1, Section 10 prohibits state governments from coining money, laying or collecting taxes, or entering into treaty obligations with foreign governments. Finally, Article 6 states that the laws passed by Congress 'shall be the supreme Law of the Land'.

However, there are also certain limitations placed on the constitutional powers of Congress. Article 1, Section 9 lists a range of areas in which Congress may not legislate. For example, Congress is prohibited from declaring a person guilty without a trial, from passing retroactive legislation, from levying duties on exports from the states and from granting any titles of nobility. Further limitations are set out in the first ten amendments to the Constitution, the 'Bill of Rights', which were passed in 1791. In particular, the first amendment states: 'Congress shall make no law respecting an establishment of religion, or prohibiting the free exercise thereof; or abridging the freedom of speech, or of the press; or the right of the people peaceably to assemble, and to petition the Government for a redress of grievances.' To these limitations should be added the involvement of the other two branches of the federal government in the affairs of Congress, such as the President's right to veto legislation and the Supreme Court's power to strike down legislation which it considers to be unconstitutional, although this power is not explicitly stated in the Constitution.

Whatever the details of the constitutional powers that Congress enjoys, it is important to appreciate that these powers are always set against equivalent powers for the other branches of the federal government and state governments as well. It is not simply that the powers of Congress are limited, it is also that they are matched by a similar set of limited presidential, judicial and state powers. Each branch of the federal government and each level of government, federal and state, has its own constitutional fiefdom. In this way, the Constitution encourages each branch and level of government to fall back on its own powers and to defend them. The result is the division of power across the set of institutions in the political system. In times of crisis, or consensus, then the interests of the branches and levels of government may temporarily unite and periods of exceptional legislative activity may occur. However, it is more normal for the institutions of government to have to coexist alongside each other, for power to be shared and for leadership to consist of a bargaining process between the members of the various institutions.

If the institutions of the political system normally operate according to a form of mutual coexistence, it is possible for such coexistence to dissolve into competition and conflict in the case of 'divided government'. 'Divided government' refers specifically to the situation where a representative of one of the country's two main parties, either the Republicans or the Democrats, controls the presidency, but where representatives of the other party control either or both of the two Houses of Congress. This situation is equivalent to the case of political 'cohabitation' in France (see Chapter 3). Unlike the situation in France, though, where 'cohabitation' results in a shift from presidential to prime ministerial leadership, in the USA, divided government is a cause of 'gridlock', or institutional and legislative stalemate. The key difference between the two countries is that France has a bicephalous executive, whereas the USA has a monocratic executive. In France, during 'cohabitation' parliament simply shifts its support from the President to the Prime Minister. By contrast, in the USA, during divided government Congress shifts from generally supporting the President to being opposed. As a result, 'gridlock' ensues (for figures on divided government, see Table 5.5).

**TABLE 5.5**

**Periods of 'unified' and 'divided' government in the United States, 1832–1994**

|  |  | Unified | Divided |
|---|---|---|---|
|  | 1832–1900 | 20 | 14 |
|  | 1900–1952 | 22 | 4 |
|  | 1952–1994 | 9 | 12 |
| *Total* | 1832–1992 | 51 | 30 |

*Note*: Congressional elections take place every two years, corresponding to one period.
*Main source*: Fiorina, 1992, p. 326.

Paradoxically, though, what it is perhaps more important to explain is not why 'gridlock' should arise during periods of divided government, but why it may also be difficult to exercise leadership during periods of 'unified government' when representatives of the same party control both the presidency and Congress. Part of the answer to this question has already been provided. Namely, the separation of powers institutionalises leadership as a bargaining process. However, as has been noted, this situation is scarcely different from the process of leadership in most of the countries considered in this book. In order to explain fully the nature of the leadership process in the USA, it is necessary to move beyond a simple presentation of the separation of powers and the constitutional relationship between the different branches of the federal government. Instead, it is necessary to examine the nature of party activity in Congress. In particular, it is necessary to examine the lack of cohesion amongst political parties in the United States. It is this factor which serves to disperse power within the legislative branch of government and to institutionalise the process of bargained leadership.

*The dispersion of power within Congress*

Leadership by the legislative branch of government is not a feature of any of the countries considered in this book. In the other five countries, this is because of the strength of disciplined party activity in the legislature, which concentrates power in the hands of party leaders, who are themselves to be found in the executive branch of government. As a result, legislative power is displaced onto the executive. In the case of the United States, the absence of programmatic legislative leadership is partly the result not of the strength, but of the weakness of disciplined party activity. Moreover, the same reason accounts for the occasional difficulties in achieving presidential leadership.

It would be misleading to believe that political parties in the United States lack a leadership structure and any internal discipline, that there are no ideological ties to bind them together and that they are entirely uncohesive. On the contrary, parties do have national, state and local organisations, which may play an important role in structuring party activity. For example, the work of the Republican National Committee in the 1970s and 1980s helped to increase party socialisation and encourage higher levels of party discipline in Congress (Reichley, 1985, p. 175). Similarly, in Congress, senior party positions in both Houses (such as the House and Senate majority leaders) are among the most coveted of positions available. Moreover, the two main parties in the party system are ideologically divided (if perhaps less so than their European counterparts) across a whole range of policy areas. Indeed, parties must be of at least some residual importance if periods of divided government are to make a difference to the leadership process when compared with periods of unified government.

However, as McSweeney and Zvesper note, the overall picture is such that, while it may be the case that '[p]arty is the single most accurate guide to how members of Congress vote', it is also the case that 'partisan voting is much more limited than in many parliamentary systems' (McSweeney and Zvesper, 1991, p. 172). Evidence of the weak cohesion of US political parties can be found in the figures for party unity in Congress (see Table 5.6). These figures suggest that on average a majority of Democrats take an opposite position to a majority of Republicans in both the House and Senate only around 50 per cent of the time. If figures are calculated which are more comparable to those used in parliamentary systems (see Chapter 2), then the lack of party unity in the US case is even more striking.

**TABLE 5.6**

Party unity in Congress, 1971–90

| Congress | Senate | House |
|---|---|---|
| 92nd (1971–72) | 39 | 33 |
| 93rd (1973–74) | 42 | 36 |
| 94th (1975–76) | 43 | 42 |
| 95th (1977–78) | 43 | 38 |
| 96th (1979–80) | 46 | 43 |
| 97th (1981–82) | 45 | 36 |
| 98th (1983–84) | 42 | 52 |
| 99th (1985–86) | 51 | 59 |
| 100th (1987–88) | 47 | 53 |
| 101st (1989–90) | 44 | 52 |

'Party unity' refers to the percentage of all votes on which a majority of voting Democrats opposed a majority of voting Republicans.
*Source*: Bailey, 1992, p. 130.

In 1988, 90 per cent of Democrats opposed 90 per cent of Republicans on only 7 per cent of all House votes and 3 per cent of all Senate votes (McSweeney and Zvesper, 1991, p. 172). As the saying goes, 'What the Constitution separates, the parties cannot unite'.

There are many historical and institutional reasons to explain the lack of party cohesion in the United States. For example, the federal system serves to decentralise power and accentuate differences within parties across wide geographical areas with many different concerns. In Congress, therefore, ideology becomes the lowest common denominator and is watered down as a consequence. Similarly, elections to the House of Representatives occur every two years, which subordinates members' concern for ideology to the desire for electoral self-preservation. Moreover, the President looks to a national constituency, while members of Congress look to more parochial ones. In many states, such as California, national and local party organisations have little control over the selection of congressional candidates. In all states, candidates can run personal campaigns and win the party's nomination in their area. Finally, the separation of powers itself acts as a disincentive to cohesive party action. The difficulty in achieving coordinated action across institutions means that there is little incentive for national programmes or strategies to be drawn up. Party organisations in each institution at each level of government are encouraged to go it alone.

Whatever the reasons for the lack of party cohesion, it has certain consequences for the operation of congressional activity and for the exercise of leadership in general. In particular, it encourages committee and subcommittee government in Congress; it encourages individualistic behaviour by members of Congress; and it entails that the President has to negotiate with members of Congress in order to pass each piece of legislation that he wants. Let us look at each of these points in turn.

• *Committee and subcommittee government in Congress*
The lack of cohesive parties has displaced power onto congressional committees and, since the 1970s, subcommittees. Bailey has summed up the argument as follows:

> Without the cement provided by unified parties, it is difficult to hold together the various stages of the legislative process over a sustained period of time. A decentralised legislative process where committee, subcommittee and individual prerogatives are stressed is the result (Bailey, 1992, p. 132).

Committee government was at its height in Congress from 1937 to 1971 (Davidson, 1981, p. 103). During this time, the legislative process was relatively predictable. The process was compartmentalised into particular policy areas and each compartment was dominated by powerful, autonomous committee chairs. Bills would be scrutinised by the appropriate committee and the chair of the committee generally had the power to ensure that each bill would pass, fail or be amended according to his or her wishes. During this time, coherent, programmatic leadership was difficult to achieve. However, policy leadership in specific areas was far from ruled out. There were few people with whom the President needed to do business and the President was aware (often well in advance) whether or not a policy proposal was likely to receive the favour of the committee chair. If the chair's favour was not immediately forthcoming, then inducements could be made to encourage a bill's passage.

Institutional reforms in the 1970s ended the era of committee government (for a list of major changes, see Exhibit 5.3). These reforms were brought about in the main either by changes being made to the rules of the Democratic party in the House or by legislation. The net effect of these reforms has been to increase the number of subcommittees and to reduce the power of committee chairs. As a

---

**EXHIBIT 5.3**

**Examples of changes to the House committee system in the 1970s**

1. Members were prohibited from chairing more than one subcommittee.
2. The 'subcommittee bill of rights'. Powers were taken away from committee chairs. These powers included the right to select subcommittee chairs, to define subcommittee jurisdictions and to determine subcommittee budgets.
3. The 'sunshine reforms'. Committee hearings were opened up to the public. Hearings became televised.
4. The 'seniority rule', by which committee chairs went to the senior serving member on the committee, was weakened. This allowed a turnover in committee chairs.
5. All committees with more than 20 members had to establish at least four subcommittees.
6. Members were limited to serving on a maximum of five subcommittees.

---

result, instead of the legislative process being controlled by a relatively small number of key individuals, power is now more dispersed, being spread across a wider range of committee and subcommittee chairs. Overall, the legislative process has become more complicated and more unpredictable. There are more access points for interest groups and Presidents have to deal with many more people than before when trying to pass their preferred policy proposals. Once again, it needs to be stressed that these reforms have not ruled out the possibility of presidential or legislative leadership. Rather, they have made such leadership more difficult to achieve.

• *Individualistic behaviour of members of Congress*
The second consequence of the lack of cohesive parties can be found in the individualism of members of Congress. In parliamentary systems, the first point of reference for members of the legislature is their own party. They owe their election and any future re-election to their party and their behaviour in the legislature shows a corresponding degree of party loyalty. In the United States, members of Congress behave differently. As was shown in the last section, it is not that party affiliation is unimportant. For example, many of the changes to the committee system were inspired by the work of a party caucus in the House, the Democratic Study Group. It is simply that party affiliation is only one determinant of behaviour alongside others which are of equal importance. For example, the personalisation of

electoral campaigns encourages members of Congress to behave independently. They do not necessarily owe their nomination as the party candidate to the local party organisation. Nor do they necessarily owe their election itself to their party label. So, in Congress, the ties that bind members to the party are weaker than in other systems.

Moreover, the incentives for individualistic behaviour by members of Congress have gradually increased. For example, staff resources have expanded. The result has been that members of Congress are better informed across a range of policy issues than before and are more likely to vote as they see fit to do so. Similarly, computer facilities in Congress have grown rapidly. Members are now in a better position to deal with incoming mail from constituents and interest groups than before and are able to send out individualised replies (Bailey, 1989, pp. 81–3). Consequently, members are able to deal individually with a large number of constituents, continually courting their vote, rather than relying on party organisations to mobilise support. Finally, the 1971 Federal Election Campaign Act and its amendments changed the nature of how election campaigns are financed. The emphasis is now on smaller, individual donations, rather than larger ones. This reform has decreased the already secondary role of political parties and increased the role of interest groups in campaign financing. Group-sponsored Political Action Committees (PACs) have arrived on the scene. Members look more towards PACs than their parties. Again, a more fluid situation is the result.

• *The need for the President to negotiate with members of Congress*
The final consequence of the lack of party cohesion is that the President has to negotiate constantly and carefully with members of Congress in order to pass legislation. Presidents cannot command or order Congress to act. They cannot draw up a policy programme and be assured of its adoption. Instead, they have to introduce legislation piecemeal. They have to pare down their policy priorities (Reagan's budget and defence programme, Clinton's budget and health reforms). They have to deal with a multitude of congressional actors. They have to be seen to lose on some issues in order to win on others. They have to be willing to cajole and be cajoled.

Overall, the level of party cohesion is sufficiently strong to present the President with difficulties in the case of divided government, but sufficiently weak to ensure that presidential success is not guaranteed in the case of unified government (refer back to Table 5.2.) Reagan and Bush were hampered in their attempts to exercise leadership, because of the opposition of the Democratic party in Congress. Carter and Clinton (from 1993–5) were also hampered because of the fluid nature of Democratic support there. True, the weakness of party identity allows Presidents in both divided and unified periods of government to seek cross-party support for their policies. For example, legislation to approve the North American Free Trade Area which Clinton supported was passed with the help of Republican party votes countering Democratic party dissensions. However, the trouble with cross-party coalitions is that they are unstable. They have to be re-formed for every bill. Popular Presidents and Presidents in the period immediately after their election may be able to achieve this task. Unpopular and lameduck Presidents, though, will be unable to do so. On these occasions, 'gridlock' sets in and a leadership gap occurs.

**The Supreme Court**

A further element in the system of the separation of powers at the federal level is the Supreme Court. Such is the Court's role that in exceptional cases it may be in a position to fill the leadership gap. The Supreme Court has two main powers in the political system. Firstly, unlike the French Constitutional Council, for example, the Supreme Court has the power of statutory interpretation. That is to say, it rules on the meaning and application of laws passed by Congress and state legislatures. The majority of its decisions are made in this domain. Secondly, since the decision which first established the principle of judicial review (*Marbury* v. *Madison*, 1803), the Court also has the power of constitutional interpretation. It decides whether or not federal and state laws are constitutional. When the Court rules on the Constitution, then the ruling may only be overturned by the Court itself or by the difficult process of passing a constitutional amendment. Over the years, both processes have occurred and Court decisions have been overturned. However, both processes usually occur only in the medium- or long-term. Consequently, the ability to issue constitutional interpretations, which are effectively binding on all protagonists at all levels in the political system, gives the Court its central role in the political process. In this sense, it is a fundamental element of the separation of powers.

There are two reasons why the Supreme Court is so central to the operation of the political system. Firstly, as has been noted, the twin principles of the separation of powers and checks and balances serve to institutionalise conflict between the different branches and levels of government. In this situation, there is a need for an arbiter to police the boundaries set out (however fuzzily) by the Constitution. As Hodder-Williams notes:

A political structure that invites contestation between state and federal government, between executive and legislative branches, between individual and government, is bound to spawn political litigation, especially when the Constitution is so revered (Hodder-Williams, 1990, p. 139).

The institution which has ultimate responsibility for handling this litigation is the Supreme Court. As such, it is bound to be brought into the political process and, given the nature of political competition, it is bound to have to make controversial decisions.

Secondly, the Supreme Court is well-placed to assume its responsibilities and to make controversial decisions. Indeed, by the very nature of the institution, it is much better placed than either the President or Congress to make such decisions. The Supreme Court consists of nine justices who are appointed by the President subject to Senate confirmation. They serve for life and may not be dismissed from their posts, nor called to account in any way, except by the highly unusual process of being impeached. As a result, they are not directly responsible for their decisions to the public. They do not have to worry about being re-elected. They can look towards the long term, rather than having to concentrate on short-term preoccupations. Consequently, the Court as a whole can enter into areas into which it would be electoral suicide for members of the other branches and levels of government to enter. In this way, the Court has the potential to fill the leadership gap.

Shapiro cites the examples of five areas in which the Supreme Court took a lead in the period 1952–77 (Shapiro, 1990, pp. 1947–8). They are: school desegregation (*Brown* v. *Board of Education, Topeka, Kansas*, 1954, *Swann* v. *Charlotte-Mecklenburg School District*, 1970); the reapportionment of electoral constituencies (*Baker* v. *Carr*, 1962, *Wesberry* v. *Sanders*, 1964, *Reynolds* v. *Sims*, 1964); the reform of the criminal justice system (*Miranda* v. *Arizona*, 1966, *Gideon* v. *Wainwright*, 1963); changes to federal and state obscenity laws (*Roth* v. *United States*, 1957); and abortion (*Roe* v. *Wade*, 1973, *Doe* v. *Bolton*, 1973). (Given the President's powers in the fields of foreign and defence policy, it is perhaps not surprising that the five areas which Shapiro identifies all concern domestic policy issues.) Some would argue that the reforms in the above areas were all ones 'whose time had come'. Be that as it may, it is undeniable that the Court was able to take a lead when Congress was unable to do so. As Shapiro notes: 'Few American politicians would care to run on a platform of desegregation, pornography, abortion, and the "coddling" of criminals' (1990, p. 48). In addition, the Court has also issued important rulings on the right of the President to withhold information from Congress (*United States* v. *Nixon*, 1974), the freedom of the press (*New York Times* v. *United States*, 1971), the death penalty (*Furman* v. *Georgia*, 1972) and affirmative action (*Regents of the University of California* v. *Bakke*, 1978).

There are, though, limits to the Court's ability to fill the leadership gap. These limits do not simply refer to the possibility of the Court overturning its own decisions or a constitutional amendment being passed. Neither do they refer to the fact that, once a decision has been made, it may take several years for it to be implemented. For example, the famous 1954 desegregation decision, *Brown* v. *Board of Education, Topeka, Kansas*, did not bring about an end to segregation overnight. Indeed, various Civil Rights Acts, further Court decisions, such as the *Swann* v. *Charlotte-Mecklenburg School District*, 1970, and the cooperation of federal and state administrators were all needed before segregation was effectively brought to an end. Instead, the chief limitation on the Court, as with the presidency and Congress, is that it is able to lead only when it is united and when it has some goals which it wishes to achieve. The pioneering decisions of the Court led by Chief Justice Earl Warren (1953–69) and those at least in the earlier years of the Court led by Chief Justice Warren Burger (1969–86) were brought about because the members of the Court had aims which they wished to pursue. Courts which are internally divided or those which have no particular place that they wish to go will be unable to fill the leadership gap. The later Burger Court and now the Court led by Chief Justice William Rehnquist both fit into this category. The absence of a national ideological consensus, a partisan realignment, or a unified system of government has left the Supreme Court as just another institution which makes only piecemeal decisions. The Court is simply another part of the division of power.

**Federalism**

As in Germany, there is a federal system of government in the United States. The framers of the US Constitution broadly agreed that such a system was necessary in order to protect the rights of the various states which were coming together to form the union. According to one of the leading proponents of federalism at the time, James Madison, the adoption of a federal structure would guarantee powers for both the federal government at the central level and state governments at the subcentral level. It would do so by creating a system in which power resided neither solely in the centre, nor solely in the localities, but in which there would be 'a composition of both' (*The Federalist Papers*, no. 39).

In fact, nowhere in the Constitution is there a list of those powers which are reserved to the state governments. Instead, the powers of the states are mainly to be found in the areas where the Constitution is silent about the powers of the federal government. For example, Congress is explicitly given the power to regulate trade *between* the states. It follows, therefore, that the states have the power to regulate trade *within* their own territorial area. The Tenth Amendment to the Constitution, passed in 1791, made this principle of constitutional silence explicit, declaring: 'The Powers not delegated to the United States by the Constitution, nor prohibited by it to the States, are reserved to the States respectively, or to the People.' Despite the Constitution's silence, therefore, the states have the right to legislate in certain matters of common law (e.g. marriage and divorce), fiscal law (e.g. taxes and duties) and criminal law. Moreover, they also have powers to organise local administrative structures and election procedures, to control state militias and maintain public order, to regulate the economy and to promote economic and social development. This system, whereby both state and federal governments have powers in separate areas, came to be known as 'dual federalism'. It is this dualism which distinguishes the US system of federalism from the German system of 'cooperative federalism'. In the United States, both federal and state level institutions have legislative powers. In Germany, legislative power is to be found mostly at the federal level, while *Land* governments are mainly responsible for implementing legislation.

However, from the 1930s onwards the US system of dual federalism came under strain. As a response to the Great Depression, the federal government started to intervene more directly in the running of the country. Particularly under the auspices of President Roosevelt's 'New Deal' programmes, measures for economic and social recovery were directed and financed by the federal authorities. Federal administrative authorities sprang up, federal regulation increased and federal grants mushroomed (see Table 5.7). On the

**TABLE 5.7**

**Federal grants to state and local governments in the United States, 1929–92**

| Year | % of GNP | % of state and local expenditure |
|------|----------|----------------------------------|
| 1929 | 0.1 | 1.5 |
| 1939 | 1.1 | 10.3 |
| 1950 | 0.8 | 10.4 |
| 1955 | 0.8 | 10.1 |
| 1960 | 1.4 | 15.0 |
| 1965 | 1.6 | 16.0 |
| 1970 | 2.4 | 20.0 |
| 1975 | 3.3 | 24.0 |
| 1980 | 3.5 | 28.0 |
| 1985 | 2.7 | 23.0 |
| 1990 | 2.5 | 20.0 |
| 1992 | 3.0 | 22.0 |

*Sources*: Adapted from Chubb, 1985, p. 280 and Stanley and Niemi, 1994, p. 323.

whole, the states were by no means unhappy with the injection of federal cash. Unable to cope with the problems of the Depression era by themselves, they needed the economic fillip being provided for them by the federal government. However, the result was that the federal government assumed effective control over areas previously left to the jurisdiction of state governments. For example, while the federal government provided grants to finance projects in the states, it also often specified how the money was to be spent. The federal system developed a 'bias for centralization' (Chubb, 1985). Moreover, this bias was deepened in the 1960s mainly as a result of President Johnson's 'Great Society' reforms, which initiated a new expansion of federal programmes. Both local élites and the public alike increasingly looked towards the centre for innovation.

Recently, this centralising process has been somewhat reversed.

Both Presidents Nixon and Reagan campaigned for a reversal of the centralising trend. In particular, President Reagan embarked upon a crusade against big government in the early 1980s in which he effectively called for a return to a system of dual federalism. As the figures in Table 5.4 testify, Reagan's crusade for the 'New Federalism' resulted in a slight downturn in the activity of the federal government. It remains, though, that this recent downturn needs to be placed in the context of around 50 years of federal government expansion. The effect of this expansion has been to focus the popular and élite desire for innovation upon the institutions of government at the central level and, in particular, the presidency. It is certainly the case that state and local governments have an important role to play in the lives of ordinary Americans. However, as the representatives of the national interest, those within the various branches of the federal government are best-placed to bring about change and the best-placed to do so within the various branches of the federal government is the President. In this sense, the federal system is part of the wider context of divided leadership, but the contemporary dynamics of federalism have not negated the need for leadership to be exercised from the centre.

**Conclusion**

In terms of the structure of resources between the different levels of government, and both within and between the different branches of the federal government, the American system is characterised by the division of leadership responsibilities. However, as in Germany, this situation does not preclude the exercise of leadership. On occasions, Presidents have been able to give a strategic impulsion to the political system. For the most part, though, the division of power rules out long periods of personalised leadership. At the same time, it is possible to exercise short-term, pragmatic and sectoral leadership. For example, in recent years, both the Congress and the President finally acted to address the problem of the budget deficit. Further back, the Supreme Court tackled certain policy areas which would otherwise have remained untouched. Similarly, the states are also able to provide some form of leadership at the subcentral level as a result of their legislative powers. As in Germany, the distribution of resources in the United States encourages a system of divided leadership. As President Clinton stated: 'Read the United States Constitution. It's about honourable compromise. And that is not weakness if you are making progress' (quoted in Greenstein, 1994, p. 601).

# 6

# Japan:
# Reactive Leadership

The current Japanese Constitution came into force on 3 May 1947. It installed a form of parliamentary government, which was apparently similar to the British system. The Constitution states that the legislature (known as the Diet) is the 'highest organ of state power' (Chapter IV, Article 41). The Diet is the sole law-making institution of the unitary Japanese state. It has the power to elect the Prime Minister and may dismiss the government from office. As with the British Parliament, though, the Japanese Diet has consistently failed to operate as the fulcrum of leadership in the country. However, in contrast to Britain, the weakness of the Diet has not been counterbalanced by a concentration of power in the executive branch of the central government. Instead, leadership in post-war Japan, as in Italy (see Chapter 7), has been characterised by the paradox of a stable system, but unstable governments. (For a list of governments since 1947, see Exhibit 6.1). An explanantion for this paradox must be sought in the leadership environment of both countries, which has centred around the actions of a hegemonic political party.

From 1955 to 1993, the Japanese political system was dominated by the Liberal Democratic Party (LDP). As with the Christian Democrats in Italy (at least until recently), the hegemonic position of the LDP in Japan meant that the country was a prime example of a one-party dominant régime (Pempel, 1990a). That is to say, over a substantial period of time, the LDP enjoyed a majority of seats in both houses of the Diet, it provided all the Prime Ministers and most of the Cabinet Ministers and it was able to shape the national political agenda. However, at the same time and, again, as in Italy, the dominant position of the LDP did not ensure strong, individual

135

---

**EXHIBIT 6.1**
**Japanese Prime Ministers and their parties since 1947**

| Prime Minister | Year | Prime Minister's party |
|---|---|---|
| Katayama Tetsu[1] | 1947–48 | Japanese Socialist party |
| Ashida Hitoshi | 1948 | Democratic party |
| Yoshida Shigeru | 1948–54 | Liberal party |
| Hatoyama Ichiro | 1954–56 | Democratic party/LDP[2] |
| Ishibashi Tanzan | 1956–57 | LDP |
| Kishi Nobusuke | 1957–60 | LDP |
| Ikeda Hayato | 1960–64 | LDP |
| Sato Eisaku | 1964–72 | LDP |
| Tanaka Kakuei | 1972–74 | LDP |
| Miki Takeo | 1974–76 | LDP |
| Fukuda Takeo | 1976–78 | LDP |
| Ohira Masayoshi | 1978–80 | LDP |
| Suzuki Zenko | 1980–82 | LDP |
| Nakasone Yasuhiro | 1982–87 | LDP |
| Takeshita Noboru | 1987–89 | LDP |
| Uno Sosuke | 1989 | LDP |
| Kaifu Toshiki | 1989–91 | LDP |
| Miyazawa Kiichi | 1991–93 | LDP |
| Hosokawa Morihiro | 1993–94 | Japan New Party |
| Hata Tsutomu | 1994 | Japan Renewal Party |
| Murayama Tomiichi | 1994 | Japanese Socialist Party |

*Notes:*
[1] Names are given in the Japanese way with the surname first.
[2] The LDP was formed in 1955 by a merger of the Liberal and Democratic parties.

---

leadership. As Pempel notes generally about one-party dominant régimes:

> The ruling party is by no means unfettered in its ability to carry out its policies; formal rules and informal norms, combined with the countervailing weight of political and societal constraints, all set limits within which such change can occur (Pempel, 1990b, p. 334).

In the case of Japan, the rules, norms and constraints in the system have been a function of two aspects of the leadership environment: first, the nature of factional conflict within the LDP and, secondly, the relationship between the LDP and other forces in the political system.

After a brief examination of the structure of resources within the executive branch of government and the role of the Japanese Prime

Minister, the major part of this chapter is devoted to an examination of the consequences of factionalism within the LDP and the relationship between the LDP and the wider political system. It will be demonstrated that the distribution of resources within and between political parties was such that successive Prime Ministers were obliged to adopt a reactive leadership style (Calder, 1988a, and Hayao, 1993). The concluding part of the chapter deals with the impact of the 1993 election on the Japanese political system. In this election, the LDP was removed from power for the first time since 1955, being replaced initially by fragile coalition governments committed, nevertheless, to bringing about fundamental political reforms. While certain of these reforms might result in a new form of decisive, individual leadership, the nature of the Japanese leadership environment is still such that the likelihood of reactive leadership remains strong.

Let us begin with an examination of the leadership process in post-war Japan in the period before the 1993 election. Following a brief examination of the powers and resources of the Prime Minister, we will analyse the so-called '1955 set-up', concentrating on the nature of factional politics in the LDP and then on the relationship between the LDP and other forces in political system.

### The Japanese Prime Minister

In Japan, as in Britain and Germany, the head of state, the Emperor, plays no active part in the policy-making process. Chapter II, Article 1 of the 1947 Constitution states that the Emperor 'shall be the symbol of the state and of the unity of the people...'. Chapter I, Article 4 further states that the Emperor 'shall not have powers related to government'. Instead, the Constitution vests executive power in the Cabinet (Chapter V, Article 65) and gives particular powers to the head of government, the Prime Minister. Unlike their counterparts in Britain and Germany, though, the structure of resources in the executive branch of government is such that Japanese Prime Ministers enjoy few formal constitutional powers. For instance, the Prime Minister has the constitutional power to appoint and dismiss government Ministers (Chapter V, Article 68). The Prime Minister also submits bills, reports on general affairs and foreign relations to the Diet and exercises control and supervision over various administrative branches of government (Chapter V, Article 72). Furthermore, Cabinet law states that the head of government has the power to decide the jurisdiction of policy issues and to suspend ministry orders temporarily pending Cabinet action (Hayao, 1993, p. 39). However, Cabinet law also fixes the number and the functions of government departments. This means that the Prime Minister does not have the power to determine which departments should exist and what their remit should be. For the most part, the constitutional and legal powers of the Japanese Prime Minister are limited and non-specific.

It is also important to note that in terms of foreign and defence policy, whereas British, French and US chief executives have enjoyed special responsibilities, the powers of the Japanese Prime Minister are relatively weak. Certain Prime Ministers have tried to play a role in foreign policy-making as a way of increasing their domestic political authority. For example, Tanaka's standing as Prime Minister in the early 1970s was partly a result of his drive to recognise the People's Republic of China. However, in general, there are few opportunities for Japanese Prime Ministers to make an impact on the world stage. As with Germany, post-war Japan has been an economic giant, but, for historical reasons, a political dwarf. Chapter II, Article 9 of the 1947 Constitution states: 'Aspiring sincerely to an international peace based on justice and order, the Japanese people forever renounce war as a sovereign right of the nation and the threat or use of force as a means of settling international disputes.' It goes on to say, '[t]he right of belligerency of the state will not be recognised.' Therefore, although Japan does have a large self-defence force (SDF), the country has not played a strategic role in matters of global defence. Indeed, only after a law was passed in 1992 did the SDF have the right even to take part in United Nations' peace-keeping operations. As a result, Japanese Prime Ministers have not derived the same political standing in defence matters as British, French and US leaders. The same is largely true of foreign affairs. In a South-east Asian context, Japan has been a major player. In a world context and, again, in contrast to some of their international counterparts, Japanese Prime Ministers have played only a minor role.

Japanese Prime Ministers have equally few administrative resources upon which to draw (see Exhibit 6.2). The Prime Minister's personal, or inner staff, is particularly light when compared with figures for certain other chief executives. However, as in Italy (see

---

**EXHIBIT 6.2**
**The administrative resources of the Japanese Prime Minister**

1. *The Inner Staff* (8 people)
   Chief Secretary
   Four Administrative Secretaries: Finance, Foreign Affairs, International Trade and Industry, National Police
   Chief Cabinet Secretary
   Parliamentary Deputy Chief Cabinet Secretary
   Administrative Deputy Chief Cabinet Secretary

2. *The Cabinet Secretariat* (176 people in six offices)
   Cabinet Advisers' Office
   Cabinet Councillors' Office on Internal Affairs
   Cabinet Councillors' Office on External Affairs
   Cabinet Security Affairs Office
   Cabinet Informational Research Office
   Cabinet Office of the Director General of Public Relations

3. *The Management and Coordination Agency*
   Three bureaux: personnel, administrative management and administrative inspection.

*Source*: Hayato, 1993, pp. 157–82.

---

Chapter 7), steps were taken in the 1980s to try to expand the administrative resources at the Prime Minister's disposal. The aim of these reforms was to try to improve the coordination and control functions of the office at the expense of the bureaucracy. In 1984, under the Nakasone premiership, the Management and Coordination Agency was established with the aim of providing 'a new structure for vigorous and effective central management' (quoted in Hayao, 1993, p. 177). In 1986, the Cabinet Secretariat was reorganised and the number of people working in it was increased. Whatever the overall aim of these reforms, their impact on the Prime Minister's power resources has been marginal. The Prime Minister 'lacks any real staff for formulating and analyzing policy' (Hayao, 1993, p. 183).

It is apparent, then, that in terms of the structure of resources within the executive branch of government, the Japanese Prime Minister is less-well placed to exercise leadership than political leaders in comparable positions in Britain, France, Germany and the USA. Instead, of all the countries considered in this book, the formal position of the Japanese Prime Minister most closely resembles that of the President of the Council of Ministers in Italy. What is true of the Japanese Prime Minister's formal and administrative powers is also true of the office's effective, political powers. The Japanese Prime Minister has only a limited capacity to influence the decision-making process in the country. In Japan, unlike the situation in Britain and France, leadership responsibilities are not displaced onto the chief executive. Indeed, unlike the situation in the United States and Germany, leadership responsibilities are not even shared formally between the principal political leader and representatives in other branches and levels of government. For instance, the role of local government in Japan is weak and the Japanese Constitutional Court has been a relatively docile political actor. Instead, the political influence of the Japanese head of government most closely resembles that of his or her Italian counterpart. In both countries, this situation is largely the result of the distribution of resources within and between political parties. In the case of Japan, it is necessary to examine two particular aspects of party politics: factional politics in the LDP; and the relationship between the LDP and other forces in political system. Let us look at each in turn.

**Factional politics within the LDP**

Despite their relatively restricted set of constitutional and administrative powers, Japanese Prime Ministers appear to have benefited from the support of a disciplined parliamentary majority from 1955 to 1993. During this time, the LDP had a consistently high degree of electoral success (see Table 6.1), failing to obtain an absolute majority of seats in the lower house of the Diet, the House of Representatives, at only three out of twelve elections from 1958 to 1990. Even on these occasions, it was usually able to secure such a majority either by attracting the support of independent members, or, following the 1983 election, by entering into a coalition with a small offshoot party, the New Liberal Club. Moreover, the LDP parliamentary party was relatively well-disciplined after 1955. From 1955 to 1990, the LDP never lost a vote in the House of Representatives as a direct result of a back-bench rebellion (Hayao, 1993, pp. 130–1). The occasional rebellion did occur and government proposals sometimes had to be withdrawn in the face of opposition from LDP Diet members, such as Kaifu's plans for electoral reform in 1991. Nevertheless, as a general

TABLE 6.1

Elections to the Japanese House of Representatives, 1958–90 (% of votes cast)

| Year | LDP | NLC | Ind. | DSP | CGP | JSP | JCP | Others |
|------|-----|-----|------|-----|-----|-----|-----|--------|
| 1958 | 57.8 | – | 6.0 | – | ˙ – | 32.9 | 2.6 | 0.7 |
| 1960 | 57.6 | – | 2.8 | 8.8 | – | 27.6 | 2.9 | 0.4 |
| 1963 | 54.7 | – | 4.8 | 7.4 | – | 29.0 | 4.0 | 0.2 |
| 1967 | 48.8 | – | 5.6 | 7.4 | 5.4 | 27.9 | 4.8 | 0.2 |
| 1969 | 47.6 | – | 5.3 | 7.7 | 10.9 | 21.4 | 6.8 | 0.2 |
| 1972 | 46.9 | – | 5.1 | 7.0 | 8.5 | 21.9 | 10.5 | 0.3 |
| 1976 | 41.8 | 4.2 | 5.7 | 6.3 | 10.9 | 20.7 | 10.4 | 0.1 |
| 1979 | 44.6 | 3.0 | 4.9 | 6.8 | 9.8 | 19.7 | 10.4 | 0.8 |
| 1980 | 47.9 | 3.0 | 3.5 | 6.6 | 9.0 | 19.3 | 9.8 | 0.9 |
| 1983 | 45.8 | 2.4 | 4.9 | 7.3 | 10.1 | 19.5 | 9.3 | 0.8 |
| 1986 | 49.4 | 1.8 | 5.8 | 6.4 | 9.4 | 17.2 | 8.8 | 1.0 |
| 1990 | 46.1 | – | 7.3 | 4.8 | 8.0 | 24.4 | 8.0 | 1.4 |

*Key*:
NLC: New Liberal Club. Centre-right, 1976–86. Offshoot from the LDP.
Ind.: Independents. They often ally with the LDP in the Diet after elections.
DSP: Democratic Socialist party. Centre. Formed in 1960. Offshoot from the JSP.
CGP: Clean Government party (*Komeito*). Centre. Formed in 1964 by representatives
of the *Soka Gakkai* Buddhist organisation.
JSP: Japanese Socialist party. Left. Formed in 1945.
JCP: Japanese Communist party. Left. Formed in 1922.

rule, the LDP parliamentary party generally supported government legislation in a relatively disciplined manner.

In Britain, the support of a disciplined parliamentary majority was one of the main reasons why leadership responsibilities were displaced upon the executive branch of government in general and the Prime Minister in particular. In Japan, the presence of a disciplined parliamentary majority for much of the post-war period did not produce the same result. Under the 1955 set-up, Japanese Prime Ministers were relatively weak figures. This point may be illustrated by examining the length of tenure of Japanese Prime Ministers when compared with other leaders. From 1955 to 1993, there were fifteen different Prime Ministers, enjoying an average term in office of just over two and a half years. By contrast, during the same period, in Britain, there were nine Prime Ministers; in Germany, there were six Chancellors; and, in the United States, there were ten Presidents. The only cases comparable to Japan are those of France, which had thirteen Prime Ministers from 1959 to 1993 but only four Presidents, and Italy, where there were 17 different heads of government from 1955 to 1993.

In Japan, as in Italy, the high degree of governmental instability was largely the result of the highly factionalised nature of the dominant party in the system. The factions which have been present within the LDP since its creation in 1955 were a determining factor in the functioning of the political system. During this time, power was largely a function not of the support that Prime Ministers might receive from a disciplined party majority, but of the relationship that they enjoyed with the LDP's various factions. In particular, factional conflict helped to determine who became Prime Minister, how long a person remained as Prime Minister and what that person was able to do as Prime Minister. After briefly sketching the reasons for the factional nature of the LDP, these three issues will be dealt with in turn.

*Factions: origins and continuity*

According to Thayer, the LDP's factions may be treated as 'formal political entities with a headquarters, regular meetings, a known membership, an established structure, and firm discipline' (Thayer, 1969, p. 15). The origins of these 'parties within a party' predate the formation of the LDP in November 1955. In the period immediately following the end of the Second World War, Japanese politics was in a state of turmoil. From 1945 to 1955, fifty-one new parties were formed. Of these, forty-five involved Diet members who ultimately joined the LDP (Calder, 1988b, p. 57). Moreover, there was conflict within the largest party on the right, the Liberal party, which split in 1954 with the formation of the Japanese Democratic party. The creation of the LDP marked the unification of the Liberal and Democratic parties and the end of inter-party competition on the Japanese right at least for several decades. Nevertheless, what this situation demonstrated was that factional conflict within the LDP was simply the latest expression of conflict which was a feature of the Japanese right in the immediate post-war period.

From 1945 to 1955 and afterwards, the main reason for this conflict lay in personal ambition, rather than ideology. On the one hand, the right was ideologically united in its opposition to socialism and communism and, under the premiership of Yoshida Shigeru, it came to develop a commitment to the so-called 'conservative policy line' based on pragmatism, economic priorities and flexibility (Muramatsu and Krauss, 1987, p. 522). On the other hand, personal rivalries were intense. For example, there were divisions between purged politicians, such as Hatoyama Ichiro, who were initially considered as 'undesirables' by the occupying Allied powers, and non-purged politicians, who saw themselves as being the new generation of political leaders. Similarly, there were divisions between professional 'career' politicians, who were well-schooled in internal party politics, and 'bureaucrats-turned-politicians' who saw themselves as representing a new approach. By the time the LDP was formed, the Japanese right was already a complex mosaic of factional conflicts based on personal rivalries.

It might be tempting to conclude that with the passage of time these two divisions would become less salient and that factional conflict would become less intense and less personalised. However, while it is certainly true that these original divisions have become less salient, factional conflict has become no less intense and no less personalised. Factions based on personalised conflict became institutionalised within the LDP and for four main reasons (Thayer, 1969, pp. 21–39).

1. Factional competition revolved around the selection of the party President. Competition was so intense for this post because, from 1955 to 1993, the party President also became the Prime Minister. Consequently, there was an incentive for faction leaders to build up a loyal band of supporters in the party and especially amongst LDP Diet members in order to maximise their chances of reaching the highest office.

2. LDP Diet members themselves had an incentive to link up with factions and faction leaders (Tsurutani, 1992, p. 213). They needed funds in order to fulfil their constituency duties, which in turn helped them to remain in office. Being a Diet member can be a very expensive occupation (Hrebenar, 1992, p. 61). One survey found that the average LDP Diet member attended over thirty ceremonies, receptions and funerals each month where 'gifts' had often to be distributed. Factions became a major source of funds for LDP Diet members. For example, faction leaders sometimes simply handed over money directly to Diet members in return for their support (Rothacher, 1993, p. 27). In addition, they also

introduced Diet members to representatives of, for example, the business community who could also be a source of funds.

3. Competition for posts in the Cabinet, party and Diet also served to institutionalise factions. As with the election of the Prime Minister, there were other political positions which faction leaders wished to see held by either themselves or representatives of their faction. From these positions, political favours could be distributed. The four Ministries with the biggest discretionary budgets were Agriculture, Construction, Defence and Transportation (Rothacher, 1993, p. 22). By holding these positions, faction representatives could offer contracts and distribute money, which could increase both their own standing and their faction's standing in the system.

4. Until recent reforms, the electoral system for the House of Representatives encouraged factional competition. It did so by encouraging conflict not only between parties, but also between candidates of the same party (see Exhibit 6.3). In the face of this intra-party competition, LDP candidates allied with factions not simply after elections but also before them, so as to utilise the (usually financial) resources that the faction possessed which could have a decisive influence on the outcome of the contest.

---

**EXHIBIT 6.3**

**The post-war system of election to the Japanese House of Representatives**

Until recently, elections to the House of Representatives were held under a system known as the Single Non-Transferable Vote. There were two key elements to this system:

1. There were multi-member constituencies, each of which returned between two and six members to the Diet. Consequently, a large party, such as the LDP, had the opportunity of winning more than one seat in the constituency and often put forward two or three candidates.

2. Each voter in the constituency had only one vote. Therefore, if a person wished to vote for the LDP, he or she had to decide which of the LDP's candidates to support.

As a result, there was competition at elections not only between candidates of different parties, but also between candidates of the same party. In this way, factionalism was encouraged as candidates would support faction leaders in order to obtain financial and material benefits which would give them an advantage in securing votes over their party rivals.

Once elected, therefore, the Diet member had a natural loyalty to the faction leader whose help was sought.

Consequently, there were various reasons as to why personalised factional conflict was present in the LDP at its foundation in 1955 and why it should have continued to exist thereafter. Moreover, there were also reasons as to why factional conflict should have encouraged corruption and dirty financial dealing. In their attempts to win and maintain support, faction leaders were driven to accept illegal payments and to engage in secret pay-offs. The uncovering of a number of financial scandals helps to account for the decline in the support for the LDP in the 1970s and 1980s. It was also one of the main reasons why LDP lost the 1993 election. Individual faction leaders and much of the LDP's leadership collectively was tainted by, amongst others, the Lockheed, Recruit and Sagawa Kyubin scandals. Nevertheless, given the permanence and the strength of factions within the party and given the dominant position of the LDP in the political system from 1955 to 1993, it is hardly surprising that factional competition should have helped to determine the nature of political leadership in Japan for much of the post-war period. Let us now look in more detail at the impact of factions upon the leadership process.

*The selection of the Prime Minister*

As a result of the LDP's parliamentary majority from 1955 to 1993, the person elected as party President also became the Prime Minister. In the selection of the party President and, hence, the Prime Minister, factional conflict was particularly rife. This was partly because of the large number of factions which existed within the LDP. Over the years, the number of factions varied from a high of eight in 1955 to a low of four in 1993, following the disintegration of the Takeshita faction. One consequence of this dispersion of LDP Diet members across many different factions was to ensure that coalitions of factions were needed in order to elect the party President. Although there were times when certain factions dominated over all others, at no time did any single faction consistently enjoy the support by itself of an absolute majority within the LDP. Instead, the balance of power within the party was relatively equal. Therefore, in the sense that, first, the highly structured organisation of factions meant that they assumed the form of parties within a party and that, secondly, coalitions of factions were needed in order to elect the party President, then what ostensibly appeared as a period of single party government in Japan from 1955 to 1993 resembled more a form of multi-party coalition government (Leiserson, 1968).

On certain occasions, particular factions were dominant and their leaders were elected as Prime Minister. In office, such leaders used their position in the party to leave their mark on government. For example, Sato's long tenure as Prime Minister was helped by the fact that he lacked any serious competitors for much of the time, three senior faction leaders having died early in his term of office. A similar situation occurred during the relatively long period of the Nakasone premiership, because of the ill health of the leading party figure at the time, Tanaka (Hayao, 1993, p. 129). For the most part, though, there was a relatively equal balance of power between the factions. As such, it was more usual for the Prime Minister to be the leader of a faction which was far from being within the party. For example, in 1974, Miki was chosen as party President and Prime Minister, even though he was the leader of only a small, centre-left faction in the LDP. He was chosen because he was untainted by the Lockheed scandal which had engulfed his predecessor, Tanaka, and because he would not be a threat to other party elders. In 1991, Miyazawa was elected as party President and Prime Minister, even though his faction had the support of only 21 per cent of all LDP Diet members (Punnett, 1992, p. 7). On this occasion, he was elected because the largest faction, the Takeshita faction, was unable to put forward a candidate of its own and because it decided to support Miyazawa ahead of either of the other two main faction leaders, Mitsuzuka and Watanabe.

Moreover, not only was it usual for Prime Ministers not to be the leader of a dominant faction, it was just as usual for them not to be a faction leader at all. If the faction leaders themselves were ineligible to stand, because of their involvement in a scandal, for example, or if they simply did not wish to stand, perhaps preferring to bide their time and wait for a more propitious occasion, then the person elected as party President and Prime Minister would inevitably be a less senior figure chosen from the ranks of one of the factions and, again, not necessarily from the ranks of the majority faction. Those chosen as party President and Prime Minister were sometimes 'everyone's second choice', rather than anyone's first choice (Fukai and Fukui, 1992, p. 30). For example, in 1989, Takeshita did not want to stand as a candidate himself, nor did he want anyone else from his faction to stand, for fear that they should challenge his position of authority. Consequently, he announced his support for Kaifu, a member of the small Komoto faction, safe in the knowledge that Kaifu had no independent power base of his own (Hayao, 1993, p. 117).

Therefore, factional competition had a great influence on the selection of the party President and the Prime Minister. One result of this competition was that at no point from 1955 to 1993 did any Japanese Prime Minister have the same control over the LDP as, for example, de Gaulle had in France over the Gaullists, or Mrs Thatcher had in Britain over the Conservative party. Instead, control was often in the hands of certain so-called 'kingmakers' in the party, rather than with the official party President and Prime Minister. In 1974, Shiina Etsusaburo was called upon to anoint Tanaka's successor and chose Miki. Then, although he was effectively excluded from formal office-holding because of the Lockheed scandal, Tanaka himself assumed the role of kingmaker and was largely responsible for determining the outcome of all party presidential elections from Ohira through to Nakasone (Hayao, 1993, p. 116). In 1987, Nakasone himself played kingmaker and, as we have seen, in 1989 and 1991, Takeshita did the same. The presence of such figures in the party served to weaken the Prime Minister's authority. As Allinson notes of Tanaka: '[his] anomalous position as a party leader and an indicted criminal ... shaped political opportunities by constraining prime ministers and the party from taking decisive leadership on many issues' (Allinson, 1993, p. 38). Prime Ministers were aware, along with the public and the party, that they owed their position not to their own strength, but to the strength of others. In this sense, LDP Prime Ministers in Japan operated in a context which was far removed from that of directly elected Presidents in France and the United States as well as that of party leaders and heads of government in Britain and Germany. Instead, as we shall see in the next chapter, their position more closely resembled that of their Christian Democratic counterparts in Italy.

Another consequence of factional competition in the selection of the party President was that LDP Prime Ministers rarely came to power with any coherent programme of their own. This was for two reasons. First, being largely based on personal ambitions, programmatic concerns were secondary to all factions. It is true that certain Prime Ministers committed themselves to introducing particular reforms. For instance, Nakasone made explicit campaign pledges to cut the country's budget deficit by reducing public spending and to privatise the national railway system. Nevertheless, in the main, policy pledges were a millstone around the neck of candidates for the party presidency. Stockwin notes: 'Political leaders realistically aspiring to party leadership have tended to dissociate themselves from policy positions that prove ideologically divisive, preferring to rely upon a general consensus so far as possible' (1982, p. 133).

Secondly, in order to become Prime Minister, it was necessary to be a skilled negotiator, a compromiser, someone who could build coalitions between the different factions and their leaders. A coherent policy programme was a disadvantage in such a situation. Hayao argues that:

> The intraparty alliances of factions needed to win the presidency are usually built more on promises of party and government posts than on policy considerations, which are generally secondary factors. This means that the prime minister generally cannot claim that he was elected to carry out specific changes (Hayao, 1993, pp. 119–20).

The election of Suzuki in 1980 was a case in point.

All things considered, the process by which the LDP selected its party President and Prime Minister did not preclude the ability to exercise leadership. A relatively dominant figure, such as Ikeda, was able to introduce economic reforms like the ten-year 'income doubling' plan. Non-dominant figures, such as Miki, Nakasone and Kaifu all tried to assert their independence, for example, in diplomatic affairs (Inoguchi, 1991, p. 188). However, the selection process did create a leadership environment which encouraged the exercise of reactive prime ministerial leadership. Prime Ministers were not insignificant, powerless individuals. They were simply faced with a leadership environment which rendered the exercise of individual political leadership very difficult to achieve.

*The dismissal of the Prime Minister*

Just as factional conflict helped to determine which people became Prime Minister, so it also helped to determine how long people remained as Prime Minister. (For the dismissal of Prime Ministers, see Exhibit 6.4). As noted above, the LDP enjoyed an absolute

EXHIBIT 6.4
Reasons why LDP Prime Ministers left office, 1955–93

| PM | Year | Reason |
|---|---|---|
| Hatoyama | 1956 | Intra-party conflict. |
| Ishibashi | 1957 | Ill-health. |
| Kishi | 1960 | Intra-party conflict. |
| Ikeda | 1964 | Ill-health. |
| Sato | 1972 | Stood down voluntarily, but under party pressure. |
| Tanaka | 1974 | Forced to resign because of scandal. |
| Miki | 1976 | LDP did badly in the lower House election. |
| Fukuda | 1978 | Intra-party conflict. |
| Ohira | 1980 | Died in office. |
| Suzuki | 1982 | Intra-party conflict. |
| Nakasone | 1987 | Stood down voluntarily. |
| Takeshita | 1989 | Forced to resign because of scandal. |
| Uno | 1989 | LDP did badly in the upper House election. |
| Kaifu | 1991 | Intra-party conflict. |
| Miyazawa | 1993 | LDP lost the lower House election. |

majority of seats in the House of Representatives from 1955 to 1993, albeit occasionally with the help of independents or the New Liberal Club. As a result, before Miyazawa's ignominious exit in 1993, LDP Prime Ministers had been forced from office as a result only of relative rather than absolute electoral defeat.

Relative electoral failure accounted directly for the dismissal of two LDP Prime Ministers before 1993. The LDP's poor performance at the 1976 House of Representatives election was the pretext for Miki's departure, while a similarly poor performance in the 1989 House of Councillors election precipitated the resignation of Uno. Of the other twelve LDP Prime Ministers from Hatoyama through to Miyazawa, two stood down voluntarily, two resigned because of ill-health, one died and the rest were forced from office, two because of financial scandals and five because of intra-party conflict (Punnett, 1992, p. 4). For example, in 1960, the Kono and Ono factions withdrew their support for the government over Prime Minister Kishi's handling of the revision of the Japan–US Security Treaty and the government collapsed.

Stockwin identifies one clear reason as to why factional conflict should have accounted directly or indirectly for the dismissal of a number of LDP Prime Ministers from office. He argues that the prime ministership was the office to which faction leaders aspired the most. Despite the office's meagre constitutional and administrative resources, despite Japan's comparatively minor strategic defence and world diplomatic role and despite the fact that the post offered fewer opportunities for patronage than, for example, the Construction Ministry, there were still incentives for individuals to seek the prime ministership. As we shall see, it gave faction leaders at least the temporary opportunity to promote certain policy preferences. Equally importantly, the publicity surrounding the office and the authority inherent in it was greater than that of any other position in the government or the party. Moreover, after serving out their time as Prime Minister, faction leaders could reasonably aspire to becoming a kingmaker. So, the prime ministership was itself a sought-after position and one from which incumbents might be able to move on to other important positions. Nevertheless, although limited, its importance meant that 'lengthy tenure by the leader of a particular faction is unpopular with other factions because it causes a log-jam in the regular process of succession and checks the claims of other factions' (Stockwin, 1988, p. 46). Faction leaders treated each new election of the party President (every two years) as an opportunity to further their own ambitions and those of their faction. Consequently and particularly in the 'civil war' period from the mid-1970s, following Sato's long premiership, until the early 1980s, after Ohira's death, LDP Prime Ministers found it increasingly difficult to remain at their post.

More insidiously, all LDP Prime Ministers lived with the constant threat of being deposed by rival faction leaders. This threat also had an impact on their ability to exercise leadership. As Krauss notes '[the Prime Minister] must always consult and reach agreement with his allies and their factions lest he jeopardize his majority coalition within the party' (Krauss, 1989, p. 48). Faction leaders defeated at one election for the party President often spent much of the inter-election period preparing for their next campaign by trying to undermine the incumbent Prime Minister. In both 1978 and 1979, Fukuda lost the battle for the party presidency and the prime ministership to Ohira. To seek his revenge, Fukuda and his supporters failed to back Ohira's (and their own) government in a motion of confidence lodged by the Socialist party in 1980. Consequently, the government was defeated and had to resign. While heads of government in all parliamentary systems face the threat of being dismissed because of intra-party rivalries, this example demonstrates that the intensity of factional rivalry in Japan meant that LDP Prime Ministers, like their Italian counterparts, had to spend much of their time worrying about their own survival at the expense of developing a strategic personal vision for the country. Once again, therefore, the nature of factional competition within the LDP helps to account for the reactive nature of prime ministerial leadership in Japan.

*The power of the Prime Minister*

From 1955 to 1993, the Prime Minister's decision-making power, already made weak because of the structure of resources within the executive, was further weakened by structure of resources within the highly factionalised LDP. One way in which factional competition impacted upon the Prime Minister's power was by the 'fair shares' rule on the basis of which Cabinet seats were allocated amongst LDP factions. Constitutionally, the Prime Minister has the power to appoint Cabinet Ministers. However, since 1968, Cabinet posts were allocated roughly proportionally according to the strength of the different LDP factions in the Diet. (For an example of this rule in action, see Table 6.2). Moreover, the people to be appointed from each faction were often chosen by the leader of that faction, rather than by the Prime Minister. The result was that, since the late 1960s, LDP Cabinets were composed of members of all the factions in the party, whether or not they had voted for the party President. Loyalty to the Prime Minister was not their main concern. Any head of government in a system where parties are strong is likely to have to

TABLE 6.2

Factional proportionality in Miyazawa's Cabinet, November 1991

| Faction | Diet membership | | Cabinet posts | |
|---|---|---|---|---|
| | Total | % | Total | % |
| Takeshita | 105 | 26.6 | 7 | 33.3 |
| Mitsuzuka | 83 | 21.0 | 4 | 19.0 |
| Miyazawa | 82 | 20.8 | 3 | 14.3 |
| Watanabe | 70 | 17.7 | 3 | 14.3 |
| Komoto | 31 | 7.8 | 3 | 14.3 |
| Independents | 24 | 6.1 | 1 | 4.8 |

*Source*: Punnett, 1992, p. 20.

appoint certain people to the Cabinet with a degree of reluctance just so as to maintain party unity. In Japan, though, the 'fair shares' rule institutionalised this practice, weakening the potential power of LDP Prime Ministers.

It might also be added that the capacity for prime ministerial leadership was also weakened because of the allocation of responsibilities between the party and government. The distribution of posts between these two organisations was decided according to the 'separation of powers' rule. That is to say, after the election of the party President, the three most senior posts in the party (the Secretary-General, the Chair of the Executive Council and the Chair of the Policy Affairs Research Council) were customarily allocated to members of different factions and, moreover, to members of factions other than that of the party President and Prime Minister (Kohno, 1992, p. 374). In this sense, not only did the 'fair shares' rule institutionalise factional conflict within the Cabinet, the 'separation of powers' rule institutionalised conflict between the Prime Minister and the party. The Prime Minister was shadowed by other senior and competing factional figures in the party organisation and, again, the power of the office was weakened.

These factors had profound consequences for prime ministerial leadership. Faced with opponents in the Cabinet and senior party organisations, the role of the Prime Minister resembled that of a coordinator, a manager, or a 'figurehead' (Tsurutani, 1992, p. 225) rather than a direction-setter. It was certainly the case that several LDP Prime Ministers enjoyed some success in particular policy areas. For instance, Ikeda played a major role in pursuing the policy of economic growth in the early 1960s. Sato concluded a treaty with Korea, which increased the level of economic cooperation between the two countries. Nakasone had a degree of success in cutting the budget deficit and in privatising various concerns. However, as Hayao notes, in recent years: 'these sorts of initiatives have been relatively few. Japanese prime ministers have not been important agenda setters' (Hayao, 1993, p. 27). Instead, most Prime Ministers spent their time reacting, rather than innovating. Like their Italian counterparts, they were the equivalent of political firefighters. This is not to say that they were unimportant figures. After all, firefighters have a particularly important job to do. For the most part, though, factional conflict was the main cause of this reactive prime ministerial leadership. As we shall see in the next section, the relationship between the LDP and other forces in political system had similar consequences.

## The LDP in the context of the political system

The study of one-party dominant régimes involves more than just the study of the one dominant party alone. In all liberal democracies, parties interact with a range of other forces in the political system. The outcome of the leadership process is partly the result of such interaction. One-party dominant régimes are no exception to this rule. For example, as we shall see in the next chapter, the political process in Italy was a function not just of the nature of the long-dominant Christian Democratic party, but also of the relationship between that party and, for example, para-public institutions. Similarly, in Japan, the political process from 1955 to 1993 was not simply determined by the nature of factional competition within the LDP. It was also partly determined by two other key relationships: first, the relationship between the LDP and forces in the Diet and, secondly, the relationship between the LDP and the bureaucracy.

### The LDP and forces in the Diet

The relationship between the LDP and opposition parties affected the nature of prime ministerial leadership. In the period immediately following the formation of the LDP, there was a highly conflictual relationship between government and opposition. Opinions within the political system were polarised. The LDP clashed with the principal opposition party, the Socialist party, over a range of issues, such as the Constitution, education, foreign and defence policy. Indeed, such was the extent of the polarisation that it was not unknown for the police to be called into the Diet to maintain order. At the same time, this period of intense cross-party conflict coincided with the LDP's absolute majority in the Diet. The party held the chairs of all parliamentary committees and had absolute majorities on all of those committees. The result was that the primary concern of senior LDP figures, including the Prime Minister, during this period was the management of intra-party conflict, rather than the construction of cross-party alliances (Krauss, 1982, p. 98). Factional politics was all-important.

However, by the mid-1970s, the relationship between the government and opposition had changed. Issues which had been so divisive in the immediate post-war period became less salient. In their place, new issues emerged, such as pollution and the quality of life, around which opposition parties were able to mobilise support and which were relatively amenable to cross-party negotiations and compromise. In addition and partly as a result of the importance of these new issues, the parliamentary position of the LDP weakened. In 1976, 1979 and 1983, the party failed to win an absolute majority of seats by itself in the House of Representatives. On these occasions, it also failed to obtain an absolute majority on all parliamentary committees and it lost control of certain committee chairs. In all, the parliamentary situation demanded that the government and opposition cooperate more in order for legislation to be passed and a new set of issues emerged on which a degree of agreement between the government and opposition could be found.

The changing relationship between the LDP and opposition forces in the Diet affected the nature of prime ministerial leadership. In the main, it ensured that LDP Prime Ministers had to balance the interests of faction leaders within their own party alongside the interests of other parties and their leaders in the Diet. In this way, LDP Prime Ministers were increasingly faced with the task of accommodating internal party interests and cross-party interests at the same time (Krauss, 1982, p. 103). For example, when he became Prime Minister in 1978, Ohira pursued a strategy of 'partial coalition', which he had previously put forward in his role as Secretary-General of the LDP. This strategy meant that the LDP still maintained a monopoly of Cabinet seats, but that it negotiated flexibly with opposition parties so as to pass legislation (Krauss and Pierre, 1990, p. 235). On the one hand, this situation increased the centrality of the Prime Minister in the political system. The Prime Minister became a key negotiator across different arenas. The importance of factional politics was now balanced by the importance of inter-party politics where the Prime Minister was a key negotiator. On the other hand, though, the process of leadership was made more difficult. The Prime Minister had to balance different interests across the various different arenas, while still remaining in power and retaining popularity. Such a task proved too difficult for most.

*The LDP and the bureaucracy*

The other key element of the Prime Minister's leadership role may be found in the relationship between the LDP and the permanent administration. Japan has a strong bureaucratic tradition. The leading position of the Japanese bureaucracy was reaffirmed in the immediate post-war period by the occupying Allied forces. For example, the bureaucracy remained relatively untouched by the post-war purges, in stark contrast to political parties which were seen as being primarily responsible for many of the negative aspects of the country's pre-war history. The permanent administration was able to fill the gap left by the weakness of political parties. Key departments, such as the highly influential Ministry of International Trade and Industry, gained a reputation for policy innovation and were highly regarded both within Japan and abroad. Indeed, even with the formation of the LDP in 1955, the influence of the bureaucracy in the policy-making process continued. The leaders of the LDP (many of whom were themselves 'bureaucrats-turned-politicians') were in harmony with the general lines of policy proposed and implemented by the bureaucracy in the process of post-war reconstuction. For example, the 'conservative policy line' was inspired by 'bureaucrats-turned-politicians' and implemented by administrators in government departments. A sign of the importance of the bureaucracy in the policy-making process may be found in the fact that, from 1955 onwards, 90 per cent of all legislation was drafted by administrators in one government agency or another (Pempel, 1984, p. 85).

There are two main reasons for the influential role of the higher administration in post-war Japan. The first concerns the frequent turnover of Ministers under LDP governments (see Table 6.3). On average, an LDP Cabinet Minister served in office for less than a year. This high level of ministerial instability ensured that Ministers were largely dependent on the advice of the permanent administration during their short stay in office (Pempel, 1984, p. 86). A key role in this respect was played by the most senior civil servant in each department, the vice-minister. It was the vice-minister, rather than the Minister, who was largely responsible for policy co-ordination within a department (Campbell, 1984, p. 318). Moreover, it was the weekly meeting of all departmental vice-ministers, rather than the Cabinet, which served as the primary site of inter-departmental policy co-ordination. Important matters would still be

**TABLE 6.3**

Average length of ministerial tenure in Japan, 1964–87

| Ministry | Average tenure |
|---|---|
| Finance | 16.4 (months) |
| Foreign Affairs | 15.9 |
| Chief Cabinet Secretary | 15.6 |
| International Trade and Industry | 13.2 |
| Economic Planning | 11.9 |
| Administrative Management | 11.9 |
| Defence | 11.4 |
| Education | 11.4 |
| Agriculture, Forestry and Fisheries | 10.9 |
| Posts and Telecommunications | 10.9 |
| Welfare | 10.5 |
| Justice | 10.5 |
| Home | 10.5 |
| Science and Technology | 10.5 |
| Labour | 10.1 |
| Construction | 10.1 |
| Transport | 10.1 |

*Source*: Stockwin, 1988, p. 43.

discussed in the Cabinet, but the vice-ministers played a key co-ordinating role.

Second, the policy-making process within the LDP brought together bureaucrats and policy experts within the party. As a result of the long period of LDP dominance, the party developed its own set of highly influential policy-making structures, the most important of which was the Policy Affairs Research Council (PARC). The PARC was composed mainly of LDP Diet members and consisted of seventeen permanent divisions, which mirrored the organisation of government Ministries and Diet committees, as well as up to seventy-five *ad hoc* research commissions and special committees covering specialised subject areas (Rothacher, 1993, p. 25). The main function of the PARC's permanent divisions was to monitor their department's work and scrutinise any pieces of draft legislation. Once a piece of legislation had been drawn up by civil servants in a particular department, it was immediately transmitted to the equivalent division of the PARC. It was then analysed within the division and meetings would take place between PARC members and members of the permanent administration as well as representatives of appropriate interest groups (Krauss, 1989, p. 52), with a view to examining the implications of the policy in question for the country and the party. The continuing presence of the LDP in government and the importance of the PARC meant that certain Diet members developed both a degree of policy expertise and close links with the bureaucracy. Once Diet members joined a particular PARC division, they tended to remain there for as long as they continued to be elected to the Diet (Tomita *et al.*, 1992, p. 277). As a result, over a period of time, the PARC became associated with policy specialists. Collectively, these specialists formed so-called 'policy tribes' (see Exhibit 6.5). These

---

**EXHIBIT 6.5**

**Definition and examples of 'policy tribes' (*zoku*)**

*Zoku* is a term [used] to describe Diet members who have a considerable amount of expertise and practical experience about a particular area of governmental policy and enough seniority in the party to have influence on a continuing basis with the ministry responsible for that policy area.

Examples: The 'big three' 'policy tribes' are construction, agriculture and commerce. Others include education, transportation and defence.

*Source*: Taken from Curtis, 1988, pp. 114–15.

---

'tribes' were unstructured organisations, which cut across factional boundaries. The people associated with them developed strong links with their counterparts in government departments and also with representatives of the interest groups, which were active in their policy area. They had an important influence on policy concerns in their area and often held senior positions in the party.

The weakness of Ministers and the Cabinet in the decision-making process and the importance of the PARC and the party's 'policy tribes' helped to determine the role of the Prime Minister in the political system. In the first place, prime ministerial intervention in interdepartmental conflicts was usually reserved for the occasions when the meetings of vice-ministers could not resolve policy problems. Within the governmental apparatus, therefore, the role of the Prime Minister was to coordinate the coordinators. Second, interdivisional conflict within the PARC and policy matters generally within the LDP were the prime responsibility of the party's most senior institutions, namely, the Deliberation Committee of the PARC and the party's Executive Council. Consequently, the Prime Minister tended to be involved only downstream of the party's policy deliberations, intervening on occasions when there was conflict between the party and the bureaucracy, or when the party itself failed to reach a decision. Once again, the role of the Prime Minister was that of a coordinator, rather than an innovator.

After this analysis, the question might be asked as to why LDP politicians should have treated the premiership as 'the jewel in the crown' (Stockwin, 1988, p. 46) of the political system. After all, as we have seen, as a result of the structure of resources within the executive, within and between political parties and between the LDP and the bureaucracy, the Prime Minister's role was essentially reactive and managerial, rather than proactive and dynamic. The answer to this question may be found in the strategic position held by the Prime Minister in the political system. As with the case of people occupying equivalent positions in other countries, the head of government was the prime focus of media and public attention. For faction leaders, such attention was an important resource as it boosted their standing and encouraged the support of potential benefactors, further securing their position within the party. Moreover, although the Prime Minister's primary role was that of a coordinator, the Prime Minister was the chief coordinator within the system, having to deal with conflict at all key points in the system: within the government and administration, between the government and parliament and within the party. Although at each of these points the Prime Minister was challenged by other powerful figures, only the Prime Minister had to deal with conflict in all of these areas at any one time. As Martin and Stronach argue:

> The role of the executive élite as a policy broker is a subtle and complex one, which involves the exercise of great manipulative skill and extremely delicate use of the prime minister's influence, with the result that his leadership is not open and explicit even though his authority may be considerable in such situations (Martin and Stronach, 1992, p. 255).

Finally, at certain times in certain policy areas, Prime Ministers were more than just reactive figures (Tsurutani, 1992, pp. 243–4). Some Prime Ministers were closely associated with particular policies, such as Tanaka and the recognition of China, Miki and clean politics, and

Takeshita and the introduction of VAT (Hayao, 1993, p. 209). In this respect, the potential for a degree of prime ministerial leadership was present in the system, even if it was not always possible for this potential to be realised.

## The end of the '1955 set-up' and the prospects for political leadership

The events surrounding the 1993 election to the House of Representatives marked a watershed in post-war Japanese politics. (For the results, see Table 6.4). In 1992 and then again in 1993, the LDP split and several new offshoot parties were formed. As a direct result of these splits, Miyazawa's government lost a vote of confidence in the House of Representatives. At the ensuing election, the LDP registered the worst result in its history. Consequently, it failed to form a government for the first time since 1955. Instead, in its place, a seven-party coalition government took office headed by Hosokawa Morihiro, the leader of one of the parties which split from the LDP, the Japan New Party (*Nihon Shinto*). Hosokawa's government then

TABLE 6.4

The 1993 election to the Japanese House of Representatives

| Party | Share of vote (%) | Seats (no.) |
|---|---|---|
| LDP | 36.6 | 223 |
| Socialists | 15.4 | 70 |
| Japan Renewal Party (*Shinseito*)[1] | 10.1 | 55 |
| Clean Government Party | 8.2 | 51 |
| Japan New Party[2] | 8.1 | 35 |
| Communists | 7.7 | 15 |
| Democratic Socialists | 3.5 | 15 |
| New Harbinger Party (*Sakigake*)[3] | 2.6 | 13 |
| Social Democratic Federation (*Shaminren*)[4] | 0.7 | 4 |
| Others | 0.2 | – |
| Independents[5] | 6.9 | 30 |
| Total | 100.0 | 511 |

[1] Centre-right. Formed 1993. Offshoot from the LDP.
[2] Centre. Formed in 1992. Offshoot from the LDP.
[3] Centre-right. Formed 1993. Offshoot from the LDP.
[4] Centre-left. Formed in 1978. Offshoot from the Socialist party.
[5] Following the 1993 election, around half of these independents supported the LDP.

embarked upon a programme of political change aimed primarily at reforming the country's electoral system and breaking the link between money and politics. Although Hosokawa himself resigned in April 1994 as a result of being implicated in a financial scandal, the events surrounding the 1993 election marked a significant change in the Japanese leadership environment in two respects.

First, one of the defining characteristics of the '1955 set-up' has disappeared. Previously, the divided nature of the opposition helped to guarantee the LDP's dominant position in the system. For example, even when the party lost its absolute majority in the Diet after 1976, opposition parties were still unable to unite so as to form an alternative government. However, following the 1993 election, the non-LDP parties were able to come to an agreement and a coalition government was formed from which only the communists were excluded. In this sense, there now appears to be an alternative to the LDP in the system, albeit a very fragile one. Yet, even this situation arguably increases the likelihood of decisive leadership. The electorate may now be faced at elections with opposing governmental programmes each of which has a realistic chance of success. In this case, new governments may be able to claim a mandate with which to initiate change. Indeed, Hosokawa's government utilised its political capital in order to draw up political reforms and, for example, to admit for the first time that Japan was the aggressor in the Pacific War (1941–5).

Second, the LDP has itself changed in various ways. The party split and its level of electoral support fell to an historic low; the previously dominant Takeshita faction disintegrated; and a new President with reformist credentials, Kono Yahei, was elected. Indeed, one of Kono's first acts as leader was to acknowledge that the party had to be reformed in order to make it eligible to return to government. Assuming that Kono was serious in his desire to initiate reform, he will be helped in his task by the fact that he is untainted by the recent wave of corruption scandals which have swept through the party. A reformed party may result in future LDP Prime Ministers enjoying a stronger power base and, again, the result may be more decisive leadership.

In both these respects, the 1993 election marked a watershed in Japanese politics. However, there are still strong continuities between the present situation and the 1955 set-up. For example, in June 1994 the LDP returned to power in a coalition headed by the socialist, Murayama Tomiichi. With the LDP holding thirteen of the twenty ministries in the new government, it operated in a manner which was reminiscent of the factional politics of the 1955–93 era. Moreover, it is unclear as to whether the LDP itself has really changed and whether it is likely to do so in the immediate future. The party is still factionalised and personalised competition continues to be intrinsic to the nature of the party. Kono himself was only elected by virtue of the fact that the Miyazawa faction supported him against Watanabe, the leader of another faction in the party. Finally, the power of the bureaucracy is unlikely to diminish, so entrenched are the interests and practices of the permanent administration.

In all, the Japanese political system since the 1993 election is marked by elements of both continuity and change. On the one hand, the LDP may be able to retain its grip on power. In this case, something approaching the 1955 set-up may reassert itself. On the other hand, with the passage of a new electoral law, one of the main factors encouraging factional competition in the party may have been removed. Like the 1994 Italian reform, the new Japanese electoral system includes a strong majoritarian element (Christensen, 1994, pp. 202–5). It is likely that this reform will weaken the role of factions in the political system and increase the authority of any future Prime Minister, LDP or otherwise. However, the jury is still out with regard to whether political leadership in Japan in the future will be more decisive or whether it will continue to be reactive. As we shall see, in this respect, as in many others, the contemporary Japanese leadership environment resembles its Italian counterpart.

# 7

# Italy:
# Acephalous Leadership

There are a number of striking similarities between the Japanese and Italian leadership environments. These similarities are derived primarily from the distribution of resources within and between political parties in the two countries. For much of the post-war period, the Italian system, like its Japanese counterpart, was characterised as a one-party dominant régime. From 1945 to 1993, the role of the Christian Democratic Party (DC) in Italy strongly resembled that of the LDP in Japan. Between these dates, the DC was permanently represented in government; it supplied sixteen of the eighteen different heads of government; it colonised the permanent administration and the state sector; and it was riven with factional conflict. Again though, in Italy, as in Japan, the presence of a hegemonic party in government over a long period of time did not ensure strong, personal leadership. In fact, the structure of resources within and between Italian political parties created a pattern of political leadership which was highly reminiscent of the leadership process in Japan. Italy had its own form of party government known pejoratively as '*partitocrazia*' (or 'partyocracy'). Heads of government were political caretakers and conflict managers, rather than mobilisers and strategic direction-setters. In the sense that decision-making responsibilities largely escaped their control, Italy may be deemed to have been an example of acephalous leadership (Cavalli, 1992).

Indeed, the comparisons between the Italian and Japanese political systems do not end there. In Italy, as in Japan, political change is currently in the air. The results of the 1992 and 1994 Italian legislative elections and the referendums which were passed in April 1993 have precipitated a political upheaval even greater than the one which has recently been witnessed in Japan. The DC no longer exists;

representatives of its former arch-enemy, the ex-communists in the Democratic Party of the Left (PDS), now play a full part in the political system; and many members of the former-DC (along with those of several other parties, most notably the Socialists) have been arrested on charges of corruption. And yet, again as in Japan, although the old Italian political system is in crisis, it has yet to be replaced by a new and stable system. Elements of a new political equilibrium are in place in which some of the conditions for strong leadership may be discerned. However, whether such leadership will be institutionalised in the new system remains to be seen.

This chapter will begin with a brief examination of the structure of resources within the executive branch of government. The formal powers of both the head of state and the head of government will be identified. Attention will then be focused on the structure of resources within and between political parties. The organisation of the country's multi-party system and the DC's multi-factional structure will be examined. The way in which both factors determined how leadership was exercised after the Constitution came into force in 1948 will be examined. The last part of the chapter briefly catalogues the changes which have been experienced by the Italian political system since the 1992 legislative election. The contours of the new leadership environment will be sketched and the prospects for lasting reform will ·be assessed. It will be argued that the momentum for change is stronger in Italy than in Japan. Nevertheless, the reform process is not yet complete and it may still falter.

## The head of state and the head of government

In Italy, as in Germany and Japan, the experience of dictatorship ensured that one of the principal desires of those drafting the post-war Constitution was to eliminate the possibility of autocratic leadership. Consequently, neither the head of state, the President of the Republic, nor the head of government, the President of the Council of Ministers, is endowed with anything approaching an extensive set of constitutional powers. In this sense, the 1948 Constitution does not create a structure of resources within the executive branch which encourages personal leadership.

The President of the Republic plays a mainly honorific role. (For a list of heads of state since 1948, see Exhibit 7.1.) Although, as in

**EXHIBIT 7.1**
**Italian heads of state since 1948**

| President | Office | Party |
|---|---|---|
| Luigi Einaudi | 1948–55 | Liberal party |
| Giovanni Gronchi | 1955–62 | Christian Democratic party |
| Antonio Segni | 1962–64 | Christian Democratic party |
| Giuseppe Saragat | 1964–71 | Social Democratic party |
| Giovanni Leone | 1971–78 | Christian Democratic party |
| Alessandro Pertini | 1978–85 | Socialist party |
| Francesco Cossiga | 1985–92 | Christian Democratic party |
| Oscar Luigi Scalfaro | 1992– | Christian Democratic party |

France, the head of state holds office for seven years, unlike France, the President of the Republic is not directly elected by the people. Instead, similar to Germany, the head of state is elected by an electoral college consisting of members of the two Chambers of parliament and representatives of regional government. The seven-year term gives Presidents of the Republic a certain independence, but the method of election gives them little popular authority. In addition, they have few constitutional prerogatives. The head of state is the commander-in-chief of the armed forces and chairs the Supreme Council of Defence (Article 87). In this capacity, past incumbents have been accused of being involved in covert military activity (Koff, 1982, p. 346). For the most part, though, strategic defence and internal security decisions are incumbent on the Defence and Interior Ministers. The head of state may send bills back to parliament for further deliberation (Article 74). From 1948 to 1985, this 'suspensive veto' was used twenty-three times, although from 1985 to 1991 President Cossiga had already used it eighteen times (Della Sala, 1993, p. 38). The President of the Republic may also dissolve either or both Chambers of parliament (Article 88). In 1979, President Pertini dissolved the lower Chamber, the Chamber of Deputies, in an attempt to resolve an ongoing governmental crisis. Finally, the head of state plays a role in nominating the head of government (Article 92). In the situation where inter- and intra-party disputes render government formation a messy and protracted business (see below), the President of the Republic may exert a degree of influence in the appointment process (Koff, 1982, pp. 344–5). All told, though, the head of state has been only a secondary political actor since 1948. At times, certain figures, such as Cossiga, have tried to emphasise their role. Indeed, Scalfaro's determination greatly helped the reform process after 1992. However, leadership responsibilities have not been incumbent on the head of state, who enjoys few constitutional powers and only limited political authority.

By contrast, the President of the Council of Ministers does play more than just an honorific role in the political process. For example, the head of government represents Italy at G7 summits of world leaders and at European Council meetings. In addition, as the principle representative of a government which is formally responsible to parliament, the President of the Council of Ministers is the focus of a considerable degree of political, media and public attention. Nevertheless, as with the head of state, the constitutional prerogatives of the head of government are meagre. (Exhibit 7.2 gives a list of Italian heads of government since 1948.) Article 95 of the Constitution states:

> The President of the Council of Ministers conducts and is responsible for the general policy of the government. He assures the unity and consistency of the political and administrative programme by promoting and coordinating the activity of the Ministers.

In its generality, the wording of this Article is not far removed from Article 65 of the German Basic Law, which sets out the so-called 'Chancellor principle'. Unlike the German Chancellor, though, the Italian head of government is not provided with any other explicit constitutional powers. The Italian Constitution states that the specific powers of the President of the Council of Ministers will be determined by a parliamentary law to be passed at a future date (Article 95). Unfortunately for the status of the office, no substantive law was forthcoming until 1988. Now, for example, the head of government does enjoy delegated powers to coordinate and simplify legislation (Furlong, 1994, p. 113). However, at least until 1988, the constitutional and legal powers of the office were extremely weak. Indeed, they were (and still are) the weakest of all the chief executives considered in this book.

Moreover, until 1988, the administrative resources at the disposal of the head of government were equally weak. Before this time, the head of government's advisory office performed only a limited set of functions. It had no formal structure of its own; no budget of its own; and no personnel of its own, having to rely on personnel being

## EXHIBIT 7.2
### Italian heads of government, 1948–94

| Office | Head of government | Party | Parties represented in the government |
|---|---|---|---|
| 5/47–5/48 | Alcide De Gasperi (IV)[1] | DC | DC, PRI, PSDI, PLI |
| 5/48–1/50 | Alcide De Gasperi (V) | DC | DC, PRI, PSDI, PLI |
| 1/50–7/51 | Alcide De Gasperi (VI) | DC | DC, PRI, PSDI |
| 7/51–6/53 | Alcide De Gasperi (VII) | DC | DC, PRI |
| 7/53 | Alcide De Gasperi (VIII) | DC | DC |
| 8/53–1/54 | Giuseppe Pella | DC | DC |
| 1/54 | Amintore Fanfani (I) | DC | DC |
| 2/54–7/55 | Mario Scelba | DC | DC, PLI, PSDI |
| 7/55–5/57 | Antonio Segni (I) | DC | DC, PLI, PSDI |
| 5/57–7/58 | Adone Zoli | DC | DC |
| 7/58–2/59 | Amintore Fanfani (II) | DC | DC, PSDI |
| 2/59–3/60 | Antonio Segni (II) | DC | DC |
| 3–7/60 | Fernando Tambroni | DC | DC |
| 7/60–2/62 | Amintore Fanfani (III) | DC | DC |
| 2/62–6/63 | Amintore Fanfani (IV) | DC | DC, PRI, PSDI |
| 6–12/63 | Giovanni Leone (I) | DC | DC |
| 12/63–7/64 | Aldo Moro (I) | DC | DC, PRI, PSDI, PSI |
| 7/64–2/66 | Aldo Moro (II) | DC | DC, PRI, PSDI, PSI |
| 2/66–6/68 | Aldo Moro (III) | DC | DC, PRI, PSDI, PSI |
| 6–12/68 | Giovanni Leone (II) | DC | DC |
| 12/68–8/69 | Mariano Rumor (I) | DC | DC, PRI, PSI |
| 8/69–3/70 | Mariano Rumor (II) | DC | DC |
| 3–8/70 | Mariano Rumor (III) | DC | DC, PRI, PSDI, PSI |
| 8/70–2/72 | Emilio Colombo | DC | DC, PRI, PSDI, PSI |
| 2–6/72 | Giulio Andreotti (I) | DC | DC |

167

**EXHIBIT 7.2** contd.

| Office | Head of government | Party | Parties represented in the government |
|---|---|---|---|
| 6/72–7/73 | Giulio Andreotti (II) | DC | DC, PSDI, PLI |
| 7/73–3/74 | Mariano Rumor (IV) | DC | DC, PSDI, PSI, PRI |
| 3–11/74 | Mariano Rumor (V) | DC | DC, PSDI, PSI |
| 11/74–2/76 | Aldo Moro (IV) | DC | DC, PRI |
| 2–7/76 | Aldo Moro (V) | DC | DC |
| 7/76–3/78 | Giulio Andreotti (III) | DC | DC |
| 3/78–3/79 | Giulio Andreotti (IV) | DC | DC |
| 3–8/79 | Giulio Andreotti (V) | DC | DC, PSDI, PRI |
| 8/79–4/80 | Francesco Cossiga (I) | DC | DC, PSDI, PLI |
| 4–10/80 | Francesco Cossiga (II) | DC | DC, PSI, PRI |
| 10/80–6/81 | Arnaldo Forlani | DC | DC, PSI, PSDI, PRI |
| 6/81–8/82 | Giovanni Spadolini (I) | PRI | DC, PSI, PSDI, PLI, PRI |
| 8–12/82 | Giovanni Spadolini (II) | PRI | DC, PSI, PSDI, PLI, PRI |
| 12/82–8/83 | Amintore Fanfani (V) | DC | DC, PSI, PSDI, PLI |
| 8/83–8/86 | Bettino Craxi (I) | PSI | DC, PSI, PSDI, PLI, PRI |
| 8/86–3/87 | Bettino Craxi (II) | PSI | DC, PSI, PSDI, PLI, PRI |
| 3/87–7/87 | Amintore Fanfani (VI) | DC | DC |
| 7/87–3/88 | Giovanni Goria | DC | DC, PSI, PSDI, PLI, PRI |
| 4/88–7/89 | Ciriaco De Mita | DC | DC, PSI, PSDI, PLI, PRI |
| 7/89–4/91 | Giulio Andreotti (VI) | DC | DC, PSI, PSDI, PLI, PRI |
| 4/91–4/92 | Giulio Andreotti (VII) | DC | DC, PSI, PSDI, PLI |
| 6/92–4/93 | Giuliano Amato | PSI | DC, PSI, PSDI, PLI |
| 4/93–4/94 | Carlo Azeglio Ciampi | no party | DC, PSI, PSDI, PLI, PDS, Greens[2] |
| 5–12/94 | Silvio Berlusconi | FI | FI, Northern League, National Alliance[3] |

*Notes:*
[1] Italian governments are referred to by the name of the head of the government and the number of times that person has formed a government. So, 'Alcide De Gasperi (IV)' indicates that this was the fourth time that De Gasperi had formed a government. De Gasperi's first three governments were formed prior to the one which was in office at the time when the Constitution was promulgated on 1st January 1948.
[2] The PDS and Green representatives resigned almost immediately.
[3] FI is Forza Italia

seconded to it from other Ministries and public corporations (Cassese, 1981, p. 184). Even then, although in 1990 5931 people were seconded to the head of government's office, 'the great majority were engaged in activities which have little relevance to the core functions of over-arching policy coordination' (Hine, 1993, p. 208). Only after the passage of the 1988 law was the office formally reorganised and given full statutory status. (For the current organisation of the office, see Exhibit 7.3.) In addition, it was given particular powers, for

---

**EXHIBIT 7.3**
**The head of government's office in Italy following the 1988 reform**

* Three key advisers: chief of staff (*capogabinetto*), the under-secretary to the office and the personal secretary.
* Various functional departments. These consist of:
  the secretariat to the Council of Ministers;
  legislative office;
  economic and social affairs section;
  press office;
  programme monitoring department;
  office of the diplomatic counsellor;
  office of the military counsellor;
  ceremonials department;
  information and archiving;
  personnel and administration.

*Source*: Hine, 1993, pp. 210–11.

---

example, with regard to regional government. In these respects, the 1988 law undoubtedly strengthened the head of government's potential to manage and coordinate government policy. However, there is little firm evidence to suggest that the head of government's formal leadership powers were significantly increased as a result.

It is apparent, therefore, that the distribution of resources within the Italian executive provides the basis neither for presidential leadership nor for the equivalent of prime ministerial leadership. Nevertheless, we must be careful as to the conclusions we draw from this situation. In none of the countries considered so far in this book is the ability to exercise leadership a function of the structure of resources within the executive branch of government alone. In all cases, these factors provide only one aspect of the environment within which leaders operate. The same is true in Italy. Here, the absence of executive leadership from 1948 to 1992 (and perhaps beyond) was only partly a result of constitutional and administrative factors and more a result of the structure of resources within and between political parties. Unlike the situation in Germany, for example, where party politics was important, but where other institutional factors were also important, such as the territorial distribution of power and the role of judicial review, in Italy party politics was the prime determinant of the leadership environment. It is true that, after the 1970s, the powers of regional governments in Italy were enhanced. Similarly, the Italian Constitutional Court has gradually developed into 'an effective policy-making body' (de Franciscis and Zannini, 1992, p. 68). Nevertheless, the nature of executive leadership and, in particular, the role of the President of the Council of Ministers (upon whom attention will be focused) was mainly determined by the distribution within and between Italian political parties. In this respect, the Italian system closely resembled the Japanese system and it is this aspect which will now be explored.

### The nature of party politics in post-war Italy

The two main determinants of the structure of resources within and between Italian political parties were Italy's multi-party system and the DC's multifactional structure. In order to understand the dynamics of political leadership in Italy from 1948 to 1992, it is necessary to appreciate that both these factors produced mutually reinforcing results, creating the conditions in which brokered and clientelistic politics could flourish and in which it was extremely difficult to achieve individual leadership. As Di Palma has written: 'one must recognize that there are few if any Western countries where politics, in fact straight party politics, as thoroughly pervades (and stalemates) every aspect of the community as in Italy' (Di Palma, 1977, p. 5). Before examining why party politics in Italy should have resulted in a form of political stalemate, it is first of all necessary to outline the basic characteristics of each of the two main determinants of party politics.

### A multi-party system

There are a number of contrasting interpretations of the Italian party system (see, for example, van Loenen, 1990). However, two general observations may be made. First , there was a relatively fragmented multiparty system. The system was dominated by confrontation between two main parties, the DC and the Communist Party (PCI), but a number of minor parties maintained a relatively consistent level of electoral support. (For election results from 1948 to 1987, see Table 7.1.) Together, the two main parties regularly won between 60 and 70

TABLE 7.1

Results of elections to the Italian Chamber of Deputies, 1948–87

| Party | 1948 | 1953 | 1958 | 1963 | 1968 | 1972 | 1976 | 1979 | 1983 | 1987 |
|---|---|---|---|---|---|---|---|---|---|---|
| DC | 48.4 | 40.1 | 42.3 | 38.3 | 39.1 | 38.8 | 38.7 | 38.3 | 32.9 | 34.3 |
| PCI | 31.0 | 22.6 | 22.7 | 25.3 | 26.9 | 27.2 | 34.4 | 30.4 | 29.9 | 26.6 |
| PSI | 1 | 12.7 | 14.2 | 13.8 | 14.5 | 9.6 | 9.6 | 9.8 | 11.4 | 14.3 |
| MSI | 2.0 | 5.8 | 4.7 | 5.1 | 4.5 | 8.7 | 6.1 | 5.3 | 6.8 | 5.9 |
| PSDI | 7.0 | 4.5 | 4.6 | 6.1 | 2 | 5.1 | 3.4 | 3.8 | 4.1 | 3.0 |
| PRI | 2.5 | 1.6 | 1.4 | 1.4 | 2.0 | 2.9 | 3.1 | 3.0 | 5.1 | 3.7 |
| PLI | 3.8 | 3.0 | 3.5 | 7.0 | 5.8 | 3.9 | 1.3 | 1.9 | 2.9 | 2.1 |
| DP | – | – | – | – | – | – | 1.5 | 1.4 | 1.5 | 1.7 |
| Radicals | – | – | – | – | – | – | 1.1 | 3.4 | 2.2 | 2.6 |
| Greens | – | – | – | – | – | – | – | – | – | 2.5 |
| SVP | 0.5 | 0.5 | 0.5 | 0.5 | 0.5 | 0.5 | 0.5 | 0.6 | 0.5 | 0.5 |
| PSdA | – | – | – | – | – | – | – | 0.2 | 0.2 | 0.4 |
| PNM | 2.7 | 6.9 | 4.8 | 1.7 | 1.3 | – | – | – | – | – |

*Key*: PCI: Communist party (left). PSI: Socialist party (centre-left). MSI: Italian Social Movement (extreme-right) – absorbed the PNM in 1972. PSDI: Social Democratic party (centre-left). PRI: Republican party (centre). PLI: Liberal party (centre-right). DP: Proletarian Democracy (extreme-left). Radicals: Post-materialist values. SVP: South Tyrol People's party (separatist). PSdA: Sardinian Action party (separatist). PNM: National Monarchist party (extreme- right) – merged with the MSI in 1972.

*Notes*:
1 PCI and PSI allied.
2 PSDI united with PSI for the 1968 elections, but separated afterwards.

per cent of the votes cast in parliamentary elections. Of these two parties, the DC was always the larger, although only on one occasion (1948–53) did it manage to win an absolute majority of seats by itself in the Chamber of Deputies. Of the minor parties, the Socialist party (PSI) was the largest, winning between 9 and 14 per cent of the vote, with the rest of the votes being distributed relatively evenly between the Liberals (PLI), the Republicans (PRI), the Social Democrats (PSDI) and the extreme right, the Italian Social Movement (MSI).

The multiparty nature of party politics was fundamental to the leadership process because the electoral system which was in operation from 1948 to 1992 ensured that all the parties in the system were able to win seats in the legislature. Between these dates, the electoral system consisted of a relatively pure form of proportional representation with a very low national threshold which parties had to achieve in order to be represented in parliament. A party had to win a total number of votes amounting to rather less than 1 per cent of the electorate to obtain representation (Furlong, 1991, p. 53). A consequence of this situation was that small parties were able to maintain a constant presence in the system. For example, the vote for the PRI from 1948 to 1987 fluctuated between a meagre 5.1 and 1.4 per cent of the votes cast. Nevertheless, the party never failed to win seats in parliament and it was also frequently represented in government. Indeed, in 1981, the first non-DC head of government since 1945, Giovanni Spadolini, came from the PRI.

The second major characteristic of the party system was that, of the two main parties, only the DC was in a position to form a government. Although the PCI was part of the governing coalition from 1944 to 1947, the onset of the Cold War and the advent of the Marshall Plan for European economic reconstruction led to the communists being effectively excluded from office. From this point on, neither the DC nor the parties allied with it considered the PCI to be eligible to join the government as a coalition partner. The party was too close to the Soviet Union, too much in favour of a command economy and insufficiently committed to a democratic system of government. Consequently, the PCI was treated as an 'anti-system' party and was condemned to political isolation. Only gradually was the party able to reintegrate itself into the mainstream of political competition. Over time, it distanced itself from the Soviet Union, demonstrated at the local level that it could govern responsibly and committed itself firmly to the constitutional process. This process of reintegration culminated in the so-called 'historic compromise' between the DC and the PCI from 1976 to 1979. During this period, DC minority governments were supported either tacitly or more openly by the PCI in parliament. In return, PCI representatives were allowed to hold positions of authority in parliament and the party was able to influence the content of government legislation. Even so, it was still the case that the PCI was excluded from government both during and after the historic compromise. Indeed, it was only after the collapse of communism in eastern Europe in 1989–90, the metamorphosis of the PCI into the PDS in 1991 and the overhaul of the party system from 1992–94 that the (now ex-)communists became eligible to play a full part in the political process.

As a result of these two basic party system characteristics, the exercise of party government from 1948 to 1992 took place under certain, highly specific conditions. In the first place, the isolation of the PCI (as well as, incidentally, the extreme-right MSI) ensured that only the parties in the centre of the political spectrum were eligible to form a government. Of these parties, the DC was by far the largest. Consequently, just as the PCI was condemned to opposition, so the DC was condemned to government. Furthermore, the fact that the DC was unable to obtain an absolute majority of seats in the legislature by itself meant that, even though the DC was condemned to govern, it was condemned to govern either alone as a minority government or in coalition with other centre(−right and −left) parties. Excluding the period of the 'historic compromise' from 1976 to 1979, there were periods of centrist governments (1947–57 and 1972–3) where the DC was in office with the support of most or all of the PLI, PRI and PSDI; periods of centre-left governments (1962–71 and 1973–5) where the DC was supported by the PRI, PSDI and PSI; and a period of five-party (*pentapartito*) government (1979–91) where the DC was in office with the PLI, PRI, PSDI and PSI. In between these distinct periods, there were transition phases usually marked by DC minority governments with the party relying on the support in parliament of shifting coalitions of various parties.

So, although the DC's constant presence in government enabled Italy to be characterised as a one-party dominant régime, the party was still obliged to share power, usually as the senior partner in a three-, four- or even five-party coalition. In this sense, the position of the DC in Italy differed somewhat from that of the LDP in Japan. Only from the late 1970s onwards did the LDP lose its absolute majority in the Diet and even then it was not forced to enter into a multiparty coalition. By contrast, in Italy, such coalitions were a constant feature of the political landscape. Indeed, even on the one occasion when the DC did enjoy an absolute majority in the Chamber of Deputies from 1948 to 1953, it still preferred to govern in alliance with other parties for fear that its majority might be eroded during the course of the legislature. As we shall see, the presence of multiparty coalition governments had important consequences for the exercise of political leadership. Before going to examine these consequences, though, it is necessary to examine the nature of factionalism within the DC.

*Factionalism within the DC*

From 1948 to 1992, Italy had a multiparty political system and the DC had a multifactional organisational structure (Leonardi and Wertman, 1989, p. 90). Like the LDP, the DC was never a monolithic party. As with the LDP, factionalism within the DC may be traced back to the very origins of the party in the period immediately following the collapse of Mussolini's fascist régime in 1943. From the outset, the DC was an inter-class party, deriving its support from a diverse set of social organisations centred primarily, but not exclusively, on the Catholic Church. The only way for the people in these diverse organisations with their different interests to work constructively together was for the party's own organisational structure to be flexible. As such, organised factions developed. The existence of factions was informally recognised by the party leadership in 1949 and then formally recognised in 1964. Gradually they developed from being loose associations of like-minded people to being formalised groups, each having their own distinct leadership, membership and organisational structure (Leonardi and Wertman, 1989, p. 17). As with the LDP in Japan, the DC's factions resembled parties within a party

Unlike the LDP, certain factions within the DC were ideologically motivated. For example, there were always important left-wing factions within the DC, such as *Forze Nuove*, *Base*, *Forze Sociali* and the *Area Zaccagnini*. At the same time, there were also right-wing factions, such as the one identified for a long time with Mario Scelba's *Centrismo Popolare*. In the main, though, and similar to the LDP, the primary motivation for factional conflict within the DC was the pursuit of personal power. Factions were often named after the faction leader (*Fanfaniani*, *Andreottiani*, *Forlaniani* and *Morotei*). Faction leaders built up powerful local bases on the basis of which they would be appointed to senior positions at the national level in governmental and party structures. In turn, from these positions, they controlled the distribution of patronage, rewarding existing followers and enticing the support of new ones in their home area and others. In this respect, factionalism came to be closely associated with clientelism (Zuckerman, 1979). As Allum notes, it also meant that factional leaders were 'often more interested in parochial issues and particular interests than broad national problems' (Allum, 1973, p. 334). Both factionalism and clientelism were encouraged by the system of preference voting at general elections (see Exhibit 7.4). In

---

**EXHIBIT 7.4**
**Preference voting and factionalism in the Italian system**

Prior to the 1994 elections, the electoral system for the Chamber of Deputies encouraged factionalism and clientelism by allowing preference voting. The country was divided up into thirty-two constituencies, each returning up to fifty deputies to parliament. In each constituency, each party produced a list of candidates. People then voted for a party list. (This was known as the list vote.) In addition, they had the right to single out up to four people (one after 1991) from the list they had chosen as the people they would prefer to see elected. (These were known as the preference votes.) Each party's proportion of the seats in each constituency was calculated according to the percentage of list votes cast for it. The candidates from each party list who were then elected were the ones who received the highest number of preference votes. Therefore, candidates had an incentive to try and maximise the number of preference votes cast for them and their supporters. As such, they developed clientelistic links with the electorate as a way of encouraging support.

---

Italy, as in Japan, there was a reciprocal relationship between faction leaders and followers. Followers were dependent upon leaders for clientelistic benefits and leaders were dependent on followers for preference votes at elections.

Another similarity between the DC and the LDP was that no single faction within the party was ever totally dominant. At times, certain faction leaders were able to guide the party in a particular direction. For example, in the late 1940s, Alcide De Gasperi helped to construct the DC's dominant position in the system, overseeing the development of Italy's long-term economic and foreign-policy priorities. However, even he was obliged to relinquish power in 1953. Similarly, Amintore Fanfani was responsible for the regeneration of the DC's organisational structure and the party's penetration of para-public organisations in the 1950s (see below) and Aldo Moro precipitated a leftward shift in coalition strategy in the 1960s. However, the degree of control enjoyed by either of these leaders was never absolute. Both had to make room for other power contenders (Pasquino, 1979, p. 89). In total, following their formal recognition in 1964, there were up to ten identifiable factions at any one time. (For the situation in 1989, see Exhibit 7.5.) These factions were represented proportionally

---

**EXHIBIT 7.5**
**Identifiable factions at the 1989 DC Party Congress**

| Centre-left | | Centre | Centre-right |
|---|---|---|---|
| De Mita | Forza | Azione Popolare | Fanfaniani (3%) |
| (35%)[1] | Nuova (7%) | (37%) | Andreottiani (18%) |

Following the Congress, 11 leadership posts went to De Mita's supporters, 11 to *Azione Popolare*, five to *Andreottiani*, two to *Forza Nuova* and one to a *Fanfaniano*.

*Notes*: [1] Figures correspond to the percentage of votes for each faction at the National Congress.
*Source*: Adapted from Caciagli, 1991, pp. 16–19.

---

on the party's ruling organisations according to their respective strengths. With no single faction being dominant, party secretaries were elected on the basis of factional alliances. The basic principle of such alliances was that, in return for helping to elect the party secretary, representatives from supporting factions would be appointed to senior positions in the party and/or positions of authority in the government or parliament. In this way, a factional balance was maintained. However, it was maintained at the expense of the party leader. DC leaders owed their appointment to fragile coalitions of factional forces. Therefore, as with the case of LDP leaders, they were never uncontested figures and, as Hine and Finocci note: '[their] legitimacy and authority [were] little greater than that of [their] challengers' (Hine and Finocci, 1991, p. 86).

**Party politics and the leadership environment**

The structure of resources within and between Italian political parties determined the precise nature of the country's leadership environment. Together, the dynamics of the multiparty system and the presence of factional conflict within the dominant party in the system combined to create a form of party government in Italy from 1948 to 1992 similar to the one which was to be found in Japan from 1955 to 1993. In particular, it created a system which encouraged both political brokerage and clientelism. Common to both countries was the fact that the dynamics of party government had an impact on three aspects of the leadership process: the selection of governments; the dismissal of governments; and the power of the head of government.

## The selection of governments

The structure of resources within and between political parties affected the selection of governments in three particular ways. First, the conditions under which party government took place diminished the link between the people and the choice of government. The PCI's exclusion from office meant that the DC had no option but to form a coalition with its smaller, centrist allies. It is true that governments were not completely impervious to election results. For example, the introduction of the PSI into government in 1963 was precipitated by a decline in support for the centrist coalition (DC, PLI, PRI, PSDI) which had previously been in office. Indeed, the 'historic compromise' itself was set in train by a loss of support for the governing block and an increase in support for the PCI at the 1976 election (Pasquino, 1987, p. 210). However, it is also true that, for want of a viable alternative government, elections generally returned the same coalition, or at least a very similar one, to office each time. As a result: '[t]he immediacy of the electoral relationship between the leader and the people was missing: the people had no means of choosing or directly controlling those who governed on their behalf' (Cavalli, 1992, p. 49). Consequently, governments had little incentive to be responsible (see below). Instead, they concentrated on the clientelistic, rather than the programmatic aspects of governing. This encouraged an incrementalist form of decision-making, rather than an emphasis on strategic planning.

Second, even when election results obliged the DC to alter its coalition strategy and to ally with a different set of coalition partners, the responsibility for choosing the new strategy was incumbent not upon the head of government, but upon the DC leadership. As a result, the choice of coalition partners was at least partly a function of the distribution of factional forces within the party itself. Coalition strategies varied as the balance of power within the DC varied. For example, in 1959, the Party Congress voted to continue excluding the PSI from the governing coalition. The outgoing party secretary, Amintore Fanfani, was in favour of extending the coalition and including the PSI, but his fortunes in the party were at least temporarily on the wane and the negative vote was partly a reflection of this situation. Instead, it was the task of the incoming party secretary, Aldo Moro, to try and convince the key *Dorotei* faction of the need for a centre-left government. At the 1962 Party Congress, the *Dorotei* faction changed its stance and decided to accept the PSI as a coalition partner. This decision paved the way for a centre-left government, which finally came about in 1963 after the DC's poor performance at the general election.

In this case, Moro, who served at the head of the newly formed centre-left coalition from 1963 to 1968, was personally identified with the change of coalition strategy. As such, he was able to able to develop a personal power base from which he was able to give the government a certain direction. Indeed, the first years of the centre-left government were marked by a number of important innovations, for example, in the organisation of local government. For the most part, though, DC heads of government were obliged to work within the confines of a coalition formula which had been chosen by their party, rather than being able to create for themselves the conditions under which they wished to operate. In this respect, it became difficult for heads of government to be personally identified with the government that they were leading. On these occasions, the lack of personal identification served to reduced their political authority and their leadership potential.

Third, inter- and intra-party politics affected the leadership process by restricting the degree of choice which heads of government could exercise over ministerial appointments. Article 92 of the 1948 Constitution gives the head of government the power to propose the names of government Ministers. However, although constitutionally this was an important power, in practice it was strictly limited. The constraints of party politics meant that heads of government could rely on the loyal support of only a handful of Ministers and Under-Secretaries (Junior Ministers) in the government. All other members of the government came either from parties opposed to the DC, or from factions opposed to the head of government's own. For example, the rules of coalition-building meant that positions in the

TABLE 7.2

The link between parliamentary seats and government posts in Italy

|  | 1963 | 1983 | 1989 |
|---|---|---|---|
| *DC:* |  |  |  |
| % seats in lower house | 67 | 61 | 62 |
| % of posts in government | 62 | 54 | 48 |
| Other parties[1]: |  |  |  |
| % of seats in lower house | 33 | 39 | 38 |
| % of posts in government | 38 | 46 | 52 |

*Note:*
[1] In 1963, the other parties in government were the PSI, PRI and PSDI. In 1983 and 1989, the PLI was included as well.
*Source:* Adapted from Hine, 1993, p. 106.

Council of Ministers were distributed on a roughly proportional basis between the DC and its coalition partners (see Table 7.2). The coalition partners themselves chose their own representatives, usually including the party leader, with the head of government being largely obliged to accept them. In this respect, the head of government had little or no control over the people who were to be appointed to up to 50 per cent of the seats in the Council of Ministers.

Similarly, ministerial portfolios were also distributed proportionally amongst the different factions within the DC. Indeed, the factional distribution of governmental positions was said to be calculated with mathematical precision in accordance with the rules laid down in the so-called 'Cencelli manual'. Named after a DC party official, Massimo Cencelli, the manual attributed values to different types of government appointments. Under-Secretaries were worth one point; full Ministers were worth three points; and the President of the Council of Ministers was worth six points (Dogan, 1989, pp. 122–3). The number of points (and, hence, portfolios) which was available to each faction corresponded to the proportional strength of that faction on the party's ruling organisations. Once the allocation of posts had been decided, then individual factions would choose which of their representatives were to be appointed to the particular posts. While Dogan has questioned whether the distribution of ministerial portfolios was strictly allocated on the basis of the mathematical formula outlined above (Dogan, 1989, p. 123), the general principle of proportionality applied and the head of government's power of appointment was limited even further.

In the allocation of portfolios, parties and factions sought to hold office not simply for its own sake, nor for purely ideological or programmatic reasons, but also because it allowed them access to government resources in the form of grants, concessions from regulations, or appointments to *sottogoverno* organisations (see below). The main patronage Ministries were Agriculture, Education, Health, Merchant Marine, Post and Telecommunications, Public Works, Southern Development, State Participation and Transport (Furlong, 1994, p. 117). By occupying Ministries such as these, parties and factions were able to win and maintain the support of particular clientèles, which in turn helped to maintain and improve their position in the system as a whole. The result, though, was that the coalition-building process was preoccupied primarily with the distribution of government posts as a method of patronage, rather than with the construction of a coherent policy programme on the basis of which the actions of the government would be judged at the next election. In this respect, Italian governments resembled their Japanese counterparts much more than they resembled either their British, French, US or German counterparts.

The need to satisfy both party and factional demands also meant that Italian governments were large, unwieldy organisations. For instance, the last *pentapartito* government (Andreotti VI, 1989) contained thirty-two full Ministers. As a result, the Council of Ministers was in no position to act as a collective decision-making body. Indeed, generally, Italian governments showed a very low degree of collegiality and cohesion (see Chapter 2). Moreover, they were uncollegial, uncohesive organisations over which the head of government had little authority. Heads of government were contested figures who were obliged to work within the confines of a coalition strategy which had often been determined for them and alongside a large number of government Ministers whose appointment they were obliged to accept. This is not to say that there was no incentive for politicians to seek to be appointed as head of government. The Presidency of the Council of Ministers was the subject of much public attention and incumbents were well-placed to demand important patronage, or status positions in future governments. (After all, the post was worth six points in the Cencelli manual.) Nevertheless, the importance of the office was not to be found in the context of strategic, direction-setting leadership, but in the context of a political system which operated on the basis of the exchange of political favours (Tarrow, 1990).

## The dismissal of governments

Party politics also helped to determine how long governments were able to remain in office. The average lifespan of a post-war Italian government was approximately 11 months. The most long-lived government survived for only three years (Craxi I, 1983–6) and the most short-lived government survived for just 12 days (De Gasperi VII, July 1953). Spadolini is quoted as saying that being the head of government was like taking part in 'a permanent obstacle race' (in Pridham, 1983, p. 209). As can be seen from Exhibit 7.6, disputes

---

**EXHIBIT 7.6**
**Motivations of government crises in Italy, 1945–89**

| | |
|---|---:|
| • Normal election timetable | 6 |
| • Inter-party dispute | 17 |
| • Intra-party dispute | 3 |
| • Both inter- and intra-party disputes | 12 |
| • Backbench revolt | 5 |
| • Programmed resignation or expected defeat | 5 |
| Total | 48 |

*Source*: Furlong, 1990, p. 58.

---

between coalition partners were the direct cause of seventeen of the forty-eight governmental crises between 1945 and 1989.

For example, in 1987, the PSI leader, Bettino Craxi, came into conflict with the DC over the question of how long he was to remain as President of the Council of Ministers. An agreement had been reached between the two parties whereby Craxi would resign from his post in March 1987, allowing a representative from the DC to take over. When Craxi started to question the agreement in February, stating that he might consider staying on as head of government, a crisis blew up and he was eventually obliged to tender his resignation (Balboni, 1989). At the same time, inter-factional disputes within the DC were the direct cause of three crises and the joint cause of twelve others. For example, shifts in the balance of power within the DC accounted directly or indirectly for the demise of the De Gasperi government in 1953, Moro in 1964 and 1966, Rumor in 1970, Andreotti in 1973 and Cossiga in 1980 (Spotts and Wieser, 1986, p. 106). In total, two-thirds (32/48) of all governmental crises from 1945 to 1989 resulted directly from the dynamics of party politics.

The main reason for the excessive level of governmental instability was that parties in the governing coalition had little incentive to be responsible. As Di Palma, writing in 1977, noted: 'Since each partner of the center coalition knows that it will continue to stay in government ... there is very little need to maintain cohesion in the coalition so as to prevent the opposition from taking over' (Di Palma, 1977, p. 251). Both the smaller parties and the individual factions within the DC were at least relatively secure in the knowledge that they would be returned to office if the government fell. Therefore, governmental crises could be tolerated. More than that, they had an incentive to create crisis situations in the hope that they might obtain more positions or more senior positions in the incoming government than they held in the outgoing one (Tarrow, 1990, pp. 325–6). In countries, such as Germany, where coalitions had at least a relatively clear programmatic content, then parties had an incentive to remain in office in order to carry through their policy commitments. By contrast, in countries, such as Italy and Japan, where parties and/or factions were motivated primarily by the desire to control government resources, no such incentive was present and governmental instability ensued.

As might be expected, the degree of governmental instability in post-war Italy affected the head of government's ability to exercise leadership. The frequency with which governmental crises occurred and with which new governments were formed reduced the head of government's status. Moreover, as Hine and Finocchi note, this reduced status was self-fulfilling: 'Because [heads of government] *can* be challenged and checked, such behaviour falls within the range of the politically acceptable' (Hine and Finocchi, 1991, p. 81). Heads of government were treated as little more than political caretakers, coming to office in the knowledge that they were unlikely to remain there for very long. They had little time to build up a personal following and little opportunity to enhance their political prestige. In the mid-1980s, Bettino Craxi tried to overcome this situation by adopting a leadership style known as '*decisionismo*'. As only the second non-DC head of government since 1945, he attempted to enhance his personal following and that of the PSI by demonstrating that strong leadership was possible. Despite remaining in office for three years, he was ultimately unsuccessful and he became one of the major victims of the *tangentopoli* corruption investigations in 1992 (see below). Therefore, the point remains that heads of government were generally unable to construct a personal rapport with the public and, like their Japanese counterparts, their authority was weak.

## The power of the head of government

In the absence of an extensive set of constitutional and administrative resources and as a result of the conditions surrounding their appointment and dismissal, heads of government had little authority with which to assert their own preferences in the decision-making process. In addition, the constraints of party politics further weakened their authority. In particular, the distribution of resources within and between political parties shifted the very centre of decision-making away from the Council of Ministers, over which heads of government might have been able to exert a degree of control, and towards party and other organisations over which they generally had much less control. It is this shift in the locus of decision-making that provides the most striking demonstration of Italy's acephalous leadership from 1948–92. It can be illustrated in two ways: *sottogoverno* and Majority Summit meetings.

### •*Sottogoverno*

According to Donovan: '[f]rom the 1960s the very basis of government moved away from parliament and cabinet into the world of "sub-government" (*sottogoverno*)' (Donovan, 1994, p. 73). The term '*sottogoverno*' refers to organisations which were formally under state and, hence, party control, but which also enjoyed a degree of independent decision-making responsibilities. The main organisations in this system were three state holding companies, IRI, ENI and EFIM and much of the banking system (see Exhibit 7.7) as well as various pensions, social security and welfare organisations. In total, there were up to 45 000 organisations in the *sottogoverno* system (Spotts and Wieser, 1986, p. 137). Of these, IRI was Europe's largest organisation and the largest single European employer. ENI was the world's ninth largest firm and the fourth largest outside the USA.

---

**EXHIBIT 7.7**

**Examples of *sottogoverno***

Three main state holding companies:

1. IRI – Institute for Industrial Reconstruction. Founded in 1933. Held stock in up to a 1000 firms involved in steel, shipbuilding, chemical, aircraft, engineering, telecommunications, credit, banking and broadcasting industries amongst others.
2. ENI – National Hydrocarbons Trust. Founded in 1953. Interests in up to 400 firms involved in petroleum, nuclear energy, textile and engineering industries.
3. EFIM – Trust for Owning and Financing Manufacturing Industries. Founded in 1964. The smallest of the three, but with interests in railway, food, aluminium and weapons industries.

The banking system:

The main commercial banks, savings banks and banks of national interest were all owned by the state.

---

Collectively, the state-controlled banking system accounted for nearly 80 per cent of Italy's banking facilities (Spotts and Wieser, 1986, pp. 137–9). Together, the *sottogoverno* organisations comprised a vast array of companies in which the state and parties had an interest.

The primary importance of *sottogoverno* was that it served as a means by which political parties could obtain access to public funds and political patronage. In the 1950s, under Fanfani's leadership, the DC deliberately began to colonise the para-public sector as a way of reducing its dependency on the Catholic church and the main employers' organisation, Confindustria. By virtue of its position as the country's hegemonic party, the DC was able to appoint the presidents and vice-presidents of the various organisations in this sector. Consequently, a symbiotic relationship developed between the DC and the para-public system, whereby 'the managers supported the DC (and the companies served as sources of patronage and sometimes resources), while the DC protected the managers' (Leonardi and Wertman, 1989, p. 237). As Spotts and Wieser note, the result of this system was that:

> *sottogoverno*, with its thousands of public entities and hundreds of thousands of jobs, was transformed by the Christian Democrats into the biggest pool of patronage in any democratic state ... the

party card became almost as important in Italy as in Communist countries (Spotto and Wieser, 1986, p. 144).

Gradually, from the 1970s onwards as the DC's hegomonic position began to weaken, the practice of *sottogoverno* was extended to include the other parties in the governing coalition. For example, after 1978, the DC retained control of IRI, the PSDI chose the president of EFIM and, after 1979, the PSI chose the president of ENI. (For the example of the banking sector, see Table 7.3.).

**TABLE 7.3**
**Party control of Italian state savings banks, 1986**

| Party | Presidencies total no. | (%) | Vice-presidencies total no. | (%) |
|-------|------------------------|-------|------------------------------|-------|
| DC    | 70 | (79.5) | 35 | (40.5) |
| PSI   | 11 | (12.5) | 36 | (41.8) |
| PSDI  | 4  | (4.5)  | 8  | (9.3)  |
| PRI   | 2  | (2.2)  | 4  | (4.6)  |
| PLI   | 1  | (1.3)  | 3  | (3.8)  |

*Source*: Pridham, 1988, p. 103.

One consequence of this situation was that all the governing parties became associated with the system of *partitocrazia*. All benefited from the system and all were punished electorally when the system started to unravel in the early 1990s. Moreover, even the PCI was implicated in the system. For example, after 1979, the PCI was allocated the third television channel (RAI 3) as well as one of the country's radio networks. Partly for this reason, the PCI and its successor, the PDS, was not in a position to profit unequivocally from the discredit of the governing parties.

A further consequence of the system of *sottogoverno* was that it discouraged 'generalised' attempts at policy-making (Hine, 1993, p. 230). Although parties controlled appointments to the many *sottogoverno* organisations, as with the case of para-public institutions in Germany, these organisations often enjoyed a considerable degree of decision-making latitude. They were in the political arena, but they operated with 'managerial autonomy in accordance with commercial criteria' (Furlong, 1994, p. 236). The government provided only 'very general policy directions' (Leonardi and Wertman, 1989, p. 237), while strategic decisions were taken by representatives in the particular organisations. In this sense, policy-making was highly sectoral, with little opportunity for the head of government to exert any degree of central control over the system. Moreover, it was also devolved down to the level of the *sottogoverno* organisations, leaving Ministers as the distributors of patronage, rather than as key decision-makers. In the sense that there was little opportunity for central direction and that decision-making responsibilities were to be found outside the governmental arena, then the *sottogoverno* system was a primary cause of Italy's acephalous leadership.

*•Majority Summit meetings*
The second illustration of acephalous leadership can be found in the increasing importance of Majority Summit meetings from the 1970s onwards. Because of the multi-party nature of the governing coalition, decisions could not be imposed upon the government by the President of the Council of Ministers. Instead, they had to be negotiated between representatives of the different coalition partners. However, rather than taking place within the formal structure of the Council of Ministers, inter-party negotiations increasingly took place in the informal arena of 'Majority Summit' meetings (Criscitiello, 1993). These meetings brought together senior representatives of the various coalition parties as well as the head of government as a way of resolving government crises or simply deciding government policy. As Criscitiello notes, the effect of Majority Summits was to ensure that 'intra-governmental coordination and collegiality [was] replaced by a method of extra-governmental party bargaining' (ibid, p. 591). By displacing decision-making from the governmental arena onto the party arena, therefore, Majority Summits again increased the role of senior party figures at the expense of the decision-making capacity of the head of government.

Moreover, although involved in Majority Summit meetings, the strategic position of the President of the Council of Ministers was weak. One of the unwritten rules of the DC was that the same person should not simultaneously hold the position of party secretary and head of government. On only four occasions did the same person occupy both posts at the same time and then for only a brief period. Moreover, on the occasions when the two positions were held by different people, those people were not necessarily close allies. Often, competitors were appointed to the two posts in an attempt to maintain the factional balance of power within the party. For example, the appointment of a reformer, Benigno Zaccagnini, as party secretary in 1975 was counterbalanced by the appointment of a right-wing figure, Giulio Andreotti, as head of government during the period of the 'historic compromise' from 1976 to 1979. So, the multi-party nature of the government and the multi-factional organisation of the DC meant that decisions were increasingly taken outside the governmental arena and that the head of government's authority in these meetings was essentially contested.

In a system dominated by the distribution of resources within and between political parties, the primary function of the head of government was to coordinate the day-to-day business of the government. Certain heads of government, such as De Gasperi and Moro, had what amounted to a programme of reforms which they wished to see enacted. Moreover, the situation was sometimes sufficiently conducive to allow some leaders to leave their mark (at least temporarily) on the political process. For instance, in the mid-1980s, Bettino Craxi benefited from the demoralised state of the DC and his appointment as only the second non-DC head of government to adopt a highly personalised, if ultimately unsuccessful, leadership style. For the most part, though, like their Japanese counterparts, Italian heads of government were managers and conflict adjusters, rather than strategic direction-setters. They derived benefits from holding office which furthered the fortunes of their own party (Spadolini and Craxi), or their own faction (Fanfani and Andreotti). More mundanely, they derived a personal prestige from meeting other leaders on the international stage and from the media attention that their position could command. Overall, however, they were far less influential than their British, French, German and US counterparts. Pridham characterises their role in the following way:

> the picture which emerges is less one of a central directing authority, the statement and pursuit of clear objectives and limited conflict over priorities, but rather one of endemic conflict, mutual adjustment with a premium on consultation and agreement and a low element of coercion (Pridham, 1988, p. 86).

In Italy, as in Japan, the nature of party politics meant that the task of exercising leadership was very difficult for heads of government to achieve.

Moreover, the nature of Italian party politics had wider

implications for the political system. It produced a system based on both brokerage, with resources being shared out amongst the competing demands of political parties, and clientelism, with parties developing a complex series of sometimes undisclosed links with patrons at all levels of government. The result of brokered and clientelistic politics, though, was an incrementalist form of sectoral, predominantly extra-governmental decision-making and a general absence of any clear link between the people and the choice of public policies. At the same time, brokerage and clientelism also led to an institutionalised network of shady dealing. It led to a world of behind-the-scenes deals, as resources were brokered, and party 'kickbacks', as clientelistic links were constructed. The DC was the main beneficiary of the system, but the other governing parties and the PCI increasingly came to benefit from it as well. In this way, the system was identified with the political class as a whole, rather with than any particular part of it (Sidoti, 1993a). Over time, as the opposition to incrementalism grew gradually stronger, and then suddenly, as some of the more corrupt aspects of party behaviour were uncovered, the public mood for reform increased. It is in this context that the events following the 1992 election transformed the nature of the Italian leadership environment and created the potential for a new form of political leadership to emerge.

**The transformation of the Italian political system**

The 1992 election to the Chamber of Deputies dealt a blow to the system of party government which had been in operation since 1948. (For the results, see Table 7.4.) Both the DC and the PDS (the ex-PCI) polled their lowest percentage of votes since the war and together they won less than half of the votes cast. At the same time, the main beneficiaries of this situation were not the other centrist parties with which the DC had been allied in government. Together, they won only 23.5 per cent of the votes cast, slightly less than their combined total in 1987. Instead, the parties that gained the most were those which had been outside the system of *partitocrazia* and which campaigned against the political class. In particular, the populist Northern League, which ran on a separatist, anti-system platform, won nearly 9 per cent of the vote. However, while this election represented a defeat for the old majority, it failed to install a new majority in its place (Sidoti, 1993b, p. 112).

**TABLE 7.4**

The 1992 election to the Italian Chamber of Deputies

| Party | Votes (%) | Seats |
|---|---|---|
| DC | 29.7 | 206 |
| PDS | 16.1 | 107 |
| PSI | 13.6 | 92 |
| Northern League[1] | 8.7 | 55 |
| RC[2] | 5.6 | 35 |
| MSI | 5.4 | 34 |
| PRI | 4.4 | 27 |
| PLI | 2.8 | 17 |
| Greens | 2.8 | 16 |
| PSDI | 2.7 | 16 |
| The Network[3] | 1.9 | 12 |
| Radicals | 1.2 | 7 |
| Other parties | 5.1 | 6 |

*Notes*:

[1] The Northern League is a right-wing, populist party, which promotes a policy of separatism for the North of Italy.

[2] RC: Communist Refoundation includes elements of the PCI which refused to join the PDS.

[3] The Network (*La Rete*) is an anti-Mafia party based in Sicily.

If the 1992 election dealt a blow to the system of *partitocrazia*, it was not a fatal blow. In the aftermath of the election, a new government was formed headed by the socialist, Giuliano Amato. Although Amato was only the third non-DC head of government since the war and although he stated that his government was committed to creating the conditions under which the political system could be reformed, he still headed a four-party coalition, consisting of DC, PLI, PSDI and PSI representatives, and containing the essential elements of that which had gone before. As a result, reform was slow to come about. At the same time, the political capital of the *partitocrazia* class started to tumble. Illegalities were discovered in the behaviour of senior politicians from all the major parties. Craxi was arrested. Andreotti was accused. Support for the established parties collapsed, while support for the Northern League and the extreme-right MSI continued to increase.

The final blow to the system came with the referendums which were held in April 1993. The most important of these referendums was the one which was originally promoted by a leading reformer within the DC, Mario Segni, and which was designed to approve a change to the system of election to the upper house of the Italian legislature, the Senate. In particular, it was designed to limit the extent of proportional representation in the Senate's electoral system. Despite the ostensibly narrow aim of the referendum, the assumption was that, if the reform was approved, then it would create an irresistible pressure to reform the system of election to the Chamber of Deputies as well (Newell and Bull, 1993, p. 609). To the extent that proportionalism ensured that the country's multi-party system was reflected in the Chamber of Deputies and that the particular form of proportionalism had long encouraged clientelism, then a vote to change the system of election to the Senate was seen as a vote against the system of party government as a whole. In the referendum, change was approved by 82.7 per cent of those who voted, confirming the anti-system feeling in the country.

Immediately, Amato resigned and made way for a 'transitional government', consisting largely of non-political figures and 'clean' politicians, which would finally be able to bring about reform. The new government was headed by Carlo Azeglio Ciampi, a former head of the Bank of Italy, one of the few state institutions which had largely escaped the effects of *sottogoverno*. One of the first acts of the government was to pass a new electoral system for the Chamber of Deputies. Under the new system 25 per cent of deputies are elected from regionally-based party lists by proportional representation, with a 4 per cent national threshold for entry into parliament, similar to the German system. The other 75 per cent of deputies are elected in single-member constituencies, similar to the British system. Thus, the new system includes a strong majoritarian element, which, it was hoped, would produce a strong government/opposition divide, and which would allow the public to make a clear choice between alternative governments. To a degree, in the first set of elections under this system in March 1994, these hopes were realised (see Table 7.5.) The disparate elements of the Italian party system were whittled down to three electoral groupings. Although many of the old parties were to be found within these groupings, the beginning of a simplified party system and one which might provide a greater opportunity for leadership was discernible. The 1994 election also produced Italy's first distinctly charismatic head of government since 1948, the media

TABLE 7.5

The 1994 election to the Italian Chamber of Deputies

| Party Grouping | Vote (%) | Seats (no. + %) | |
|---|---|---|---|
| Freedom Alliance[1] | 42.9 | 366 | 58.1 |
| Progressives[2] | 34.4 | 213 | 33.8 |
| Centrists[3] | 15.7 | 46 | 7.3 |
| Others | 7.0 | 5 | 0.8 |

*Notes*:
[1] Main components: Forza Italia (Silvio Berlusconi's party); Northern League; National Alliance (ex-MSI); PLI/Union of the Centre (ex-PLI); Christian Democrat Centre (ex-DC); Pannella List (ex-Radicals); Socialists (ex-PSI and PSDI).
[2] PDS; RC; Rete; Greens; PSI; Socialist Renewal (ex-PSI); Democratic Alliance (ex-PSI and PRI); Social Christians (ex-DC).
[3] PPI (ex-DC); Segni Pact (ex-DC): PRI.

tycoon, Silvio Berlusconi, although his coalition itself collapsed in December 1994.

It appears, therefore, that in Italy, as in Japan, the old political system has been replaced by a new one. In Italy, however, the reform process has been even stronger than in Japan. In Italy, the whole of the old political class has been discredited, the old parties which previously dominated the political system are now moribund and the opportunity for the forces associated with the old system to reassert themselves, at least in an unreconstructed form, is small. In all these respects, the degree of continuity between the old and the new systems is much less pronounced in Italy than in Japan. Nevertheless, the contours of the new Italian system are still unclear. It will take a number of years and a number of elections for the transformation of the Italian system to be completed and only then will it be possible to give a definitive judgement about the new dynamics of the country's leadership environment.

# 8

# The Institutional Basis of Political Leadership

In the opening chapter, political leadership was identified as a process of interaction between leaders and the leadership environment with which they are faced. It was demonstrated that the nature of this interaction determines the ways in which and the extent to which heads of state and heads of government are able to affect the outcome of the decision-making process in a country. It was also demonstrated that there are many different elements to the interaction process. These elements were analysed under three separate headings: the ambitions and styles of political leaders; institutional structures; and the needs of the society. (To recap on the various elements under these headings, see Exhibit 8.1.)

Following the six country-study chapters, we are now in a position to see that each of the different elements under these headings was salient to the interaction process. We are also in a position to confirm that in all six countries the leadership process was influenced most significantly by the set of elements under the heading of institutional structures. These elements were at least partly responsible for determining the ambitions and styles of political leaders and for mediating the impact of the needs of the society upon the leadership process. In sum, they were largely responsible for creating the particular patterns of leadership that were identified in each of the six countries that were studied.

In the first part of this chapter, we will demonstrate the impact of institutional structures upon the leadership process. In the second part, we will account for why they should have had such an impact. We will do so by examining the institutional approach to politics. In this way, we will place what so far has been a highly empirical study of political leadership in the context of a wider, theoretical approach to

---

**EXHIBIT 8.1**
**Elements in the interactionist approach to political leadership**

*Leaders*
1  *Ambitions*
   Focus of aims
   Scope of aims
2  *Styles*
   e.g., Uncompromising,
   or malleable,
   assertive, or
   responsive

*The leadership environment*
1  *Institutional structures:*
   (i)  Within the executive branch of the central
        government, e.g.,
        Different ways of taking and leaving
        office.
        Constitutional and procedural powers.
        Staff resources and relationship with the
        permanent administration.
        International position of the country.

   (ii) Between the executive branch of govern-
        ment and other branches and levels of
        government, e.g.,
        Executive/legislative relations.
        Role of the Supreme Court
        (or equivalent).
        Relations between central and
        subcentral units of government.

   (iii) Within and between political parties, e.g.,
        Party leadership.
        Organisational structure of party.
        Nature of party support in
        the legislature.

2  *The need of the society:*
   (i)   Historical legacy.
   (ii)  Societal attitudes, e.g.,
         Partisan affiliation of the electorate.
         Interest group activity.
   (iii) Popular desires.

---

political science. We will examine the advantages and disadvantages
of the institutional approach to politics and show how this study of
political leadership may add to our appreciation of this approach.

## Political leadership in six liberal democracies

### Ambitions and styles

The country studies demonstrated that political leaders harboured
various kinds of ambitions and that they exhibited different types and

forms of leadership styles. In terms of the former, one of the most ambitious leaders was Charles de Gaulle. He had a particular vision of executive leadership, which he tried to realise in office. He also tried to create a system in which his successors would be able to exercise leadership in a similar way. Slightly less grandly, it was also shown that German Chancellors developed particular interests in certain policy areas. For example, Adenauer and Brandt had ambitions in foreign policy, Schmidt in monetary and economic policy and Kohl in German unification. Indeed, even in systems where executive leadership was difficult to achieve, heads of government were still personally associated with certain policies. In Japan, Ikeda was identified with the 'income doubling' plan and Nakasone pledged to cut the country's budget deficit. In Italy, De Gasperi oversaw the development of foreign policy in the immediate post-war period and Fanfani encouraged the colonisation of the para-public sector by the DC in the 1950s.

In terms of leadership styles, a distinction was made between the malleable and managerial behaviour of certain British Prime Ministers, such as Attlee, Macmillan, Home, Wilson and Major, and the uncompromising and mobilising behaviour of both Heath and Thatcher. In France, the charismatic presence of de Gaulle contrasted sharply with the reassuring tones of Pompidou and Mitterrand and the technocratic loftiness of Giscard d'Estaing. In the United States, Franklin D. Roosevelt's agenda-setting leadership style served as the model for many of the Presidents who succeeded him. In Italy, Craxi developed a personalistic and direct style of leadership, known as '*decisionismo*', during the mid-1980s.

In these ways, the country studies indicated that both the ambitions and styles of political leaders had an impact on the conduct of the decision-making process. For example, in Britain, the leadership process during the Thatcher prime ministership was different from that under the Wilson prime ministership. In France, under the de Gaulle presidency, it was different from that under the Giscard presidency. In this sense, they indicated that leaders made a difference. And yet, as foreseen in the opening chapter, the country studies also indicated that leaders only made a difference up to a point. These chapters indicated that their ambitions and styles were at least partly determined by the leadership environment (and, in particular, by institutional structures) with which they were faced. For example, they suggested that, as their term in office developed, US Presidents tended to develop ambitions in foreign policy at the expense of domestic policy-making. They did so, because they enjoyed a greater room for manœuvre in the former than in the latter. Similarly, the fact that most Japanese and Italian heads of government adopted a reactive style of leadership was not coincidental. They did so, because the system in which they operated discouraged the exercise of strategic, personal leadership. These examples do not suggest that the ambitions and styles of all political leaders in any given country were indistinguishable. They simply indicate that the motivations and actions of political leaders were at least partly structured by the prevailing leadership environment and, as we shall see, by institutional structures in particular. In the second part of this chapter, we will explain why this should be the case.

*The needs of the society*

The country studies also demonstrated that the leadership process was partly determined by the needs of the society. It was shown that there were historical reasons which influenced the exercise of political leadership. For example, in Germany, the instability of the Weimar Republic and the dictatorship of the Third Reich created conflicting leadership tensions. The system encouraged personalised leadership, but also set distinct limits within which such leadership could take place. By contrast, in Italy and Japan, historical factors meant that there was a similar fear of dictatorship, but this fear was countered by few encouragements for personalised leadership. In this way, historical reasons helped to account for there being a greater potential for individual leadership in post-war Germany than in either Italy or Japan. It was also shown that societal attitudes influenced the leadership process. For example, party identification in post-war Britain was split along class lines, which favoured a relatively balanced two-party system. This system encouraged a form of executive leadership by creating the conditions both for single party majority governments and for regular alternations in power. By contrast, in Italy, party identification was fragmented and polarised, which led to a multi-party system with anti-system parties on both the left and the right. This system discouraged executive leadership by making coalition governments inevitable and alternations in power almost impossible. Finally, short-term popular desires were also seen to affect the leadership process. For example, the US depression in the

1930s allowed President Roosevelt to take emergency measures to relieve the crisis and to lay the foundations of the 'modern presidency'. Similarly, the recent changes undergone by both the Japanese and the Italian systems were caused by a swift and overwhelming public rejection of traditional political practices. In both these cases, the effect on the leadership process has yet to be seen.

In these ways, it is apparent that along with the ambitions and styles of political leaders the needs of the society had an impact on the decision-making process. The leadership process cannot be divorced from the historical and social context in which it takes place. Again, though, the six country studies also indicated that the way in which the needs of the society affected the leadership process was often partly determined by the other aspect of the leadership environment, namely, institutional structures. For example, in Germany, Italy and Japan, historical factors were significant, because of the ways in which they fed into the institutional environment. They resulted in institutional opportunities, or constraints, which political leaders could mobilise, or which they had to overcome. Similarly, the partisan affiliation of the electorate was important not just in itself, but also by virtue of the way in which it was mediated through the system of election to the national legislature. In Britain, the plurality electoral system favoured the two large parties, rendering the likelihood of single-party majority governments and alternations in power much greater. By contrast, in Italy, the proportional electoral system favoured the smaller parties, increasing the likelihood of coalition governments and decreasing the potential for any alternation in power. As a result, it may be concluded that, as one aspect of the leadership environment, the needs of the society did have an impact upon the nature of the leadership process. However, it may also be concluded that the key aspect of the leadership environment was to be found under the heading of institutional structures. Once again, in the second part of this chapter, we will account for some of the reasons why this should be the case.

*Institutional structures*

In all, the country studies demonstrated that institutional structures had the greatest impact on the leadership process. The set of elements under this heading helped to determine the ambitions and styles of political leaders and to mediate the impact of the needs of the society.

Before we go on to explain why this set of elements should have had such an impact on the leadership process, let us first of all illustrate some of the ways in which it was significant. Let us do so by considering it under the three sub-headings that were identified in the opening chapter:

1. the structure of resources within the executive branch of the central government;
2. the structure of resources between the executive branch of the central government and other branches and levels of government;
3. the structure of resources within and between political parties.

As we shall see, the combination of the various elements under these sub-headings was largely responsible for determining the particular patterns of leadership that were identified in the six country chapters. (To recap on these patterns, see Exhibit 8.2.)

*•The structure of resources within the executive branch of central government*
In terms of the structure of resources within the executive branch of the central government, the ways in which leaders assumed and left office had significant consequences for the exercise of leadership. For example, in France and the USA, the direct election of the President created an unambiguous focus for leadership, personalising the leadership process and providing a mandate for government. Presidents in these countries also enjoyed a security of tenure, allowing them to concentrate on both the policy process and securing re-election. In Germany and Britain, the conduct of parliamentary elections created a similar focus for leadership, although the intermediary role of political parties reduced the extent to which the leadership process was personalised. Moreover, although German Chancellors enjoyed a considerable degree of job security, British Prime Ministers were vulnerable to party challenges and one of their continuing tasks was to secure their position within the party. By contrast, in Japan and Italy, heads of government were pure party creations, enjoying little direct popular support, possessing only a limited capacity for personal action and facing the constant threat of dismissal. In such a context, personal leadership was difficult to achieve.

The leadership process was also affected by the distribution of constitutional and procedural powers within the executive. In formal terms, the powers of the British Prime Minister, the German

## EXHIBIT 8.2
## Patterns of political leadership

### Britain: prime ministerial leadership

Strong prime ministerial powers countered by Cabinet collegiality, departmentalism and party constraints, in a unitary and centralised state, with no judicial review and weak Parliament.

### Germany: dispersed leadership

Strong Chancellor countered by Minister and Cabinet principles, coalition politics, an influential legislature, active Constitutional Court, strong para-public institutions and federalism.

### Japan: reactive leadership

Weak prime ministerial powers, in the context of a dominant and highly factionalised party, a clientelistic electoral system, an important role for the Diet and an influential bureaucracy.

### France: presidential leadership

Presidentialisation of the system countered by the role of the Prime Minister, in a unitary and centralised state, with limits to the role of the Constitutional Council and the decline of the legislature.

### United States: divided leadership

Presidential powers, in the context of strong congressional powers, weak parties, a potentially active Supreme Court and a federal system.

### Italy: acephalous leadership

Weak prime ministerial powers, in the context of a dominant and highly factionalised party, a clientelistic electoral system, multi-party coalition politics with anti-system parties and para-public organisations.

Chancellor, the US President and both the French President and Prime Minister were relatively great. Considerable leadership responsibilities were incumbent upon all these leaders. By contrast, few such responsibilities were incumbent upon either the Japanese or the Italian head of government. Within the executive, their position was weak. All the same, British and German heads of government were faced with countervailing pressures from both collective and departmental interests. Moreover, the lack of collegiality within the US executive meant that Cabinet members had little incentive to be loyal to the President's programme. Finally, the dualism of the French executive meant that there was both a certain tension within the system and the potential for presidential government to be replaced by prime ministerial government. Consequently, although certain leaders enjoyed not inconsiderable powers, in no country did the principal political leader enjoy an absolute set of powers with which to exercise leadership over the executive.

In the opening chapter, it was noted that there is no clear relation between staff size and the ability to exercise leadership. The six country studies confirmed the validity of this assertion. For example, in Italy and Japan, where the head of government enjoyed few staff resources, the potential for personalised leadership within the executive was constrained. And yet, in the United States, where the President enjoyed considerable administrative backing, the capacity for presidential leadership was also constrained. This was because of the complexities involved in controlling and coordinating the many presidential advisory structures. Indeed, this point applies to the President's relations with the permanent administration as well. By contrast, in Britain, Germany and France, the head of government controlled a relatively efficient set of advisory units. In these cases, the existence of such units did not guarantee that the head of government could impose a direction on the government. However, it did increase the likelihood that the head of government's leadership style would filter through the executive as a whole.

Finally, the international position of the country was shown to affect the leadership process. In this respect, it was significant whether or not the country in question possessed nuclear weapons. In the case of those countries which did, Britain, France and the United States, the responsibility for strategic defence and foreign-policy decisions lay unambiguously with the principal political leader. This situation increased the leader's authority within the executive and encouraged other actors to exhibit a degree of political deference. By contrast, in those countries which did not possess nuclear weapons, Germany, Italy and Japan, the authority of the principal political leader was not as great. In these countries, decision-making in the field of foreign and defence policy was shared rather more equally between the head of government and responsible Ministers. The status of the head of government was less elevated and leadership expectations were less extensive.

•*The structure of resources between the executive branch of central government and other branches and levels of government*
In addition to the structure of resources within the executive branch of the central government, the leadership process was also affected by the structure of resources between this branch of government and the other branches and levels of government. In terms of the executive's relationship with the legislature, it was noticeable that the former dominated the latter in both Britain and France. In these two countries, the legislature exercised only a residual influence over the decision-making process. By contrast, in the United States, the twin principles of the separation of powers and checks and balances ensured that there was a more even distribution of responsibilities. Although Congress was rarely in a position to set and realise the leadership agenda itself, its formal powers meant that the executive and legislative branches had to work together, necessitating a system of bargaining and compromise. In Germany and Japan (at least since the mid-1970s), a similar system occurred. In sum, the legislature constrained political leaders in the executive branch of the British and French governments the least. Consequently, their room for manoeuvre was the greatest in this respect.

The role of the highest court of the land also varied across the six countries. Once again, consistent with the principles of the separation of powers and checks and balances, the US Supreme Court played a significant part in the decision-making process. Indeed, during the 1950s and 1960s, it assumed a key leadership role in certain issue areas. By contrast, in the UK, the judiciary had no power to review the constitutionality of statute law and played only a minor role in the policy process. In the other four countries under consideration, constitutional courts were active, but to different degrees. Amongst this set of countries, the role of the German Constitutional Court was the most highly developed. Here, the Court was regularly called upon to provide a judicial solution to a political problem. By contrast, in France, the Constitutional Council has only recently frustrated attempts to pass reform-minded legislation. Overall, the judiciary's role in the decision-making process was the least significant in Britain and the most significant in the United States.

With regard to the prerogatives of central and subcentral units of government, the country studies suggested that political leaders at the central level of government enjoyed the greatest degree of autonomy in Britain and France. In these countries, there was a unitary system of government. Consequently, there was a centralisation of leadership responsibilities and a nationalisation of the political process. This situation contrasted sharply with the situation in both Germany and the United States where there was a federal system of government. In these countries, although many important leadership functions were incumbent solely upon political leaders at the federal level, other such functions were devolved down to leaders at the subcentral level. Consequently, the sovereignty of political leaders at the central level was not absolute. Instead, in contrast to their British and French counterparts, their influence on the decision-making process was necessarily limited.

*•The structure of resources within and between political parties*
Finally, the country studies demonstrated that the leadership process was affected by the structure of resources within and between political parties. In certain countries, Presidents and Prime Ministers were also party leaders. The British Prime Minister, the French President, the German Chancellor and the Japanese Prime Minister all simultaneously occupied the post of head of state or head of government and (at least *de facto*) party leader. In the first three cases, this situation provided the leader with a considerable degree of political authority, or at least a greater degree of authority than any of their party colleagues. In the last case, the combination of being Prime Minister and party leader meant that the Japanese head of government occupied a strategic position within the political system, but the organisation of the LDP ensured that other senior party and government figures were also strategically placed (see below). In this sense, the position of LDP leaders was similar to that of DC leaders in Italy. Here, it was unusual for the head of government to hold the position of party leader as well. Instead, the President of the Council of Ministers occupied a position more akin to that of *primus inter pares*

within the party. In the United States, where the role of political parties was weak (see below), the President's position as party leader was not institutionalised. Consequently, the President gained little benefit from being the party's most visible representative. From these examples, it is apparent that political leaders in Britain, France and Germany derived a greater benefit from the position they occupied within their own party than did their counterparts in either Italy, Japan or the United States.

The internal organisational structure of parties was also shown to be a significant determinant of the leadership process. In Britain, Germany and, especially, France, the centralisation of power in the hands of the party leader was a key element in ensuring a degree of personal leadership. Differences were noted, though, between the organisation of both the Conservative and Labour parties in Britain and the CDU and the SPD in Germany. In Italy and Japan, factionalism within the dominant party determined much of the nature of the political system. The large number of heads of government and the relative weakness of their powers were both largely a result of the extremely divided nature of the LDP and the DC. Furthermore, the lack of cohesion within US political parties was a major reason why presidential success rates in Congress were comparatively low and why representatives of the executive and legislative branches of government were obliged to engage in a process of extensive and ongoing negotiation. Once again, therefore, it may be concluded that leaders in Britain, France and Germany headed parties whose internal organisation was more conducive to personal leadership than their counterparts in either Italy, Japan or the United States.

In terms of the level of party support in the legislature, a slightly different picture emerged. In the opening chapter, it was noted that governments which enjoy majority support in the legislature are usually best placed to pass their legislative programme. The country studies demonstrated that governments in Britain, France, Germany and Japan were regularly in this position. By contrast, in Italy, governments with minority support were not unknown, although they tended to presage a realignment of coalition partners. In the United States, the equivalent of minority government, namely, divided government, occurred frequently. In both cases, the passage of a coherent legislative programme was made more difficult because of this situation. It was also noted in the opening chapter that single-party governments are generally better placed to pass their legislative programme than coalition governments. The evidence showed that Britain, Japan and the United States were the only countries consistently to experience single party governments. Even then, the presidential system in the United States made comparisons difficult and factionalism within the LDP meant that governments often behaved as if they were a coalition of parties. Consequently, only British governments regularly enjoyed the benefit of this important leadership resource. In France, Germany and Italy, coalition governments were the norm. In France, the primacy of presidential politics did tend to diminish the problems normally associated with coalition government. Nevertheless, there were still severe difficulties between Gaullist and Giscardian parties in the late 1970s. In Germany, Chancellors were regularly obliged to act within the confines of coalition politics. This meant that their power of appointment was reduced and that they had to act within the limits of the agreed coalition programme. In Italy, heads of government regularly headed three-, four-, or even five party-coalition governments. As a result, their room for individual initiative was small and the necessity of negotiation absolute.

In all these ways, the six country studies confirmed that the leadership process was a product of the interaction between the ambitions and styles of political leaders, the needs of the society and institutional structures. However, they also confirmed that institutional structures had the most significant impact on the interaction process. The set of elements under this heading was at least partly responsible for determining the ambitions and styles of political leaders, for mediating the impact of the needs of the society upon the decision-making process and for creating the particular patterns of political leadership that were identified in the six country studies. These observations imply neither that leaders were unimportant, nor that the needs of the society were irrelevant, nor again that the patterns of political leadership were a function of institutional structures alone. Instead, they simply suggest that institutional structures had the greatest impact upon the leadership process in a country.

And yet, having demonstrated the significance of this point, certain questions remain to be answered. Why are institutional structures so important to the leadership process? Why are the elements under this heading so significant? Why should they create relatively stable patterns of leadership? Why should these patterns differ from one country to the next? Why should these differences be greater between some countries than others? In order to provide some of the answers to these questions and to place this study of political leadership in a wider, more theoretical context, it is necessary to examine the nature of institutional structures. In the next section, we will examine the institutional approach to politics.

## The institutional approach to politics

In recent years, there has been a reappraisal of the role played by institutions in the political process. (See, for example, Hall, 1986; and March and Olsen, 1984 and 1989). In his highly regarded book, Peter Hall used the term 'institution' to refer to 'the formal rules, compliance procedures, and standard operating practices that structure the relationship between individuals in various units of the polity and the economy' (Hall, 1986, p. 19). Whether or not Hall's definition is taken on board, as Thelen and Steinmo note, 'institutionalists are interested in the whole range of state and societal institutions that shape how political actors define their interests and that structure their relations of power to other groups' (Thelen and Steinmo, 1992, p. 2). This means that institutions are deemed to include presidencies, prime ministerships, Ministries, Cabinets, advisory units, bureaucracies, para-public agencies, legislatures, electoral systems, courts, systems of local government, interest groups and political parties. In this sense, they include many of those elements which were previously categorised under the heading of institutional structures.

The institutional approach to politics is derived from the appreciation that institutions, such as the ones identified above, play a fundamental part in structuring the nature of political competition. It is derived from the appreciation that institutional variables explain political outcomes (Thelen and Steinmo, 1992, p. 1). In the context of political leadership, this approach indicates that institutions help to determine the nature of the leadership process. It indicates that they are primarily responsible for structuring the interaction between leaders and the leadership environment. At the outset, though, it must be stressed that the institutional approach does not indicate that institutions themselves exercise leadership. Individuals exercise leadership and it is for this reason that it is necessary to study the ambitions and styles of individual political leaders. Moreover, institutions operate within the context of complex social forces and historical traditions and, likewise, it is for this reason that it is equally necessary to study the needs of the society. Instead, to say that institutions help to determine the nature of the leadership process is simply to say that this process is structurally suggested (Dowding, 1991, p. 16). In short, the institutional approach indicates that the ways in which and the extent to which Presidents and Prime Ministers can influence the outcome of the decision-making process is in part determined by the role of institutions in the political system.

Institutions are significant for two main reasons: they affect both the degree of pressure that political actors can bring to bear on the decision-making process and the likely direction of that pressure (Hall, 1986, p. 19). In the first place, institutions are significant because they affect the degree of pressure that political actors can apply to the leadership process. Institutions define the rules of the political game. They mark out certain boundaries within which the decision-making process operates. They do so, because they provide political leaders with potential leadership resources and constraints. Such resources and constraints include the presence of constitutional and procedural prerogatives, or their absence; the strength of formal and informal compliance mechanisms, or their weakness; and the abstract authority of a particular position, or its contestability. In sum, these resources and constraints may provide office-holders with the opportunities to achieve power (Blondel, 1990, p. 279), but they also place obstacles in the way of achieving such power. As a general rule, the greater the set of resources that are concentrated upon a particular office, the more likely it is that the incumbent of that office will be able to exercise personal and strategic leadership. The greater the set of constraints, the less likely it is that such leadership will be forthcoming.

The corollary of this point is that, by mapping the institutional structure of a particular country, it is possible to indicate the fundamental pattern of that country's decision-making process. In any particular country at any one time, many institutions are operational. This means that the leadership process is shaped not by a single institution (such as the prime ministership), nor by a single set of institutions (such as the executive). Instead, the leadership process is shaped by a combination of interlocking institutions and sets of institutions (Hall, 1986, p. 260). The relationship between these institutions is complex and their effects are almost always countervailing. And yet, the sum of these relationships and their effects produces a distinctive pattern of political leadership. Such patterns were identified in each of the six country studies. For example, in Britain, the configuration of the country's many different institutional structures meant that leadership resources were concentrated upon the prime ministership. By contrast, in Japan, there was no such concentration of resources. Instead, the configuration of institutional structures meant that Prime Ministers adopted a reactive style of leadership. These observations imply neither that the power of British Prime Ministers was absolute, nor that the behaviour of Japanese Prime Ministers was indistinguishable. They simply suggest that institutional structures were responsible for providing particular distributions of leadership resources and constraints and for creating patterns of political leadership.

Second, institutions affect the direction of the pressure that political actors can apply, because they help to shape political behaviour. As noted above, institutions are collections of rules, procedures and standard operating practices. As such, they produce certain duties and obligations by which office-holders have to abide. This means that leaders cannot simply assume office and behave in any way they may wish. Instead, they have to play out certain roles which the institution creates for them. Leaders are obliged to behave in ways which are appropriate to these institutional roles (March and Olsen, 1984, p. 741). There are incentives for leaders to behave appropriately (such as cooperation from other members of the group) as well as sanctions for not doing so (such as rejection through not being seen to fit in). Moreover, these roles are 'relatively invariant in the face of turnover of individuals and relatively resilient to the idiosyncratic preferences and expectations of individuals' (March and Olsen, 1984, p. 741). That is to say, when a new leader takes office, that leader will be obliged to play a similar role to that of his or her predecessor. In this way, institutions develop a memory. They induce repeated patterns of behaviour. They create relatively stable patterns of political leadership.

For both these reasons, institutionalism helps to explain the nature of the leadership process. Political leadership consists of a process of interaction between leaders and the leadership environment in which they operate. At the same time, this interaction process takes place within the context of institutional structures, which help to determine where power lies and what roles political leaders have to play. And yet, this is not to say that institutions predetermine political outcomes, nor that they fix leadership behaviour in advance. Institutionalism is neither deterministic nor reductionist. It is simply to say that they construct a strategic context within which political leaders make their choices (Immergut, 1992, p. 239). Political leaders still express their own ambitions and exhibit their own styles, but their behaviour is not a totally independent variable. Instead, it is shaped by the particular institution in which the leader is operating and by the general institutional configuration of the polity. The free will of political leaders is channelled through such institutional mechanisms (Hall, 1986, p. 259). In this way, the institutional approach to politics avoids the problems associated with both methodological individualism and structural determinism. It avoids the reductionism of the theories put forward by both Thomas Carlyle and Herbert Spencer (see Chapter 1). In short, it is perfectly compatible with the interactionist approach to the study of political leadership.

### Political leadership and the institutional approach to politics

It is apparent, therefore, that the institutional approach to politics helps to explain why institutional structures had such a significant impact on the decision-making process in the six countries that were studied. As a result, this approach can provide a useful insight into the study of political leadership. However, the reverse is also true. The study of political leadership can itself provide a useful insight into our understanding of the institutional approach to politics. This can be seen by briefly examining the advantages and disadvantages of this approach. As we shall see, there are two main advantages to the institutional approach:

1. it provides an explanation of historical continuities
2. it also accounts for variations in the decision-making processes of individual countries (Hall, 1986, p. 19).

However, there are also two main disadvantages:

1. it creates a strong tendency towards 'static' institutional analyses (Thelen and Steinmo, 1992, p. 13)
2. it encourages a degree of 'exceptionalism' in comparative studies.

In this final section, we will briefly examine both these advantages and disadvantages and see how the study of political leadership relates to them.

The first main advantage of the institutional approach is that it explains continuities in both the decision-making process and political behaviour. By their very nature, institutions are relatively durable. As we demonstrated above, they consist of rules, which cannot be simply broken, compliance procedures, which are not easily set aside, and standard operating practices, which are not open to instantaneous change or alteration (March and Olsen, 1989, p. 55). In short, institutions induce a strong tendency towards stability, or 'fixity' in the political process. In this way, as we also demonstrated above, the institutional approach provides the opportunity for understanding the persistence across time of certain patterns of power relations and forms of political leadership. For example, they help to explain not just why there may be presidential government in France, but also why there has been a general tendency towards this form of government since 1958. They account for why US Presidents have consistently had to engage in a bargaining process with other political actors. They show why successive heads of government have been unable to provide personal leadership in post-war Italy.

However, this advantage is matched by an equivalent disadvantage. The institutional approach is so convincing in explaining continuity that it sometimes fails to indicate that change may occur. As Thelen and Steinmo note, the issue of dynamism is often neglected in institutional analyses (Thelen and Steinmo, 1992, p. 13). This is because the desire to account for decision-making regularities and routine behaviour is at the heart of the institutional approach. In this way, there is a tendency to exaggerate that which is stable and to overlook that which is shifting. And yet, the previous chapters demonstrated that although countries exhibited relatively fixed patterns of leadership these patterns were not invariable. They were subject to change. For example, the tendency towards presidential government in France was matched by the potential for prime ministerial leadership. Similarly, the pattern of divided leadership in the United States did not rule out periods of presidential initiative. Finally, the structural weakness of the head of government in Italy did not eliminate the possibility that individual leaders could leave a certain mark upon the system. In this way, the study of political leadership helps to increase our understanding of the institutional approach to politics, because it underscores the fact that there are elements of both continuity and change to the decision-making process.

More fundamentally, though, the study of political leadership also indicates where these elements of continuity and change may lie. As might be expected, the former are mainly to be found under the heading of institutional structures. For the reasons considered above, these elements create a relatively fixed aspect to the leadership environment. The latter, though, may be found in both the behaviour of political leaders and the needs of the society. In the sense that their ambitions and styles are not predetermined and that they enjoy a degree of free will, leaders can act as catalysts of change. For example, Franklin D. Roosevelt, Konrad Adenauer, Charles de Gaulle and Margaret Thatcher are all associated with variations in the regular patterns of their country's leadership process. Similarly, in the opening chapter, it was noted that patterns of party identification are not immutable and that popular desires are subject to short-term fluctuations. Both elements introduce a degree of dynamism into the leadership process. For example, in France, relatively small shifts in partisan support induced a change from presidential to prime ministerial leadership in both 1986 and 1993. In Germany, the collapse of communism created expectations upon which Helmut Kohl was able to capitalise, so increasing his authority. By indicating that decision-making processes are marked by elements of continuity and change and by indicating where such elements are to be found, the study of political leadership provides an insight into the institutional approach to politics.

The second main advantage of the institutional approach is that it accounts for variations in the decision-making processes of individual countries. This is because institutions vary from one country to the next. For example, the country studies demonstrated that the prime ministership was not the same in Britain as in Japan and that the role of the legislature was not the same in France as in Germany. It is also because the configuration of institutions varies from one country to the next. For example, even though both Germany and Italy were shown to possess a similar set of institutions, the ways in which these institutions intertwined with each other in the former was different from the ways in which they did so in the latter. In the context of her study, examples of such variations led Immergut to conclude that there are 'different democracies whose specific institutional designs have affected the rules of the game for specific political contests' (Immergat, 1992, p. 231). In the context of political leadership, these institutional variations led us to conclude that there was a distinctiveness to each country's decision-making process and to the behaviour of its political leaders. Again, though, this advantage is matched by an equivalent disadvantage. By stressing the individuality of institutions and sets of institutional structures, the institutional approach sometimes encourages too great a degree of specificity when comparing countries. It produces a misleading tendency in which each country is considered to be exceptional. This tendency results from the observations that institutions and sets of institutions do not operate in exactly the same way in any two countries. Rather, each country's institutions are different. Each country's leadership process is unique. However, this is a misleading tendency, because, in its most extreme form, it means that comparisons between countries become futile. If each country is different, then comparisons are trivial. All that can be said is that French institutions are different from Japanese institutions, British institutions are different from US institutions and German institutions are different from Italian institutions. Once again, though, the country chapters demonstrated that comparisons were possible. In terms of political leadership, Britain was shown to be similar to France, Germany was similar to the United States and Japan was similar to Italy. In this way, the study of political leadership once again provides an insight into our appreciation of the institutional approach to politics. It does so, because it indicates that it is possible to adopt such an approach without falling into the trap of exceptionalism. It indicates that it is possible to make comparisons across countries.

More fundamentally again, though, the study of political leadership also indicates the various respects in which the institutions and institutional structures of countries are similar. Although equivalent institutions are not exactly the same in any two countries, there are sufficient similarities in certain cases for comparisons to be made. For example, the country studies demonstrated that the role of the German head of state is sufficiently close to that of the Italian head of state for them to be treated as playing a similar role in the decision-making process. Furthermore, although the configuration of institutions is not precisely the same in any two countries, once again, there are sufficient similarities in certain cases for comparisons to be made. For example, the identification of three sets of countries in which the individual patterns of leadership closely resembled each other demonstrated that essentially unique decision-making processes could be considered together. In this way, by indicating that decision-making processes were marked by elements of both difference and similarity and by identifying where such elements may lie, the study of political leadership provides a futher insight into the institutional approach to politics.

## Conclusion

This has been a study of the way that political leadership is exercised in liberal democracies. In particular, it has been a study of the ways in which and the extent to which heads of state and heads of government were able to control the decision-making process in six liberal democracies: Britain, France, Germany, Italy, Japan and the United States. It has shown that what these leaders can and cannot do is primarily determined by the institutional structures of their countries. It has also explained why this should be the case. Overall, this book has provided a framework which could also be applied to other liberal democracies, such as Australia, Canada, the Netherlands, the Republic of Ireland, Spain and Sweden. At the same time, it has also indicated certain areas where research into the institutional approach to politics may be conducted. In these ways, it is hoped that this book has provided a modest contribution to contemporary leadership studies.

# Bibliography

Allinson, Gary D. (1993) 'Citizenship, Fragmentation, and the Negotiated Polity', in Gary D. Allinson and Yasunori Stone (eds), *Political Dynamics in Contemporary Japan* (Ithaca: Cornell University Press) pp. 17–49.

Allum, P. A. (1973) *Politics and Society in Post-war Naples* (Cambridge: Cambridge University Press).

Avril, Pierre (1986) 'Présidentialisme et contraintes de l'exécutif dual', in J-L. Seurin, *La Présidence en France et aux Etats-Unis* (Paris: Economica) pp. 237–45.

Bailey, Christopher J. (1989) *The US Congress* (Oxford: Basil Blackwell).

Bailey, Christopher J. (1992) 'Congress and Legislative Activism', in Gillian Peele, Christopher J. Bailey and Bruce Cain (eds) *Developments in American Politics* (London: Macmillan) pp. 115–37.

Baker, David, Gamble, Andrew and Ludlam, Steve (1993) '1846 ... 1906 ... 1996? Conservative Splits and European Integration', in *Political Quarterly*, vol. 64, no. 4, Oct.–Dec. 1993, pp. 420–34.

Balboni, Enzo (1989) 'Who governs? The Crisis over the Craxi Government and the Role of the President of the Republic', in Robert Leonardi and Piergiorgio Corbetta (eds) *Italian Politics: A Review*, vol. 3 (London: Pinter) pp. 11–24.

Barber, James D. (1977) *The Presidential Character: Predicting Performance in the White House* (Englewood Cliffs, New Jersey: Prentice-Hall).

Baylis, Thomas C. (1989) *Governing by Committee: Collegial Leadership in Advanced Societies* (Albany: State University of New York Press).

Beloff, Max, and Peele, Gillian (1985) *The Government of the UK: Political Authority in a Changing Society* (London: Weidenfeld and Nicolson).

Berman, Larry (1987) *The New American Presidency* (Boston: Little, Brown).

Bessette, Joseph M. and Tulis, Jeffrey (1981) 'The Constitution, Politics, and the Presidency', in Joseph M. Bessette and Jeffrey Tulis (eds) *The Presidency in the Constitutional Order* (Baton Rouge: Louisiana State University Press) pp. 3–30.

Blondel, Jean (1980) *World Leaders* (London: Sage).

Blondel, Jean (1987) *Political Leadership. Towards a General Analysis* (London: Sage).

Blondel, Jean (1990) *Comparative Government. An Introduction* (London: Philip Allan).

Blondel, Jean and Müller-Rommel, Ferdinand (1993) 'Introduction', in Jean Blondel and Ferdinand Müller-Rommel (eds) *Governing Together. The Extent and Limits of Joint Decision-Making in Western European Cabinets* (London: Macmillan) pp. 1–19.

Brand, Jack (1992) *British Parliamentary Parties. Policy and Power* (Oxford: Clarendon Press).

Bulmer, Simon (1989a) 'Unity, Diversity and Stability: the "Efficient Secrets" behind West German Public Policy', in Simon Bulmer (ed.) *The Changing Agenda of West German Public Policy* (Aldershot: Dartmouth) pp. 13–39.

Bulmer, Simon (1989b) 'Territorial Government', in Gordon Smith, William E. Paterson and Peter H. Merkl (eds) *Developments in West German Politics* (London: Macmillan) pp. 40–59.

Bulmer, Simon (1991) 'Efficiency, Democracy and West German Federalism: a Critical Analysis', in Charlie Jeffery and Peter Savigear (eds), *German Federalism Today* (New York: St. Martin's Press) pp. 103–19.

Bulpitt, Jim (1983) *Territory and Power in the United Kingdom* (Manchester: Manchester University Press).

Burch, Martin (1988) 'The British Cabinet: A Residual Executive', in *Parliamentary Affairs*, vol. 41, no. 1, January, pp. 34–48.

Burnham, June, and Jones, G. W. (1993) 'Advising Margaret Thatcher: the Prime Minister's Office and the Cabinet Office Compared', in *Political Studies*, vol. 41, no. 2, June, pp. 299–314.

Burns, James MacGregor (1978) *Leadership* (New York: Harper & Row).

Caciagli, Mario (1991) 'The 18th DC Congress: from De Mita to Forlani and the Victory of 'Neodoroteism', in Filippo Sabetti and Raimondo Catanzaro (eds) *Italian Politics: A Review*, vol. 5 (London, Pinter), pp. 8–22.

Calder, Kent E. (1988a) 'Japanese Foreign Economic Policy: Explaining the Reactive State', in *World Politics*, vol. 40, no. 4, July, pp. 517–41.

Calder, Kent E. (1988b) *Crisis and Compensation, Public Policy and Political Stability in Japan, 1949–1986* (Princeton: Princeton University Press).

Campbell, Colin (1992) 'Presidential Leadership', in Gillian Peele, Christopher J. Bailey and Bruce Cain (eds) *Developments in American Politics* (London: Macmillan) pp. 83–114.

Campbell, John Creighton (1984) 'Policy Conflict and its Resolution within the Governmental System', in Ellis S. Krauss, Thomas P. Rohlen and Patricia G. Steinhoff (eds) *Conflict in Japan* (Honolulu: University of Hawaii Press), pp. 294–328.

Carcassonne, Guy (1988) 'France (1958): The Fifth Republic after Thirty Years', in Vernon Bogdanor (ed.) *Constitutions in Democratic Politics* (Aldershot: Gower) pp. 241–56.

Cassese, Sabino (1981) 'Is There a Government in Italy? Politics and Administration at the Top', in Richard Rose and Ezra Suleiman (eds) *Presidents and Prime Ministers* (Washington: American Enterprise Institute) pp. 171–202.

Cavalli, Luciano (1992) *Governo del Leader e Regime dei Partiti* (Bologna: Il Mulino).

Chandler, William M. (1993) 'The Christian Democrats and the Challenge of Unity', in Stephen Padgett (eds) *Parties and Party Systems in the New Germany* (Aldershot: Dartmouth) pp. 129–46.

Charlot, Jean and Charlot, Monica (1992) 'France', in David Butler and Austin Ranney (eds), *Electioneering: A comparative study of continuity and change* (Oxford: Clarendon Press) pp. 133–55.

Christensen, Raymond V. (1994) 'Electoral Reform in Japan, How It Was Enacted and Changes It May Bring', in *Asian Survey*, vol. 34, no. 7, July, pp. 589–605.

Chubb, John E. (1985) 'Federalism and the Bias for Centralization', in John E. Chubb and Paul E. Peterson (eds), *The New Direction in American Politics* (Washington DC: The Brookings Institution) pp. 273–306.

Clarke, Peter (1991) *A Question of Leadership: From Gladstone to Thatcher* (Harmondsworth: Penguin).

Cole, Alistair (1994) *François Mitterrand: A Study in Political Leadership* (London: Routledge).

Criddle, Byron (1987) 'France: Parties in a Presidential System', in Alan Ware (ed.) *Political Parties: Electoral Change and Structural Response* (Oxford: Basil Blackwell) pp. 137–57.

Criscitiello, Annarita (1993) 'Majority Summits: Decision-Making Inside the Cabinet and Out: Italy, 1970–1990', in *West European Politics*, vol. 16, no. 4, October, pp. 581–94.

Crossman, Richard (1972) 'Introduction', in Walter Bagehot, *The English Constitution* (London: Harper) pp. 1–57.

Curtis, Gerald L. (1988) *The Japanese Way of Politics* (New York: Columbia University Press).

Davidson, Roger H. (1981) 'Subcommittee Government: New Channels for Policy Making', in Thomas E. Mann and Norman J. Ornstein (eds), *The New Congress* (Washington DC: American Enterprise Institute) pp. 99–133.

de Franciscis, Maria Elisabetta and Zannini, Rosella (1992) 'Judicial Policy-Making in Italy: the Constitutional Court', in *West European Politics*, vol. 15, no. 3, July, pp. 68–79.

de Gaulle, Charles (1971), *Memoirs of Hope* (London: Weidenfeld & Nicolson).

Della Sala, Vincent (1993) 'The Cossiga Legacy and Scalfaro's Election: in the Shadow of Presidentialism', in Stephen Hellman and Gianfranco Pasquino (eds), *Italian Politics: A Review*, vol. 8 (London: Pinter) pp. 34–49.

Di Palma, Giuseppe (1977) *Surviving Without Governing: The Italian Parties in Parliament* (Berkeley: University of California Press).

Dogan, Mattei (1989) 'How to Become a Cabinet Minister in Italy: Unwritten Rules of the Political Game', in Mattei Dogan (ed.) *Pathways to Power. Selecting Rulers in Pluralist Democracies* (Boulder: Westview Press) pp. 99–139.

Dönhoff, Marion (1982) *Foe into Friend: The Makers of the New Germany from Konrad Adenauer to Helmut Schmidt* (London: Weidenfeld & Nicolson).

Donovan, Mark (1994) 'Democrazia Cristiana: Party of Government' in David Hanley (ed.) *Christian Democracy in Europe. A Comparative Perspective* (London: Pinter) pp. 71–86.

Dowding, Keith M. (1991) *Rational Choice and Political Power* (London: Edward Elgar).

Drewry, Gavin (1992) 'Judicial Politics in Britain: Patrolling the Boundaries', in *West European Politics*, vol. 15, no. 3, July, pp. 9–28.

Duhamel, Olivier (1987) 'The Fifth Republic under François Mitterrand, Evolution and Perspectives', in George Ross, Stanley Hoffman and Sylvia Malzacher (eds), *The Mitterrand Experiment* (Oxford: Polity Press) pp. 140–60.

Duhamel, Olivier (1993) *Les Démocraties, régimes, histoires, exigences* (Paris: Editions du Seuil).

Dunleavy, Patrick, Jones, G. W. and O'Leary, Brendan (1990) 'Prime Ministers and the Commons: Patterns of Behaviour, 1868 to 1987', in *Public Administration*, vol. 68, Spring, pp. 123–140.

Dunleavy, Patrick, and Jones, G. W. with Burnham, June, Elgie, Robert and Fysh, Peter (1993) 'Leaders, Politics and Institutional Change: The Decline of Prime Ministerial Accountability to the House of Commons, 1868–1990', in *British Journal of Political Science*, vol. 23, pp. 267–298.

Dunleavy, Patrick and Rhodes, R. A. W. (1990) 'Core Executive Studies in Britain', in *Public Administration*, vol. 68, Spring, pp. 3–28.

Dupuy, François (1985), 'The Politico-Administrative System of the Département in France', in Yves Mény and Vincent Wright (eds), *Centre–Periphery Relations in Western Europe* (London: Allen & Unwin) pp. 79–103.

Edinger, Lewis J. (1975) 'The Comparative Analysis of Political Leadership', in *Comparative Politics*, vol. 7, no. 2, January, pp. 253–69.

Edinger, Lewis J. (1990) 'Approaches to the Comparative Analysis of Political Leadership', in *Review of Politics*, vol. 52, no. 4, Fall, pp. 509–23.

Edinger, Lewis J. (1993) 'A Preface to Studies in Political Leadership', in Gabriel Sheffer (ed.) *Innovative Leadership in International Politics* (Albany: State University of New York Press) pp. 3–20.

Elgie, Robert (1993a) 'From the Exception to the Rule: the Use of Article 49–3 of the Constitution since 1958', in *Modern and Contemporary France*, vol. NS1, no. 1, January, pp. 17–26.

Elgie, Robert (1993b) *The Role of the Prime Minister in France, 1981–91* (London: Macmillan).

Fiorina, Morris P. (1992) 'An Era of Divided Government', in Gillian Peele, Christopher J. Bailey and Bruce Cain (eds) *Developments in American Politics* (London: Macmillan) pp. 324–54.

Frears, John (1990) 'The French Parliament: Loyal Workhorse, Poor Watchdog', in *West European Politics*, vol. 13, no. 3, July, pp. 32–51.

Frognier, André-Paul (1993) 'The Single-Party/Coalition Distinction in Cabinet Decision-Making', in Jean Blondel and Ferdinand Müller-Rommel (eds) *Governing Together: The Extent and Limits of Joint Decision-Making in Western European Cabinets* (London: Macmillan) pp. 43–73.

Fukai, Shigeko N. and Fukui, Haruhiro (1992) 'Elite Recruitment and Political Leadership', in *PS: Political Science and Politics*, vol. 25, no. 1, March, pp. 25–36.

Furlong, Paul (1990) 'Parliament in Italian Politics', in *West European Politics*, vol. 13, no. 3, July, pp. 52–67.

Furlong, Paul (1991) 'Government Stability and Electoral Systems: the Italian Example', in *Parliamentary Affairs*, vol. 44, no. 1, January, pp. 50–59.

Furlong, Paul (1994) *Modern Italy: Representation and Reform* (London: Routledge).

Gaffney, John (1988) 'French Socialism and the Fifth Republic', in *West European Politics*, vol. 11, no. 3, July, pp. 42–56.

Gardner, John (1990) *On Leadership* (New York: The Free Press).

George, Alexander L. (1974) 'Assessing Presidential Character', in *World Politics*, vol. 26, pp. 234–82.

Greenstein, Fred I. (1992) 'Can Personality and Politics be Studied Systematically?', in *Political Psychology*, vol. 13, no. 1, pp. 105–128.

Greenstein, Fred I. (1994) 'The Presidential Leadership Style of Bill Clinton: An Early Appraisal', in *Political Science Quarterly*, vol. 108, no. 4, pp. 589–601.

Hah, Chong-Do and Bartol, Frederick C. (1983) 'Political Leadership as a Causative Phenomenon: Some Recent Analyses', in *World Politics*, vol. 36, no. 1, October, pp. 100–120.

Hall, Peter A. (1986) *Governing the Economy: The Politics of State Intervention in Britain and France* (Cambridge: Polity Press).

Hart, John (1987) 'The President and his Staff', in Malcolm Shaw (ed.) *Roosevelt to*

*Reagan. The Development of the Modern Presidency* (London: C. Hurst) pp. 159–205.

Hayao, Kenji (1993) *The Japanese Prime Minister and Public Policy* (Pittsburgh: University of Pittsburgh Press).

Heclo, Hugh (1983) 'One Executive Branch or Many', in Anthony King (ed.), *Both Ends of the Avenue: The Presidency, the Executive Branch and Congress in the 1980s* (Washington DC: American Enterprise Institute) pp. 26–58.

Hine, David (1993) *Governing Italy: The Politics of Bargained Pluralism* (Oxford: Clarendon Press).

Hine, David and Finocchi, Renato (1991) 'The Italian Prime Minister', in G. W. Jones (ed.) *West European Prime Ministers* (London: Frank Cass) pp. 79–96.

Hockin, Thomas A. (1977) 'Preface', in Thomas A. Hockin (ed.) *Apex of Power: The Prime Minister and Political Leadership in Canada* (Scarborough, Ontario: Prentice-Hall) pp. ix–xv.

Hodder-Williams, Richard (1981) 'Courts of Last Resort', in Richard Hodder-Williams and James Ceasar (eds) *Politics in Britain and the United States* (London: Duke University Press) pp. 142–72.

Hodder-Williams, Richard (1990) 'Litigation and Political Action: Making the Supreme Court Activist', in Robert Williams (ed.) *Explaining American Politics. Issues and Interpretations* (London: Routledge) pp. 116–43.

Hodgson, Godfrey (1984) *All Things to All Men: The False Promise of the Modern American Presidency* (Harmondsworth: Penguin).

Howorth, Jolyon (1993) 'The President's Special Role in Foreign and Defence Policy', in Jack Hayward (ed.) *De Gaulle to Mitterrand, Presidential Power in France* (London: Hurst) pp. 150–89.

Hrebenar, Ronald J. (1992) 'The Money Base of Japanese Politics', in Ronald J. Hrebenar (ed.) *The Japanese Party System*, 2nd edn (Boulder: Westview Press) pp. 54–78.

Immergut, Ellen M. (1992) *Health Politics: Interests and Institutions in Western Europe* (Cambridge: Cambridge University Press).

Ingle, Stephen (1989) *The British Party System* (Oxford: Basil Blackwell).

Inoguchi, Takashi (1991) 'The Nature and Functioning of Japanese Politics', in *Government and Opposition*, vol. 26, no. 2, pp. 185–98.

James, Simon (1992) *British Cabinet Government* (London: Routledge).

Jones, Charles O. (1990) 'The Separated Presidency – Making it Work in Contemporary Politics', in Anthony King (ed.) *The New American Political System* (Washington DC: American Enterprise Institute) pp. 1–28.

Jones, George (1990) 'Mrs. Thatcher and the Power of the PM', in *Contemporary Record*, vol. 3, no. 4, April, pp. 2–6.

Jones, George W. (1991) 'Presidentialization in a Parliamentary System?', in Colin Campbell, S. J., and Margaret Jane Wyszomirski (eds) *Executive Leadership in Anglo-American Systems* (Pittsburgh: University of Pittsburgh Press) pp. 111–37.

Jones, G. W. (1969) 'The Prime Minister's Power', in Anthony King (ed.) *The British Prime Minister: A Reader* (London: Macmillan) pp. 195–220.

Jones, G. W. (1991) 'West European Prime Ministers in Perspective', in G. W. Jones (ed.) *West European Prime Ministers* (London: Frank Cass) pp. 163–78.

Judge, David (1992) 'The "Effectiveness" of the post-1979 Select Committee System:

the Verdict of the 1990 Procedure Committee', in *Political Quarterly*, vol. 63, pp. 91–100.

Katz, Daniel (1973) 'Patterns of Leadership', in Jeanne N. Knutson (ed.) *Handbook of Political Psychology* (San Francisco: Jossey-Bass) pp. 203–33.

Katzenstein, Peter J. (1987) *Politics and Policy in West Germany: The Growth of a Semisovereign State* (Philadelphia: Temple University Press).

Kavanagh, Dennis (1990) 'From Gentlemen to Players: Changes in Political Leadership', in Dennis Kavanagh, *Politics and Personalities* (London: Macmillan) pp. 246–71.

Keeler, John T. S. (1993a) 'Opening the Window for Reform: Mandates, Crises and Extraordinary Policy-Making', in *Comparative Political Studies*, vol. 25, no. 4, January, pp. 433–86.

Keeler, John T. S. (1993b) 'Executive Power and Policy-Making Patterns in France: Gauging the Impact of the Fifth Republic Institutions', in *West European Politics*, vol. 16, no. 4, October, pp. 518–44.

Keeler, John T. S. and Stone, Alec (1987) 'Judicial–political Confrontation in Mitterrand's France: The Emergence of the Constitutional Council as a Major Actor in the Policy-making Process', in George Ross, Stanley Hoffman and Sylvia Malzacher (eds), *The Mitterrand Experiment. Continuity and Change in Modern France* (Cambridge: Polity Press) pp. 161–81.

Kellerman, Barbara (1984) 'Leadership as a Political Act', in Barbara Kellerman (ed.) *Leadership: Multidisciplinary Perspectives* (Englewood Cliffs, New Jersey: Prentice-Hall) pp. 63–89.

Kellerman, Barbara, (ed.) (1986) *Political Leadership: A Source Book* (Pittsburgh: University of Pittsburgh Press).

Kennedy, Ellen (1991) *The Bundesbank: Germany's Central Bank in the International Monetary System* (London: Pinter).

Kernell, Samuel (1991) 'New and Old Lessons on White House Management', in Colin Campbell, S.J. and Margaret Jane Wyszomirski (eds) *Executive Leadership in Anglo-American Systems* (Pittsburgh: University of Pittsburgh Press) pp. 341–60.

King, Anthony (1976) 'Modes of Executive–Legislative Relations: Great Britain, France and West Germany', in *Legislative Studies Quarterly*, vol. 1, no. 1, pp. 11–36.

King, Anthony (1991) 'The British Prime Ministership in the Age of the Career Politician', in G. W. Jones (ed.) *West European Prime Ministers* (London: Frank Cass) pp. 25–47.

King, Anthony (1993) 'Foundations of Power', in George C. Edwards III, John H. Kessel and Bert A. Rockman (eds) *Researching the Presidency. Vital Questions, New Approaches* (Pittsburgh: University of Pittsburgh Press) pp. 415–51.

King, Anthony (1994) '"Chief Executives" in Western Europe', in Ian Budge and David McKay (eds) *Developing Democracy. Comparative Research in Honour of J.F.P. Blondel* (London: Sage) pp. 150–63.

Klatt, Hartmut (1992) 'German Unification and the Federal System', in *German Politics*, vol. 1, no. 3, December, pp. 1–21.

Koff, Stephen P. (1982) 'The Italian Presidency: Constitutional Role and Political Practice', in *Presidential Studies Quarterly*, vol. 12, no. 3, Summer, pp. 337–51.

Kohno, Masaru (1992) 'Rational Foundations for the Organization of the Liberal Democratic Party in Japan', in *World Politics*, vol. 44, April, pp. 369–97.

Kommers, Donald P. (1994) 'The Federal Constitutional Court in the German Political System', in *Comparative Political Studies*, vol. 26, no. 4, January, pp. 470–91.

Krauss, Ellis S. (1982) 'Japanese Parties and Parliament: Changing Leadership Roles and Role Conflicts', in Terry Edward MacDougall (ed.) *Political Leadership in Contemporary Japan* (Ann Arbor, Michigan: Papers in Japanese Studies) no. 1, pp. 93–113.

Krauss, Ellis S. (1989) 'Politics and the Policymaking Process', in Takeshi Ishida and Ellis S. Krauss (eds) *Democracy in Japan* (Pittsburgh: University of Pittsburgh Press) pp. 39–64.

Krauss, Ellis S. and Pierre, Jon (1990) 'The Decline of Dominant Parties: Parliamentary Politics in Sweden and Japan in the 1970s', in T. J. Pempel (ed.) *Uncommon Democracies: The One-Party Dominant Regimes* (Ithaca: Cornell University Press) pp. 226–59.

Lagroye, Jacques, and Wright, Vincent (1979) 'Introduction: Local Government in Britain and in France – the Problems of Comparisons and Contrasts', in Jacques Lagroye and Vincent Wright (eds) *Local Government in Britain and France. Problems and Prospects* (London: George Allen & Unwin) pp. 1–9.

Landfried, Christine (1992) 'Judicial Policy-Making in Germany: The Federal Constitutional Court', in *West European Politics*, vol. 15, no. 3, July, pp. 50–67.

Leiserson, Michael (1968) 'Factions and Coalitions in One-Party Japan: An Interpretation Based on the Theory of Games', in *American Political Science Review*, vol. 62, no. 3, September, pp. 770–787.

Leonardi, Robert and Wertman, Douglas A. (1989) *Italian Christian Democracy: the Politics of Dominance* (London: Macmillan).

Lipset, Seymour M. and Rokkan, Stein (1967) 'Cleavage Structures, Party Systems, and Voter Alignments: An Introduction', in Seymour M. Lipset and Stein Rokkan (eds) *Party Systems and Voter Alignments: Cross-national Perspectives* (New York: Free Press) pp. 1–64.

McSweeney, Dean and Zvesper, John (1991) *American Political Parties: The Formation, Decline and Reform of the American Party System* (London: Routledge).

Machin, Howard, and Wright, Vincent (1982) 'Why Mitterrand Won: The French Presidential Elections of April–May 1981', in *West European Politics*, vol. 5, no. 1, pp. 5–35.

March, James G. and Olsen, Johan P. (1984) 'The New Institutionalism: Organizational Factors in Political Life', in *American Political Science Review*, vol. 78, no. 3, September, pp. 734–49.

March, James G. and Olsen Johan P. (1989) *Rediscovering Institutions: The Organizational Basis of Politics* (New York: The Free Press).

Martin, Curtis H. and Stronach, Bruce (1992) *Politics East and West: A Comparison of Japanese and British Political Culture* (New York: M. E. Sharpe).

Massot, Jean (1991) 'Le Président de la République et le Premier ministre', in Dominique Chagnollaud (ed.) *Bilan Politique de la France, 1991* Paris: Hachette) pp. 21–7.

Massot, Jean (1993) *Chef de l'Etat et Chef du Gouvernement: Dyarchie et hiérarchie* (Paris: La Documentation française).

Mayntz, Renate (1980) 'Executive Leadership in Germany: Dispersion of Power or "Kanzlerdemokratie"', in Richard Rose and Ezra N. Suleiman (eds), *Presidents and Prime Ministers* (Washington, DC: American Enterprise Institute), pp. 139–70.

Mayntz, Renate (1987) 'West Germany', in William Plowden (ed.) *Advising the Rulers* (Oxford: Blackwell) pp. 3–17.

Mughan, Anthony and Patterson, Samuel C., (eds) (1992) *Political Leadership in Democratic Societies* (Chicago: Nelson-Hall).

Müller, Wolfgang (1993) 'The Relevance of the State for Party System Change', in *Journal of Theoretical Politics*, vol. 5, no. 4, pp. 419–54.

Müller-Rommel, Ferdinand (1988a) 'The Centre of Government in West Germany: Changing Patterns under 14 Legislatures (1949–1987)', in *European Journal of Political Research*, vol. 16, no. 2, March, pp. 171–90.

Müller-Rommel, Ferdinand (1988b) 'Federal Republic of Germany: a System of Chancellor Government', in Jean Blondel and Ferdinand Müller-Rommel (eds) *Cabinets in Western Europe* (London: Macmillan).

Müller-Rommel, Ferdinand (1994) 'The Chancellor and his Staff', in Stephen Padgett (ed.) *Adenauer to Kohl: The Development of the German Chancellorship* (London: Hurst) pp. 106–26.

Muramatsu, Michio, and Krauss, Ellis S. (1987) 'The Conservative Policy Line and the Development of Patterned Pluralism', in Kozo Yamamura & Yasukichi Yasuba (eds), *The Political Economy of Japan, vol. 1: The Domestic Transformation* (Stanford: Stanford University Press) pp. 516–54.

Murphy, Arthur B. (1984) 'Evaluating the Presidents of the United States', in *Presidential Studies Quarterly*, vol. 14, no. 1, pp. 117–26.

Neustadt, Richard (1965) *Presidential Power* (New York: John Wiley).

Newell, James L. and Bull, Martin J. (1993) 'The Italian Referenda of April 1993: Real Change at Last?', in *West European Politics*, vol. 16, no. 4, October, pp. 607–15.

Niclauss, Karlheinz (1993) 'Le gouvernement fédéral', in *Pouvoirs*, no. 66, pp. 99–109.

Norton, Philip (1980) *Dissension in the House of Commons 1974–1979* (Oxford: Oxford University Press).

Norton, Philip (1985) 'Behavioural Changes: Backbench Independence in the 1980s', in Philip Norton (ed.) *Parliament in the 1980s* (Oxford: Basil Blackwell) pp. 22–47.

Norton, Philip (1987) 'Mrs Thatcher and the Conservative Party: Another Institution Handbagged?', in Kenneth Minogue and Michael Biddiss (eds) *Thatcherism: Personality and Politics* (London: Macmillan) pp. 21–37.

Norton, Philip (1990) 'Parliament in the United Kingdom: Balancing Effectiveness and Consent', in *West European Politics*, vol. 13, no. 3, July, pp. 10–32.

Padgett, Stephen (1994) 'Chancellors and the Chancellorship', in Stephen Padgett (ed.) *Adenauer to Kohl: The Development of the German Chancellorship* (London: Hurst) pp. 1–19.

Padgett, Stephen and Burkett, Tony (1986) *Political Parties and Elections in West Germany: The Search for a New Stability* (London: Hurst).

Paige, Glenn D. (1977) *The Scientific Study of Political Leadership* (New York: The Free Press).

Parodi, Jean-Luc (1988) 'Imprévisible ou inéluctable. L'évolution de la Cinquième République?', in Olivier Duhamel and Jean-Luc Parodi (eds) *La Constitution de la Cinquième République* (Paris: Presses de la Fondation nationale des Sciences politiques) pp. 24–43.

Pasquino, Gianfranco (1979) 'Italian Christian Democracy: A Party for all Seasons?', in *West European Politics*, vol. 2, no. 3, pp. 88–109.

Pasquino, Gianfranco (1987) 'Party Government in Italy: Achievements and Prospects', in Richard Katz (ed.) *The Future of Party Government, vol. 2: Party Governments: European and American Experience* (Berlin: Walter de Gruyter) pp. 202–42.

Paterson, William E. (1981) 'The Chancellor and his Party: Political Leadership in the Federal Republic', in William E. Paterson and Gordon Smith (eds) *The West German Model: Perspectives on a Stable State* (London: Frank Cass) pp. 3–17.

Paterson, William E. and Southern, David (1991) *Governing Germany* (Oxford: Basil Blackwell).

Pempel, T. J. (1984) 'Organizing for Efficiency, The Higher Civil Service in Japan', in Ezra N. Suleiman (ed.) *Bureaucrats and Policy Making, A Comparative Overview* (London: Holmes & Meier) pp. 72–106.

Pempel, T. J. (1990a) 'Introduction', in T. J. Pempel (ed.) *Uncommon Democracies: The One-Party Dominant Regimes* (Ithaca: Cornell University Press) pp. 1–32.

Pempel, T. J. (1990b) 'Conclusion. One-Party Dominance and the Creation of Regimes', in T. J. Pempel (ed.) *Uncommon Democracies: The One-Party Dominant Regimes* (Ithaca: Cornell University Press) pp. 333–60.

Pious, Richard M. (1991) 'Presidential War Powers, the War Powers Resolution, and the Persian Gulf', in Martin L. Fausold and Alan Shank (eds) *The Constitution and the American Presidency* (Albany: State University of New York Press) pp. 195–210.

Polsby, Nelson (1990) 'Political Change and the Character of the Contemporary Congress', in Anthony King (ed.) *The New American Political System* (Washington, DC: American Enterprise Institute) pp. 29–46.

Pridham, Geoffrey (1983) 'Party Politics and Coalition Government in Italy', in Vernon Bogdanor (ed.) *Coalition Government in Western Europe* (London: Heinemann).

Pridham, Geoffrey (1988) *Political Parties and Coalitional Behaviour in Italy* (London: Routledge).

Punnett, Malcolm (1992) *The Selection of the Party Leader – Japanese Style* (Glasgow: Strathclyde Papers on Government & Politics, no. 85).

Reichley, A. James (1985) 'The Rise of National Parties', in John E. Chubb and Paul E. Peterson (eds) *The New Direction in American Politics* (Washington, DC: The Brookings Institute) pp. 175–200.

Reif, Karlheinz (1987) 'Party Government in the Fifth French Republic', in Richard Katz (ed.) *The Future of Party Government, vol. 2: Party Governments: European and American Experiences* (New York: Walter de Gruyter) pp. 27–77.

Rhodes, R.A.W. (1987) 'Territorial Politics in the United Kingdom: The Politics of Change, Conflict and Contradiction', in *West European Politics*, vol. 10, no. 4, October, pp. 21–51.

Ridley, F. F. (1966) 'Chancellor Government as a Political System and the German Constitution', in *Parliamentary Affairs*, vol. 19, pp. 446–61.

Rockman, Bert A. (1984) *The Leadership Question: The Presidency and the American System* (New York: Praeger).

Rockman, Bert A. (1988) 'The American Presidency in Comparative Perspective: Systems, Situations and Leaders', in Michael Nelson (ed.) *The Presidency and the Political System* (Washington, DC: Congressional Quarterly Press) pp. 55–79.

Rose, Richard (1991) 'Prime Ministers in Parliamentary Democracies', in G W. Jones (ed.) *West European Prime Ministers* (London: Frank Cass) pp. 9–24.

Rost, Joseph C. (1991) *Leadership for the Twenty-First Century* (New York: Praeger).

Rothacher, Albrecht (1993) *The Japanese Power Elite* (London: Macmillan).

Saalfeld, Thomas (1990) 'The West German Bundestag after 40 Years: The Role of Parliament in a "Party Democracy"', in *West European Politics*, vol. 13, no. 3, July, pp. 68–89.

Seldon, Anthony (1990) 'The Cabinet Office and Coordination 1979–87', in *Public Administration*, vol. 68, Spring, pp. 103–21.

Shapiro, Martin (1990) 'The Supreme Court from Early Burger to Early Rehnquist', in Anthony King (ed.) *The New American Political System* (Washington, DC: American Enterprise Institute) pp. 47–85.

Sheffer, Gabriel, (ed.) (1993) *Innovative Leadership in International Politics* (Albany: State University of New York Press).

Sheffer, Gabriel (1993) 'Introduction: In Search of Innovative Leadership in World Politics', in Gabriel Sheffer (ed.) *Innovative Leadership in International Politics* (Albany: State University of New York Press) pp. vii–xviii.

Sidoti, Francesco (1993a) 'The Italian Political Class', in *Government and Opposition*, vol. 28, no. 3, pp. 339–52.

Sidoti, Francesco (1993b) 'Italy: A Clean-up after the Cold War', in *Government and Opposition*, vol. 28, no. 1, pp. 105–14.

Sinclair, Barabara (1991) 'Governing Unheroically (and Sometimes Unappetizingly): Bush and the 101st Congress', in Colin Campbell, S.J. and Bert A. Rockman (eds), *The Bush Presidency: First Appraisals* (Chatham, New Jersey: Chatham House Publishers) pp. 155–84.

Smith, Gordon (1986) *Democracy in Western Germany: parties and politics in the Federal Republic*, 3rd edn (Aldershot: Gower).

Smith, Gordon (1991) 'The Resources of a German Chancellor', in G. W. Jones (ed.) *West European Prime Minister* (London: Frank Cass) pp. 48–61.

Smith, Gordon (1992) 'The Nature of the Unified State', in Gordon Smith, William E. Paterson, Peter H. Merkl and Stephen Padgett (eds) *Developments in German Politics* (London: Macmillan) pp. 37–51.

Spotts, Frederic and Wieser, Theodor (1986) *Italy: A Difficult Democracy. A Survey of Italian Politics* (Cambridge: Cambridge University Press).

Stanley, Harold W. and Niemi, Richard G. (1994) *Vital Statistics on American Politics*, 4th edn (Washington, DC: Congressional Quarterly Press).

Stern, Geoffrey (1993) *Leaders and Leadership* (Oxford: LSE and the BBC).

Stockwin, J. A. A. (1982) *Japan: Divided Politics in a Growth Economy* (London: Weidenfeld & Nicolson).

Stockwin, J. A. A. (1988) 'Parties, Politicians and the Political System', in J. A. A. Stockwin (ed.) *Dynamic and Immobilist Politics in Japan* (London: Macmillan) pp. 22–53.

Stone, Alec (1989) 'In the Shadow of the Constitutional Council: The 'Juridicisation' of the Legislative Process in France', in *West European Politics*, vol. 12, no. 2, April, pp. 12–34.

Stone, Alec (1992a) 'Where Judicial Politics are Legislative Politics: The French Constitutional Council', in *West European Politics*, vol. 15, no. 3, July, pp. 29–49.

Stone, Alec (1992b) *The Birth of Judicial Politics in France: The Constitutional Council in Comparative Perspective* (Oxford: Oxford University Press).

Stone, Alec (1994) 'Judging Socialist Reform. The Politics of Coordinate Construction in France and Germany', in *Comparative Political Studies*, vol. 26, no. 4, January, pp. 443–69.

Sturm, Roland (1994) 'The Chancellor and the Executive', in Stephen Padgett (ed.) *Adenauer to Kohl: The Development of the German Chancellorship* (London: Hurst) pp. 78–105.

Suleiman, Ezra N. (1980) 'Presidential Government in France', in Richard Rose and Ezra N. Suleiman (eds), *Presidents and Prime Ministers* (Washington, DC: American Enterprise Institute) pp. 94–138.

Taras, David and Weyant, Robert (1991) 'Dreamers of the Day: A Guide to Roles, Character and Performance on the Political Stage', in Leslie A. Pal and David Taras (eds) *Prime Ministers and Premiers: Political Leadership and Public Policy in Canada* (Ontario: Prentice-Hall) pp. 2–15.

Tarrow, Sidney (1990) 'Maintaining Hegemony in Italy: "The softer they rise, the slower they fall!"', in T. J. Pempel (ed.) *Uncommon Democracies: The One-Party Dominant Regimes* (Ithaca: Cornell University Press) pp. 306–32.

Thayer, Nathaniel B. (1969) *How the Conservatives Rule Japan* (Princeton: Princeton University Press).

Thelen, Kathleen and Steinmo, Sven (1992) 'Historical institutionalism in comparative politics', in Sven Steinmo, Kathleen Thelen and Frank Longstreth (eds) *Structuring Politics* (Cambridge: Cambridge University Press) pp. 1–32.

Tomita, Nobuo, Akira, Nakamura and Hrebenar, Ronald J. (1992) 'The Liberal Democratic Party: The Ruling Party of Japan', in Ronald J. Hrebenar (ed.) *The Japanese Party System*, 2nd edn (Boulder: Westview Press) pp. 237–84.

Tsurutani, Taketsugu (1992) 'Japan's Chief Executive', in Taketsugu Tsurutani and Jack B. Gabriel (eds) *Chief Executives: National Political Leadership in the United States, Mexico, Great Britain, Germany and Japan* (Pullman: Washington, Washington State University Press) pp. 209–49.

Tucker, Robert C. (1981) *Politics as Leadership* (Columbia: University of Missouri Press).

van Loenen, Gerbert (1990) 'Weimar or Byzantium: Two Opposing Approaches to the Italian Party System', in *European Journal of Political Research*, vol. 18, pp. 241–56.

Vickers, John and Wright, Vincent (1988) 'The Politics of Industrial Privatisation in Western Europe: An Overview', in *West European Politics*, vol. 11, no. 4, October, pp. 1–30.

Weaver, R. Kent and Rockman, Bert A. (1993) 'Assessing the Effects of Institutions', in R. Kent Weaver and Bert A. Rockman (eds) *Do Institutions Matter? Government Capabilities in the United States and Abroad* (Washington, DC: The Brookings Institution) pp. 1–41.

Wehling, Hans-Georg (1989) 'The Bundesrat', in *Publius: The Journal of Federalism*, vol. 19, no. 4, Fall, pp. 53–64.

Weller, Patrick (1985) *First Among Equals. Prime Ministers in Westminster Systems* (London: George Allen & Unwin).

Wildavsky, Aaron (1975) 'The Two Presidencies', in Aaron Wildavsky (ed.) *Perspectives on the Presidency* (Boston: Little, Brown) pp. 448–61.

Williams, Philip (1968) *The French Parliament 1958–67*, (London: George Allen & Unwin).

Wright, Vincent (1978) 'France', in David Butler and Austin Ranney (eds) *Referendums, A Comparative Study of Practice and Theory* (Washington, DC: American Enterprise Institute) pp. 139–68.

Wright, Vincent (1989) *The Government and Politics of France* (London: Unwin Hyman).

Wright, Vincent (1993) 'The President and the Prime Minister: subordination, conflict, symbiosis or reciprocal parasitism', in Jack Hayward (ed.) *De Gaulle to Mitterrand: Presidential Power in France* (London: Hurst) pp. 101–19.

Zuckerman, Alan S. (1979) *The Politics of Faction: Christian Democratic Rule in Italy* (New Haven: Yale University Press).

# Index

226 *Index*